TEACHER'S GUIDE

Connected Mathematics 2

Frogs, Fleas, and Painted Cubes

Quadratic Relationships

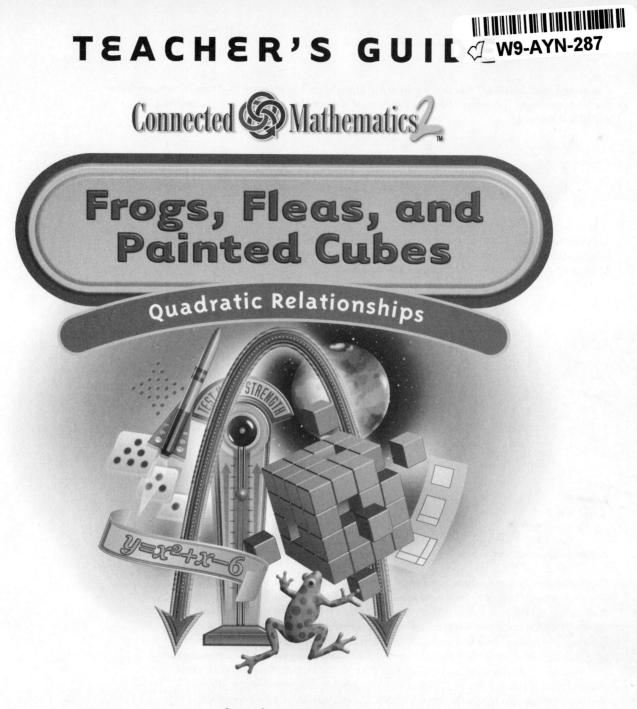

Glenda Lappan

James T. Fey

William M. Fitzgerald

Susan N. Friel

Elizabeth Difanis Phillips

PEARSON

Prentice
Hall

Boston, Massachusetts
Upper Saddle River, New Jersey

Connected Mathematics™ was developed at Michigan State University with financial support from the Michigan State University Office of the Provost, Computing and Technology, and the College of Natural Science.

This material is based upon work supported by the National Science Foundation under Grant No. MDR 9150217 and Grant No. ESI 9986372. Opinions expressed are those of the authors and not necessarily those of the Foundation.

The Michigan State University authors and administration have agreed that all MSU royalties arising from this publication will be devoted to purposes supported by the Department of Mathematics and the MSU Mathematics Enrichment Fund.

Acknowledgments appear on page 168, which constitutes an extension of this copyright page.

PEARSON

Prentice Hall

ISBN 0-13-165680-5

2 3 4 5 6 7 8 9 10   09 08 07 06

Authors of Connected Mathematics

(from left to right) Glenda Lappan, Betty Phillips, Susan Friel, Bill Fitzgerald, Jim Fey

Glenda Lappan is a University Distinguished Professor in the Department of Mathematics at Michigan State University. Her research and development interests are in the connected areas of students' learning of mathematics and mathematics teachers' professional growth and change related to the development and enactment of K–12 curriculum materials.

James T. Fey is a Professor of Curriculum and Instruction and Mathematics at the University of Maryland. His consistent professional interest has been development and research focused on curriculum materials that engage middle and high school students in problem-based collaborative investigations of mathematical ideas and their applications.

William M. Fitzgerald (*Deceased*) was a Professor in the Department of Mathematics at Michigan State University. His early research was on the use of concrete materials in supporting student learning and led to the development of teaching materials for laboratory environments. Later he helped develop a teaching model to support student experimentation with mathematics.

Susan N. Friel is a Professor of Mathematics Education in the School of Education at the University of North Carolina at Chapel Hill. Her research interests focus on statistics education for middle-grade students and, more broadly, on teachers' professional development and growth in teaching mathematics K–8.

Elizabeth Difanis Phillips is a Senior Academic Specialist in the Mathematics Department of Michigan State University. She is interested in teaching and learning mathematics for both teachers and students. These interests have led to curriculum and professional development projects at the middle school and high school levels, as well as projects related to the teaching and learning of algebra across the grades.

CMP2 Development Staff

Teacher Collaborator in Residence
Yvonne Grant
Michigan State University

Administrative Assistant
Judith Martus Miller
Michigan State University

Production and Field Site Manager
Lisa Keller
Michigan State University

Technical and Editorial Support
Brin Keller, Peter Lappan, Jim Laser,
Michael Masterson, Stacey Miceli

Assessment Team
June Bailey and Debra Sobko (Apollo Middle School, Rochester, New York), George Bright (University of North Carolina, Greensboro), Gwen Ranzau Campbell (Sunrise Park Middle School, White Bear Lake, Minnesota), Holly DeRosia, Kathy Dole, and Teri Keusch (Portland Middle School, Portland, Michigan), Mary Beth Schmitt (Traverse City East Junior High School, Traverse City, Michigan), Genni Steele (Central Middle School, White Bear Lake, Minnesota), Jacqueline Stewart (Okemos, Michigan), Elizabeth Tye (Magnolia Junior High School, Magnolia, Arkansas)

Development Assistants
At Lansing Community College *Undergraduate Assistant:* James Brinegar

At Michigan State University *Graduate Assistants:* Dawn Berk, Emily Bouck, Bulent Buyukbozkirli, Kuo-Liang Chang, Christopher Danielson, Srinivasa Dharmavaram, Deb Johanning, Kelly Rivette, Sarah Sword, Tat Ming Sze, Marie Turini, Jeffrey Wanko; *Undergraduate Assistants:* Daniel Briggs, Jeffrey Chapin, Jade Corsé, Elisha Hardy, Alisha Harold, Elizabeth Keusch, Julia Letoutchaia, Karen Loeffler, Brian Oliver, Carl Oliver, Evonne Pedawi, Lauren Rebrovich

At the University of Maryland *Graduate Assistants:* Kim Harris Bethea, Kara Karch

At the University of North Carolina (Chapel Hill) *Graduate Assistants:* Mark Ellis, Trista Stearns; *Undergraduate Assistant:* Daniel Smith

Advisory Board for CMP2

Thomas Banchoff
Professor of Mathematics
Brown University
Providence, Rhode Island

Anne Bartel
Mathematics Coordinator
Minneapolis Public Schools
Minneapolis, Minnesota

Hyman Bass
Professor of Mathematics
University of Michigan
Ann Arbor, Michigan

Joan Ferrini-Mundy
Associate Dean of the College of
Natural Science; Professor
Michigan State University
East Lansing, Michigan

James Hiebert
Professor
University of Delaware
Newark, Delaware

Susan Hudson Hull
Charles A. Dana Center
University of Texas
Austin, Texas

Michele Luke
Mathematics Curriculum
Coordinator
West Junior High
Minnetonka, Minnesota

Kay McClain
Assistant Professor of
Mathematics Education
Vanderbilt University
Nashville, Tennessee

Edward Silver
Professor; Chair of Educational
Studies
University of Michigan
Ann Arbor, Michigan

Judith Sowder
Professor Emerita
San Diego State University
San Diego, California

Lisa Usher
Mathematics Resource Teacher
California Academy of
Mathematics and Science
San Pedro, California

Field Test Sites for CMP2

During the development of the revised edition of *Connected Mathematics* (CMP2), more than 100 classroom teachers have field-tested materials at 49 school sites in 12 states and the District of Columbia. This classroom testing occurred over three academic years (2001 through 2004), allowing careful study of the effectiveness of each of the 24 units that comprise the program. A special thanks to the students and teachers at these pilot schools.

Arkansas
Magnolia Public Schools
Kittena Bell*, Judith Trowell*; *Central Elementary School:* Maxine Broom, Betty Eddy, Tiffany Fallin, Bonnie Flurry, Carolyn Monk, Elizabeth Tye; *Magnolia Junior High School:* Monique Bryan, Ginger Cook, David Graham, Shelby Lamkin

Colorado
Boulder Public Schools
Nevin Platt Middle School: Judith Koenig

St. Vrain Valley School District, Longmont
Westview Middle School: Colleen Beyer, Kitty Canupp, Ellie Decker*, Peggy McCarthy, Tanya deNobrega, Cindy Payne, Ericka Pilon, Andrew Roberts

District of Columbia
Capitol Hill Day School: Ann Lawrence

Georgia
University of Georgia, Athens
Brad Findell

Madison Public Schools
Morgan County Middle School: Renee Burgdorf, Lynn Harris, Nancy Kurtz, Carolyn Stewart

Maine
Falmouth Public Schools
Falmouth Middle School: Donna Erikson, Joyce Hebert, Paula Hodgkins, Rick Hogan, David Legere, Cynthia Martin, Barbara Stiles, Shawn Towle*

Michigan
Portland Public Schools
Portland Middle School: Mark Braun, Holly DeRosia, Kathy Dole*, Angie Foote, Teri Keusch, Tammi Wardwell

Traverse City Area Public Schools
Bertha Vos Elementary: Kristin Sak; *Central Grade School:* Michelle Clark; Jody Meyers; *Eastern Elementary:* Karrie Tufts; *Interlochen Elementary:* Mary McGee-Cullen; *Long Lake Elementary:* Julie Faulkner*, Charlie Maxbauer, Katherine Sleder; *Norris Elementary:* Hope Slanaker; *Oak Park Elementary:* Jessica Steed; *Traverse Heights Elementary:* Jennifer Wolfert; *Westwoods Elementary:* Nancy Conn; *Old Mission Peninsula School:* Deb Larimer; *Traverse City East Junior High:* Ivanka Berkshire, Ruthanne Kladder, Jan Palkowski, Jane Peterson, Mary Beth Schmitt; *Traverse City West Junior High:* Dan Fouch*, Ray Fouch

Sturgis Public Schools
Sturgis Middle School: Ellen Eisele

Minnesota
Burnsville School District 191
Hidden Valley Elementary: Stephanie Cin, Jane McDevitt

Hopkins School District 270
Alice Smith Elementary: Sandra Cowing, Kathleen Gustafson, Martha Mason, Scott Stillman; *Eisenhower Elementary:* Chad Bellig, Patrick Berger, Nancy Glades, Kye Johnson, Shane Wasserman, Victoria Wilson; *Gatewood Elementary:* Sarah Ham, Julie Kloos, Janine Pung, Larry Wade; *Glen Lake Elementary:* Jacqueline Cramer, Kathy Hering, Cecelia Morris, Robb Trenda; *Katherine Curren Elementary:* Diane Bancroft, Sue DeWit, John Wilson; *L. H. Tanglen Elementary:* Kevin Athmann, Lisa Becker, Mary LaBelle, Kathy Rezac, Roberta Severson; *Meadowbrook Elementary:* Jan Gauger, Hildy Shank, Jessica Zimmerman; *North Junior High:* Laurel Hahn, Kristin Lee, Jodi Markuson, Bruce Mestemacher, Laurel Miller, Bonnie Rinker, Jeannine Salzer, Sarah Shafer, Cam Stottler; *West Junior High:* Alicia Beebe, Kristie Earl, Nobu Fujii, Pam Georgetti, Susan Gilbert, Regina Nelson Johnson, Debra Lindstrom, Michele Luke*, Jon Sorensen

Minneapolis School District 1
Ann Sullivan K–8 School: Bronwyn Collins; Anne Bartel* (Curriculum and Instruction Office)

Wayzata School District 284
Central Middle School: Sarajane Myers, Dan Nielsen, Tanya Ravnholdt

White Bear Lake School District 624
Central Middle School: Amy Jorgenson, Michelle Reich, Brenda Sammon

New York
New York City Public Schools
IS 89: Yelena Aynbinder, Chi-Man Ng, Nina Rapaport, Joel Spengler, Phyllis Tam*, Brent Wyso; *Wagner Middle School:* Jason Appel, Intissar Fernandez, Yee Gee Get, Richard Goldstein, Irving Marcus, Sue Norton, Bernadita Owens, Jennifer Rehn*, Kevin Yuhas

* indicates a Field Test Site Coordinator

Ohio

Talawanda School District, Oxford
Talawanda Middle School: Teresa Abrams, Larry Brock, Heather Brosey, Julie Churchman, Monna Even, Karen Fitch, Bob George, Amanda Klee, Pat Meade, Sandy Montgomery, Barbara Sherman, Lauren Steidl

Miami University
Jeffrey Wanko*

Springfield Public Schools
Rockway School: Jim Mamer

Pennsylvania

Pittsburgh Public Schools
Kenneth Labuskes, Marianne O'Connor, Mary Lynn Raith*; *Arthur J. Rooney Middle School:* David Hairston, Stamatina Mousetis, Alfredo Zangaro; *Frick International Studies Academy:* Suzanne Berry, Janet Falkowski, Constance Finseth, Romika Hodge, Frank Machi; *Reizenstein Middle School:* Jeff Baldwin, James Brautigam, Lorena Burnett, Glen Cobbett, Michael Jordan, Margaret Lazur, Tamar McPherson, Melissa Munnell, Holly Neely, Ingrid Reed, Dennis Reft

Texas

Austin Independent School District
Bedichek Middle School: Lisa Brown, Jennifer Glasscock, Vicki Massey

El Paso Independent School District
Cordova Middle School: Armando Aguirre, Anneliesa Durkes, Sylvia Guzman, Pat Holguin*, William Holguin, Nancy Nava, Laura Orozco, Michelle Peña, Roberta Rosen, Patsy Smith, Jeremy Wolf

Plano Independent School District
Patt Henry, James Wohlgehagen*; *Frankford Middle School:* Mandy Baker, Cheryl Butsch, Amy Dudley, Betsy Eshelman, Janet Greene, Cort Haynes, Kathy Letchworth, Kay Marshall, Kelly McCants, Amy Reck, Judy Scott, Syndy Snyder, Lisa Wang; *Wilson Middle School:* Darcie Bane, Amanda Bedenko, Whitney Evans, Tonelli Hatley, Sarah (Becky) Higgs, Kelly Johnston, Rebecca McElligott, Kay Neuse, Cheri Slocum, Kelli Straight

Washington

Evergreen School District
Shahala Middle School: Nicole Abrahamsen, Terry Coon*, Carey Doyle, Sheryl Drechsler, George Gemma, Gina Helland, Amy Hilario, Darla Lidyard, Sean McCarthy, Tilly Meyer, Willow Nuewelt, Todd Parsons, Brian Pederson, Stan Posey, Shawn Scott, Craig Sjoberg, Lynette Sundstrom, Charles Switzer, Luke Youngblood

Wisconsin

Beaver Dam Unified School District
Beaver Dam Middle School: Jim Braemer, Jeanne Frick, Jessica Greatens, Barbara Link, Dennis McCormick, Karen Michels, Nancy Nichols*, Nancy Palm, Shelly Stelsel, Susan Wiggins

---

* indicates a Field Test Site Coordinator

Reviews of CMP to Guide Development of CMP2

Before writing for CMP2 began or field tests were conducted, the first edition of *Connected Mathematics* was submitted to the mathematics faculties of school districts from many parts of the country and to 80 individual reviewers for extensive comments.

School District Survey Reviews of CMP

Arizona
Madison School District #38 (Phoenix)

Arkansas
Cabot School District, Little Rock School District, Magnolia School District

California
Los Angeles Unified School District

Colorado
St. Vrain Valley School District (Longmont)

Florida
Leon County Schools (Tallahassee)

Illinois
School District #21 (Wheeling)

Indiana
Joseph L. Block Junior High (East Chicago)

Kentucky
Fayette County Public Schools (Lexington)

Maine
Selection of Schools

Massachusetts
Selection of Schools

Michigan
Sparta Area Schools

Minnesota
Hopkins School District

Texas
Austin Independent School District, The El Paso Collaborative for Academic Excellence, Plano Independent School District

Wisconsin
Platteville Middle School

Individual Reviewers of CMP

Arkansas
Deborah Cramer; Robby Frizzell *(Taylor)*; Lowell Lynde *(University of Arkansas, Monticello)*; Leigh Manzer *(Norfork)*; Lynne Roberts *(Emerson High School, Emerson)*; Tony Timms *(Cabot Public Schools)*; Judith Trowell *(Arkansas Department of Higher Education)*

California
José Alcantar *(Gilroy)*; Eugenie Belcher *(Gilroy)*; Marian Pasternack *(Lowman M. S. T. Center, North Hollywood)*; Susana Pezoa *(San Jose)*; Todd Rabusin *(Hollister)*; Margaret Siegfried *(Ocala Middle School, San Jose)*; Polly Underwood *(Ocala Middle School, San Jose)*

Colorado
Janeane Golliher *(St. Vrain Valley School District, Longmont)*; Judith Koenig *(Nevin Platt Middle School, Boulder)*

Florida
Paige Loggins *(Swift Creek Middle School, Tallahassee)*

Illinois
Jan Robinson *(School District #21, Wheeling)*

Indiana
Frances Jackson *(Joseph L. Block Junior High, East Chicago)*

Kentucky
Natalee Feese *(Fayette County Public Schools, Lexington)*

Maine
Betsy Berry *(Maine Math & Science Alliance, Augusta)*

Maryland
Joseph Gagnon *(University of Maryland, College Park)*; Paula Maccini *(University of Maryland, College Park)*

Massachusetts
George Cobb *(Mt. Holyoke College, South Hadley)*; Cliff Kanold *(University of Massachusetts, Amherst)*

Michigan
Mary Bouck *(Farwell Area Schools)*; Carol Dorer *(Slauson Middle School, Ann Arbor)*; Carrie Heaney *(Forsythe Middle School, Ann Arbor)*; Ellen Hopkins *(Clague Middle School, Ann Arbor)*; Teri Keusch *(Portland Middle School, Portland)*; Valerie Mills *(Oakland Schools, Waterford)*; Mary Beth Schmitt *(Traverse City East Junior High, Traverse City)*; Jack Smith *(Michigan State University, East Lansing)*; Rebecca Spencer *(Sparta Middle School, Sparta)*; Ann Marie Nicoll Turner *(Tappan Middle School, Ann Arbor)*; Scott Turner *(Scarlett Middle School, Ann Arbor)*

Minnesota
Margarita Alvarez *(Olson Middle School, Minneapolis)*; Jane Amundson *(Nicollet Junior High, Burnsville)*; Anne Bartel *(Minneapolis Public Schools)*; Gwen Ranzau Campbell *(Sunrise Park Middle School, White Bear Lake)*; Stephanie Cin *(Hidden Valley Elementary, Burnsville)*; Joan Garfield *(University of Minnesota, Minneapolis)*; Gretchen Hall *(Richfield Middle School, Richfield)*; Jennifer Larson *(Olson Middle School, Minneapolis)*; Michele Luke *(West Junior High, Minnetonka)*; Jeni Meyer *(Richfield Junior High, Richfield)*; Judy Pfingsten *(Inver Grove Heights Middle School, Inver Grove Heights)*; Sarah Shafer *(North Junior High, Minnetonka)*; Genni Steele *(Central Middle School, White Bear Lake)*; Victoria Wilson *(Eisenhower Elementary, Hopkins)*; Paul Zorn *(St. Olaf College, Northfield)*

New York
Debra Altenau-Bartolino *(Greenwich Village Middle School, New York)*; Doug Clements *(University of Buffalo)*; Francis Curcio *(New York University, New York)*; Christine Dorosh *(Clinton School for Writers, Brooklyn)*; Jennifer Rehn *(East Side Middle School, New York)*; Phyllis Tam *(IS 89 Lab School, New York)*; Marie Turini *(Louis Armstrong Middle School, New York)*; Lucy West *(Community School District 2, New York)*; Monica Witt *(Simon Baruch Intermediate School 104, New York)*

Pennsylvania
Robert Aglietti *(Pittsburgh)*; Sharon Mihalich *(Freeport)*; Jennifer Plumb *(South Hills Middle School, Pittsburgh)*; Mary Lynn Raith *(Pittsburgh Public Schools)*

Texas
Michelle Bittick *(Austin Independent School District)*; Margaret Cregg *(Plano Independent School District)*; Sheila Cunningham *(Klein Independent School District)*; Judy Hill *(Austin Independent School District)*; Patricia Holguin *(El Paso Independent School District)*; Bonnie McNemar *(Arlington)*; Kay Neuse *(Plano Independent School District)*; Joyce Polanco *(Austin Independent School District)*; Marge Ramirez *(University of Texas at El Paso)*; Pat Rossman *(Baker Campus, Austin)*; Cindy Schimek *(Houston)*; Cynthia Schneider *(Charles A. Dana Center, University of Texas at Austin)*; Uri Treisman *(Charles A. Dana Center, University of Texas at Austin)*; Jacqueline Weilmuenster *(Grapevine-Colleyville Independent School District)*; LuAnn Weynand *(San Antonio)*; Carmen Whitman *(Austin Independent School District)*; James Wohlgehagen *(Plano Independent School District)*

Washington
Ramesh Gangolli *(University of Washington, Seattle)*

Wisconsin
Susan Lamon *(Marquette University, Hales Corner)*; Steve Reinhart *(retired, Chippewa Falls Middle School, Eau Claire)*

Table of Contents

Frogs, Fleas, and Painted Cubes

Frogs, Fleas, and Painted Cubes
Quadratic Relationships

Goals of the Unit

- Recognize the patterns of change for quadratic relationships

- Write equations for quadratic relationships represented in tables, graphs and problem situations

- Connect quadratic equations to the patterns in tables and graphs of quadratic relationships

- Use a quadratic equation to identify the maximum or minimum value, the x- and y-intercepts, and other important features of the graph of the equation

- Recognize equivalent quadratic expressions

- Use the Distributive Property to write equivalent quadratic expressions in factored and expanded form

- Use tables, graphs, and equations of quadratic relationships to solve problems in a variety of situations from geometry, science, and business

- Compare properties of quadratic, linear, and exponential relationships

Developing Students' Mathematical Habits

As students work on the problems in this unit, they learn to ask themselves questions about problem situations that involve non-linear relationships:

- *What are the variables?*

- *How can I recognize whether the relationship between the variables is quadratic?*

- *What equation models a quadratic relationship in the table, graph, or problem context?*

- *How can I answer questions about the situation by studying a table, graph, or equation of the quadratic relationship?*

Overview

The fundamental goal of the *Connected Mathematics* algebra units is to develop students' abilities to describe and analyze relationships between variables. This goal encompasses gaining an understanding of and skill in using tabular (tables), graphic (graphs), and symbolic (equations) modes of representing and reasoning about such relationships. It also includes developing familiarity with several of the most common patterns of variation.

In the grade 7 units *Variables and Patterns* and *Moving Straight Ahead,* students were introduced to basic concepts and representations of algebra, focusing on linear functions. In the grade 8 unit *Thinking with Mathematical Models*, they revisited linear models (as in the bridge-thickness experiment) and investigated several examples of inverse variation (as in the bridge-length experiment and distance-rate-time problems). In *Growing, Growing, Growing*, students explored exponential models. In *Frogs, Fleas, and Painted Cubes*, the focus switches to a nonlinear polynomial relationship—the second-degree polynomial, or the quadratic function. By investigating a variety of problem situations, students learn about the characteristics of quadratic relationships, as represented in tables, graphs, and equations.

The relationships in this unit are all functions. Through their work with these relationships, students continue to develop an intuitive understanding of the term *function*. For example, the height of a jumping frog or flea is a function of, or depends on, the amount of time the jumper has been in the air. The area of a rectangle with a fixed perimeter is a function of, or depends on, its side length. The number of painted faces on the small cubes that comprise a larger cube is a function of, or depends on, the edge length of the large cube. Some examples of cubic functions, or third-degree polynomials, are included for comparison and contrast.

Each of the three types of representations of quadratic functions—graphs, tables, and equations—gives important information about the situation being modeled. Students look for commonalities and differences among the three representations, and use them to answer questions.

Questions related to the graphs of quadratic relationships emphasize their shape (parabolas), the location and interpretation of intercepts and lines of symmetry, and the presence and location of maximum or minimum points.

Questions related to tables of quadratic relationships focus on patterns in the rate of change in y-value as the x-value increases (or decreases), and contrast those patterns with the constant rate of change that characterizes linear functions. Patterns in tables can also reveal to students the locations of intercepts and maximum or minimum points.

Questions about equations of quadratic relationships focus on connecting the symbolic form to tabular and graphic forms, and determining significant intercepts. The problems in the unit lead to both the factored and expanded forms of quadratic equations. Through their work, students will discover the equivalence of the two forms and learn that each is convenient for gathering different types of information. While there is some simple symbol manipulation of quadratic expressions, students are not expected to master the traditional symbol manipulation procedures associated with a traditional polynomial algebra course. In the next two algebra units, students will have additional opportunities to determine and use factored and expanded forms of quadratic equations and to solve quadratic equations by factoring the symbolic form of the equation. In this unit, they use graphs and tables to solve quadratic equations by finding the x-intercepts.

Summary of Investigations

Investigation 1

Introduction to Quadratic Relationships

Students look at the area of rectangles with a fixed perimeter to discover that within the family of rectangles with a fixed perimeter, a square has the greatest (maximum) area. Using tables and graphs to represent the data, they learn to recognize the shape of a quadratic function (a parabola), connect the shape to patterns in the table, and describe special features of the quadratic relationship, such as intercepts and maximum points. Students write an equation for the relationship between the area and length of rectangles with a fixed perimeter, P. The relationship is a quadratic function of the length, ℓ, or width, w.

$$A = \ell\left(\frac{P}{2} - \ell\right) \text{ or } A = w\left(\frac{P}{2} - w\right)$$

Investigation 2
Quadratic Expressions

Students investigate how increasing one dimension of a square (with sides of length n) by 2 and decreasing the other dimension by 2 affects the area. The area of the rectangle is $(n + 2)(n - 2)$. Students discover that the area of the square is always 4 units greater than the area of the rectangle, so the area of the rectangle is $n^2 - 4$. Students explore a visual representation of the Distributive Property. They discover that they can represent quadratic relationships as the product of two linear expressions, called *factored form*, or as the sum of one or more terms, called *expanded form*. For example, if one dimension of a square of length n is increased by 2 and the other dimension is increased by 3, then the area of the rectangle can be written as $(n + 2)(n + 3)$ or as $n^2 + 5n + 6$. Students use the Distributive Property to write quadratic expressions in equivalent forms from expanded form to factored form and from factored form to expanded form. Students make connections among tables, graphs, and equations to learn which form of a quadratic equation provides specific information about the relationship.

Investigation 3
Quadratic Patterns of Change

Students investigate quadratic relationships in sequences of triangular, square, and rectangular numbers. They discover that the model for the number of handshakes is the same as for other problems, including triangular numbers. Students consider variations on the handshake problem, exploring questions such as: when two athletic teams each with n members line up to shake hands after a game, how many handshakes take place? How many handshakes take place among teams with different numbers of players? What if members of a single n-member team exchange "high fives" after a win? By comparing and analyzing patterns in tables, graphs, and equations, they express these quadratic relationships with equivalent expressions and predict whether variations in the handshake problem are quadratic.

Investigation 4
What Is a Quadratic Function?

This investigation uses the classic projectile motion problems to extend students' understanding of quadratic polynomials and their graphs. Students find significant intercepts, and maximum or minimum points, from quadratic relationships given in standard form. Investigating patterns of change in quadratic equations more closely, students discover that differences between consecutive y values, called *first differences*, are constant for linear relationships, and that *second differences* are constant for quadratic relationships. They also discover that in cubic relationships, *third differences* are constant.

Mathematics Background

The word "quadratic" can be misleading, because it seems to imply a connection to the number four. The prefix *quad* relates to the classic problem of trying to find a square with the same area as a given circle. This is known as finding the *quadrature* of the circle. So the name refers to finding the area, x^2, of a square with a side length of x.

Representing Quadratic Functions with Equations

Quadratic relationships are defined as relationships of the form $y = ax^2 + bx + c$, in which a, b, and c are constants and $a \neq 0$. This form of the equation is called *expanded form*. This definition emphasizes that the independent variable is raised to the second power. While this is a useful definition, it is also important to understand the *factored form* of quadratic equations.

Quadratic functions arise from situations with an underlying multiplicative relationship, such as the area of rectangles. So quadratic relationships can also be defined as functions whose y-value is the product of two linear factors—the form

$y = (ax + c)(bx + d)$, where $a \neq 0$ and $b \neq 0$. The power of this form is that it connects polynomials to products of linear factors. For example, you can also represent $y = 2x^2 + 3x - 2$ as $y = (2x - 1)(x + 2)$. The factored form can help you determine x-intercepts and the location of the maximum and minimum points.

The first context students explore is finding the maximum area for a rectangle with a fixed perimeter. This situation allows students to look at characteristic patterns of change for quadratic functions in a table, graph, and equation.

If the perimeter of a rectangle is 20 meters, then the area A of the rectangle can be represented as $A = \ell w$, where ℓ is the length and w is the width. Since $2(\ell + w) = 20$ or $\ell + w = 10$, w can be written as $(10 - \ell)$ and the area can be written in terms of one of its dimensions, $A = \ell(10 - \ell)$.

Examining the table, graph, and equation for this relationship provides an introduction to quadratic functions.

Areas of Rectangles With Perimeter 20 Meters

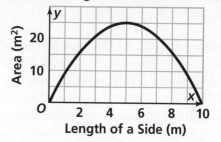

This situation provides an opportunity to explore the pattern of change in the table and how it relates to the graph and equation. As length increases by 1, area increases to a certain point, and then at a fixed point (maximum), area starts to decrease. The maximum area occurs halfway between the x-intercepts [$(0, 0)$ and $(10, 0)$], at the point $(5, 25)$, on the line of symmetry. The line of symmetry is a vertical line through the maximum point; it divides the graph into two congruent parts. So the shape of the rectangle with a maximum area of 25 square units is a square with side lengths of 5 meters.

Representing Quadratic Patterns of Change with Tables

In this unit, students often make tables to represent quadratic equations. Patterns of change in quadratic relationships are most readily observed in tables.

In linear relationships, as the x-values increase by one in the *"first" differences*—the difference between consecutive y-values—are constant, indicating a constant rate of change. In quadratic relationships, "second" differences—the differences between successive first differences—are constant. (Figure 1)

First differences represent the rate at which y is changing with respect to x. That is, the first difference gives the change in y-values between x and $x + 1$. Second difference indicates the rate at which the first difference is changing. If all of

Rectangles With Perimeters of 20 m

Length of Base	Width	Area
0	10	0
1	9	9
2	8	16
3	7	21
4	6	24
5	5	25
6	4	24
7	3	21
8	2	16
9	1	9
10	0	0

Figure 1

$y = 6(x - 2)^2$

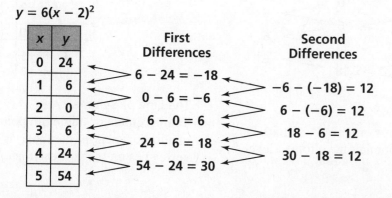

the second differences are the same, then the relationship is quadratic.

Connecting Patterns of Change to Calculus

Finding successive differences of polynomials relates to derivatives in calculus. The first derivative, y', of $y = ax^2 + bx + c$ is $y' = 2ax + b$, which means that this rate is still dependent on x and changes with x. The second derivative is $2a$, which is no longer dependent on x but is constant. For linear functions, the first derivative is a constant.

The following argument shows why the second difference for quadratic relationships is $2a$.

For quadratic equations of the form $y = ax^2 + bx + c$, the second difference between two successive values of y is constant and it is equal to $2a$. This can be seen by picking three successive values for x.

x	$ax^2 + bx + c$	first difference	second difference
0	c		
		$a + b$	
1	$a + b + c$		$2a$
		$3a + b$	
2	$4a + 2b + c$		

Note this argument will work for any three consecutive values of x.

One way students can detect whether a pattern is quadratic is by calculating second differences.

Extending Patterns of Change to Cubic Functions or Polynomial Functions

In cubic functions, such as $y = (x - 2)^3$, students make another interesting discovery—third differences are constant. This is a characteristic of cubic relationships, also called third-degree polynomials.

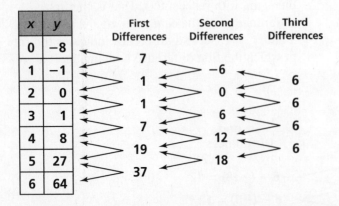

x	y	First Differences	Second Differences	Third Differences
0	−8			
		7		
1	−1		−6	
		1		6
2	0		0	
		1		6
3	1		6	
		7		6
4	8		12	
		19		6
5	27		18	
		37		
6	64			

Similar relationships hold for other polynomials. For example, fourth-degree polynomials have fourth-level

differences constant, and so on. Polynomial rela[...] with different degrees all have characteristic gra[...] tabular patterns.

Representing Quadratic Patterns of Chang[...] with Graphs

The values of a, b, and c in the general equation $y = ax^2 + bx + c$ affect the shape, orientation location of the graph of a quadratic function, a [...]

Maximum/Minimum Points

If the parameter a (the coefficient of the x^2 term quadratic is positive, the curve opens upward an minimum point, as shown below.

$$y = x^2 - x + 6$$

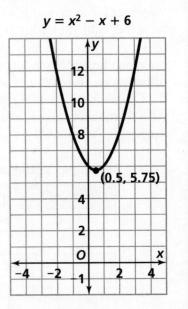

$(0.5, 5.75)$

If a is negative, the curve opens downward a maximum point, as shown below.

$$y = -x^2 - x + 6$$

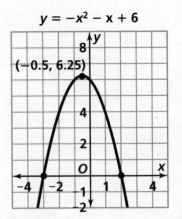

$(-0.5, 6.25)$

The Line of Symmetry

The maximum or minimum point of the graph [...] quadratic function (parabola) is called the *verte[...]* vertex lies on the vertical *line of symmetry* tha[...]

the parabola into halves that are mirror images. The vertex is located halfway between the *x-intercepts*, if the *x*-intercepts exist. The *y-intercept* is the point where the parabola crosses the *y*-axis.

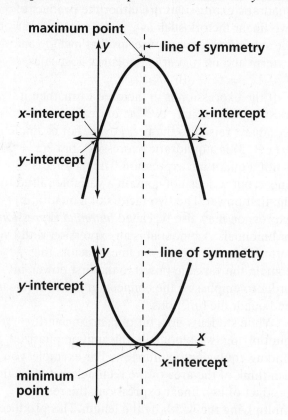

To find the maximum or minimum points and the intercepts of a parabola, students can make a table of values or trace the parabola on their calculators. More sophisticated methods for locating these features are outlined later. It is important for students to understand that a quadratic relationship is the result of multiplying two linear factors—factors in which the variable is raised to the first power.

Note: In this unit, when writing a quadratic expression in factored form is called for, the quadratic expression is factorable over rational numbers. However, not all quadratic expressions are factorable over rational numbers. For example, $-x^2 - x + 6$ *can* be written as a product of linear factors with rational coefficients $(-x + 2)(x + 3)$ while $x^2 - x + 6$ can *not*. In future algebra classes students learn other strategies for working with quadratic expressions such as these which are factorable over real numbers. The real numbers are the union of rational and imaginary numbers.

x-Intercepts

One way to find the *x*-intercepts is to set *y* equal to 0 and solve for *x*. For example, to find the *x*-intercepts of the equation $y = -x^2 - x + 6$, set *y* equal to 0 and solve for *x*.
$$0 = -x^2 - x + 6$$
$$0 = x^2 + x - 6$$
$$0 = (x + 3)(x - 2)$$
Note that the expression is now in factored form. $x = -3$ or 2 are both solutions of this equation. So the *x*-intercepts are the points $(-3, 0)$ and $(2, 0)$. The vertex, which is a maximum point in this case, is be located halfway between the *x*-values at -0.5. To find the *y*-value of the vertex, substitute -0.5 for *x* in the equation and solve for *y*.
$$y = -(-0.5)^2 - (-0.5) + 6 = 6.25$$
The maximum point is $(-0.5, 6.25)$. The equation of the line of symmetry is $x = -0.5$.
Here is a graph of the equation:

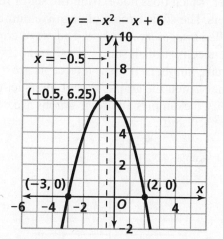

Most of the time it is not possible to factor a quadratic equation. You can also solve quadratic equations by applying the *quadratic formula*.

The quadratic formula is:
$$x = \frac{-b \pm \sqrt{(b^2 - 4ac)}}{2a}$$

For example, applying the quadratic formula to the equation $y = -2x^2 + 3x + 4$ gives the following:
$$0 = -2x^2 + 3x + 4$$
$$x = \frac{-3 \pm \sqrt{(9 - 4(-2)(4))}}{2(-2)}$$
$$x = -0.85 \text{ or } 2.35.$$

In general, the x-intercepts are located at $(\frac{-b + \sqrt{(b^2 - 4ac)}}{2a}, 0)$ and $(\frac{-b - \sqrt{(b^2 - 4ac)}}{2a}, 0)$. The x value of the vertex lies halfway between these x values at $\frac{-b}{2a}$. This can be substituted into the original equation to determine the corresponding y value.

In this unit, students do not need to know how to use the quadratic formula. They can use a table or trace a graph on the calculator to read the maximum, and the intercepts.

The expression under the radical sign, $b^2 - 4ac$, is called the **discriminant**. Many times the discriminant is an irrational number such as $\sqrt{2}$. In this case, the quadratic expression is not factorable. If the discriminant is negative, then the situation yields the square root of a negative number, which does not exist in the set of real numbers. The square roots of negative numbers are called *imaginary numbers*. The set of *complex numbers* consist of all sums of real numbers and imaginary numbers. If the x-intercepts are imaginary, then the graphs do not intersect the x-axis. Two examples and their graphs are $y_1 = x^2 + 1$ and $y_2 = -x^2 - 1$.

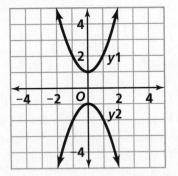

This unit includes only quadratic expressions that can be easily factored, so that students can develop an understanding of equivalent forms for a quadratic expression and the information that each expression offers.

The Distributive Property and Equivalent Quadratic Expressions

Students explore quadratic equations in both factored form and expanded form. They learn that quadratic expressions are either the product of two linear factors, such as $y = (x + 1)(x - 1)$, or the sum or difference of terms that include an x^2 term and no higher exponent of x, such as $y = 2x^2 + 6x - 10$.

If the expression is in factored form, then it must contain exactly two factors, each with the variable x raised to the first power. For example, $2x(x + 3)$ is a quadratic expression, but $2(x + 3)$ is not a quadratic expression. The factor 2 is linear, but it does not contain a variable raised to the first power. The two factors of a quadratic expression may also be called *binomial expressions* or binomials. A binomial is an expression with two terms. This unit focuses on linear factors that contain the variable raised to the first power, in order to emphasize the connection between linear and quadratic functions.

While students do a bit of factoring and multiplying two binomials, this unit emphasizes finding equivalent expressions. For example, you can think of the area of the rectangle below as the product of two linear expressions, the result of multiplying the width by the length. This produces the *factored form* of a quadratic expression. You can also think of the area as the sum of the areas of the subparts of the rectangle. This generates the *expanded form* of a quadratic expression.

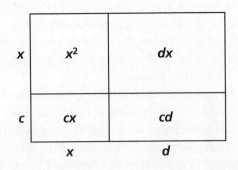

$A = (x + c)(x + d)$ factored form
$A = x^2 + cx + dx + cd$ expanded form

In *Say It With Symbols*, students address multiplying binomials and factoring quadratic expressions in greater detail.

A Note on Terminology

To introduce quadratic expressions, this unit uses the term *expanded form* instead of *standard form* to help students remember that expanded form represents the sum of the areas of the smaller rectangles that compose the large rectangle. Also, the word *standard* implies a preferred form. Students should be able to build on prior learning by identifying factored and expanded forms as examples of the distributive property, as discussed in earlier units: *Accentuate the Negative, Moving Straight Ahead,* and *Thinking with Mathematical Models.*

This unit also briefly exposes students to cubic equations, which are either the product of three linear factors, such as $y = (x - 2)(x - 2)(x - 2)$, or a sum or difference of terms that include an x^3 term and no higher exponent of x, such as $y = x^3 - 6x^2 + 12x - 8$.

Other Contexts for Quadratic Functions

Counting Handshakes

The classic handshake problem and variations on it offer an interesting context for students to explore quadratic functions.

When a team of n members exchanges high fives at the end of a game, how many high fives take place?

Students can draw diagrams, look for patterns in tables, or use reasoning, as follows:

- Each person high fives with $(n - 1)$ people, so there are $n(n - 1)$ high fives. But this counts each high five twice, so we must divide by two. The number of high fives, h, is $h = \frac{n(n - 1)}{2}$.
- The first person high fives $n - 1$ people; the second person high fives $n - 2$ people, the third person high fives $n - 3$ people, and so on. The total number of high fives, h, is $h = 1 + 2 + 3 + \ldots + n - 1$.

Sum of the First *n* Counting Numbers

If both examples of reasoning above are valid, then we can claim that $1 + 2 + 3 + \ldots + n - 1 = \frac{n(n - 1)}{2}$. This gives a formula for finding the sum of the first $n - 1$ counting numbers. If we add n to both sides, we

have a formula for finding the sum of the first n counting numbers:
$$1 + 2 + 3 + \ldots + n - 1 + n$$
$$= \frac{n(n - 1)}{2} + n = \frac{n(n + 1)}{2}.$$

In the ACE for Investigation 3, there is a Did You Know? feature about Carl Gauss, a famous mathematician who discovered this formula when he was a young student. Gauss' method works for any arithmetic sequence. An *arithmetic sequence* is a sequence of numbers in which the difference between any two consecutive terms is constant. Below is a generalization of his method, which works for any arithmetic sequence.

Generalization of Gauss's Method

The sequence of counting numbers,
$1, 2, 3, 4, 5, 6, \ldots$
is an arithmetic sequence (the difference is 1); so is the sequence $60, 65, 70, 75, 80, 85, \ldots$ (the difference is 5). Notice that the sequence does not have to start with 1.

For example, here's how to find the sum of the odd whole numbers from 5 to 13:

$$5 + 7 + 9 + 11 + 13 = \frac{5}{2} \times (5 + 13) = 45$$

Another way to express the sum is $\frac{n}{2}$(first + last), where n is the number of terms being added, "first" is the first number in the sequence, and "last" is the last number in the sequence.

Triangular Numbers

Triangular numbers are numbers that can be represented by a triangular array of dots:

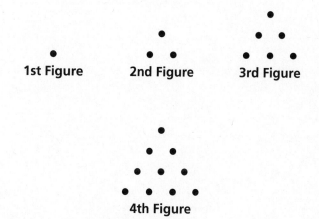

1st Figure　　**2nd Figure**　　**3rd Figure**

4th Figure

You can think of each figure as the sum of the first n whole numbers. For example, in the

3rd Figure, the number of dots is $1 + 2 + 3$ or 6. In the 4th Figure the number of dots is $1 + 2 + 3 + 4$ or 10. The sequence $1, 3, 6, 10, 15, 21, \ldots$ represents triangular numbers. The equation for the nth triangular number, is $T_n = \dfrac{n(n + 1)}{2}$. It is similar to the equation for the number of high fives for a team of n members. The number of high fives for n people is actually the $(n - 1\text{th})$ triangular number.

It is interesting for students to observe that the equation $y = \dfrac{n(n - 1)}{2}$ could represent the number of high fives, y, that are exchanged among n people; or the $(n - 1\text{th})$ triangular number; or the sum of the first $(n - 1)$ counting numbers.

The first few contexts in Investigations 1−3 can be represented by equations of the form $y = x(x + a)$ or $y = x(a - x)$. In Investigation 4, students explore classic projectile problems that are represented by $y = ax^2 + bx + c$.

Equations Modeling Projectile Motion

Equations such as $h = -16t^2 + 64t + 6$ model one-dimensional projectile motion. They are based on the principles of mechanics. These equations assume that motion occurs in a vacuum, but you can make reasonably accurate predictions about the motion for modest speeds in normal air. The general form is $h = -16t^2 + v_0t + h_0$, in which the coefficient -16 is determined by the Earth's gravitational pull on the flying body; v_0 is the initial velocity of the projectile, and h_0 is the initial height of the projectile.

In the problems involving basketball players, fleas, and frogs jumping, students may bring up the topic of the speed at which the jumpers jump. Speed is associated with change in distance—in this case, a change in height. The jumper's speed decreases en route to the maximum height and increases on the return trip to the ground. The change in speed is reflected in the tables by the increasingly smaller change in y-value as the x-value increases, until the maximum y-value is reached. At the top of the jump, the speed is 0 for an instant. After the maximum height is attained, y-values decrease by increasing increments, reflecting the change in speed as the jumper returns to the ground.

Patterns of change is a unifying theme for looking at linear, exponential, and quadratic functions in *Connected Mathematics*. As with linear and exponential relationships, students explore the patterns of change that characterize quadratic relationships and learn to recognize these patterns of change in tabular, graphical, or symbolic representations.

Content Connections to Other Units

Big Idea	Prior Work	Future Work
Analyzing quadratic relationships by examining patterns of change in table, graph, and symbolic representations	Analyzing linear and exponential relationships among quantitative variables *(Variables and Patterns, Moving Straight Ahead, Thinking With Mathematical Models,* and *Growing, Growing, Growing)*	Reviewing and extending the analysis of quadratic relationships, with more emphasis on symbolic methods *(high school)*
Comparing characteristics of table and graph for quadratic relationships with tables and graphs for linear and exponential relationships; using these characteristics to predict next entries	Comparing pattern of change in tables and graphs for linear and exponential relationships *(Moving Straight Ahead, Thinking With Mathematical Models* and *Growing, Growing, Growing)*	Extending the analysis of patterns of change to other polynomial and trigonometric functions *(high school)*
Understanding the significance of *x*- and *y*-intercepts, maximum, minimum, and symmetry of a graph	Understanding the significance of *x*- and *y*-intercepts of a linear function *(Moving Straight Ahead and Thinking With Mathematical Models);* understanding the significance of *y*-intercept in exponential functions *(Growing, Growing, Growing)*	Understanding the significance of zeroes in solving equations and of maximum and minimum in applications; using symbolic methods for finding zeroes, maximum, minimum; and applying the quadratic formula *(high school)*
Understanding, writing, and interpreting equivalent quadratic expressions	Recognizing equivalent forms of rational numbers *(Bits and Pieces I, Bits and Pieces II, Accentuate the Negative)*	Using Distributive Property (and other rearrangement properties) to write equivalent forms of symbolic expressions *(Say It With Symbols, The Shapes of Algebra,* and high school)
Attaching contextual meaning to equations	Attaching contextual meaning to *m* and *b* in linear relationships $y = mx + b$, and to *a* and *b* in exponential relationships, $y = a(b)^x$ *(Moving Straight Ahead, Thinking With Mathematical Models,* and *Growing, Growing, Growing)*	Attaching contextual meaning to **different forms** of linear and quadratic relationships *(Say It With Symbols);* extending symbol sense about quadratics to include meaning and use of quadratic formula, formula for vertex; attaching contextual meaning to different symbolic forms of polynomial and trigonometric functions *(high school)*
Informally recognizing that altering the domain and range, or scale, potentially alters the shape or view of the resulting graph	Understanding the significance of scale in constructing and interpreting graphs from data *(Data About Us, Data Around Us 2004, Moving Straight Ahead, Thinking With Mathematical Models,* and *Growing, Growing, Growing)*	Exploring issues of practical and theoretical domain and range, formally treated *(high school)*

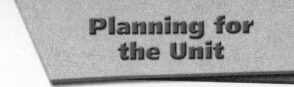

Pacing Suggestions and Materials

Investigations and Assessments	Pacing 45–50 min. classes	Materials for Students	Materials for Teachers
1 Introduction to Quadratic Relationships	3 days	Grid paper (1 per student), 20-cm length string (optional, 1 per group), square tiles (optional, 50 per group), poster paper (optional)	Transparent grid paper, overhead graphing calculator, Transparencies 1.2A-D, 1.3
Mathematical Reflections	$\frac{1}{2}$ day		
Assessment: Check Up 1	$\frac{1}{2}$ day		
2 Quadratic Expressions	7 days	poster paper (optional), Labsheet 2.5	Transparent grid paper, overhead graphing calculator, Transparencies 2.1A, 2.1B, 2.2, 2.3A, 2.3B, 2.5A, 2.5B
Mathematical Reflections	$\frac{1}{2}$ day		
Assessment: Check Up 2	$\frac{1}{2}$ day		
3 Quadratic Patterns of Change	3 days	Labsheet 3.3, poster paper (optional)	Overhead graphing calculator (optional), Transparency 3.1
Mathematical Reflections	$\frac{1}{2}$ day		
Assessment: Partner Quiz	1 day		
4 What Is a Quadratic Function?	4 days	Labsheets 4.3A and B, base ten thousands blocks (optional, 1 per group), centimeter or other unit cubes poster paper (optioinal)	Overhead graphing calculator (optional), motion detector, ball and stopwatch (optional), Rubik's cube, base ten thousands block, or other large cube (optional), Transparencies 4.1, 4.2A, 4.2B, 4.3, 4.4
Looking Back and Looking Ahead	$\frac{1}{2}$ day		
Mathematical Reflections	$\frac{1}{2}$ day		
Assessment: Self Assessment	Take Home		
Assessment: Unit Test	1 day		

Total Time	**$22\frac{1}{2}$ days**	**Materials for Use in All Investigations**	
For detailed pacing for Problems within each Investigation, see the Suggested Pacing at the beginning of each Investigation.

For pacing with block scheduling, see next page. | | Graphing calculators, blank transparencies and transparency markers (optional), student notebooks | Blank transparencies and transparency markers (optional) |

Pacing for Block Scheduling (90-minute class periods)

Investigation	Suggested Pacing	Investigation	Suggested Pacing	Investigation	Suggested Pacing
Investigation 1	**2 days**	**Investigation 3**	**2 days**	**Investigation 4**	$2\frac{1}{2}$ **days**
Problem 1.1	$\frac{1}{2}$ day	Problem 3.1	$\frac{1}{2}$ day	Problem 4.1	$\frac{1}{2}$ day
Problem 1.2	$\frac{1}{2}$ day	Problem 3.2	$\frac{1}{2}$ day	Problem 4.2	$\frac{1}{2}$ day
Problem 1.3	$\frac{1}{2}$ day	Problem 3.3	$\frac{1}{2}$ day	Problem 4.3	$\frac{1}{2}$ day
Math Reflections	$\frac{1}{2}$ day	Math Reflections	$\frac{1}{2}$ day	Problem 4.4	$\frac{1}{2}$ day
Investigation 2	**3 days**			Math Reflections	$\frac{1}{2}$ day
Problem 2.1	$\frac{1}{2}$ day				
Problem 2.2	$\frac{1}{2}$ day				
Problem 2.3	$\frac{1}{2}$ day				
Problem 2.4	$\frac{1}{2}$ day				
Problem 2.5	$\frac{1}{2}$ day				
Math Reflections	$\frac{1}{2}$ day				

Vocabulary

Essential Terms Developed in This Unit		Useful Terms Referenced in This Unit	Terms Developed in Previous Units
Constant term	Term	Equation	Cubic relationships
Expanded form	Triangular numbers	Exponential relationship	Distributive Property
Factored form		Like terms	First differences
Function		Linear relationship	Second differences
Line of symmetry		Linear term	Third differences
Maximum value		Relationship	
Minimum value		Quadratic term	
Parabola			
Quadratic expressions			

Components

Use the chart below to quickly see which components are available for each Investigation.

Investigation	Labsheets	Additional Practice	Transparencies		Formal Assessment		Assessment Options	
			Problem	Summary	Check Up	Partner Quiz	Multiple-Choice	Question Bank
1		✔	1.2A–D, 1.3		✔		✔	✔
2	2.5	✔	2.1A, 2.1B, 2.2, 2.3A, 2.3B, 2.5A, 2.5B		✔		✔	✔
3	3.3	✔	3.1			✔	✔	✔
4	4.3A, 4.3B	✔	4.1, 4.2A, 4.2B, 4.3, 4.4				✔	
For the Unit		*ExamView* CD-ROM, Web site	LBLA		Unit Test, Notebook Check, Self Assessment		Multiple-Choice, Question Bank, *ExamView* CD-ROM	

Also Available For Use With This Unit

- Parent Guide: take-home letter for the unit
- Implementing CMP
- Spanish Assessment Resources
- Additional online and technology resources

Technology

The Use of Calculators

The graphing calculator is used throughout the unit. Its purpose is to provide students with a useful method for finding information about a situation by examining its graph. In addition, the graphing calculator allows students to look at a lot of examples quickly. This helps students to observe patterns and make conjectures about relations. **Note:** The instructions below may not match the particular calculator your students are using.

Graphing Quadratic Equations

Graphing calculators can be used to investigate quadratic relations in much the same way they are used to study linear or exponential relations. The starting point is usually to enter the rule for the relation in the $Y =$ menu. Then use the table set

menu to determine a starting point and increment for the generation of an (x, y) table and the table command to actually produce the table.

To make a suitable graph for any quadratic, set the window boundaries so that you get a full view of the quadratic shape (and adjust if needed after a first look). Pressing the $\boxed{\text{GRAPH}}$ key will produce a graph that can be traced to read off coordinates of interesting points like intercepts or maximum or minimum points. The viewing window can be magnified around a specific location.

It is important to note that restricting the window to show only values that make sense in a given situation is sometimes useful but can be deceiving. Viewed only in the first quadrant, for example, a parabola that opens upward can seem to be a simple increasing curve. It is often necessary to adjust the window settings to make the characteristic shape apparent. For example, both of the following screens display a graph of the equation $y = 0.5x^2 + 0.2$.

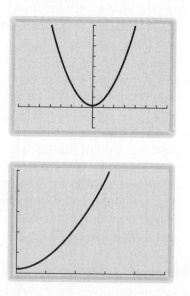

As another example, consider the following situation: When one or more of the parameters a, b, or c is held constant while the others are varied, the result is a family of related curves. For example, keeping a constant (the quadratic term constant) in each of the following, we obtain the graphs on the right:

$y = 2x^2 + 3x + 4$
$y = 2x^2 - x + 6$
$y = 2x^2 - 10$

These graphs are all exactly the same shape (or "widths"), but they have different locations. With a common viewing window, one could get a misleading impression of those graphs, because the same portion of each graph is not in view or only a piece of each graph is showing.

Adjusting Table Settings

Once an equation has been entered, (x, y) pairs that satisfy the equation can be shown in a table. The increments by which the values in a table are displayed can be adjusted by changing the settings in the TABLE SETUP menu.

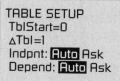

Press $\boxed{\text{2nd}}$ $\boxed{\text{WINDOW}}$ to access the TABLE SETUP menu and enter a new value for $\triangle$TBL. Then press $\boxed{\text{2nd}}$ $\boxed{\text{GRAPH}}$ to display the table. Shown below is a table relating to the equation $y = x^2 + 2x + 4$.

X	Y1
0	4
1	7
2	12
3	19
4	28
5	39
X=0	

Entering Data

In this unit, some students may want to look at tables and graphs of values given in tables. Data given as (x, y) pairs can be entered into the calculator and plotted.

To enter a list of (x, y) data pairs, press $\boxed{\text{STAT}}$ to access the STAT EDIT menu. Press $\boxed{\text{ENTER}}$ to select the Edit mode. Then, enter the data pairs into the L1 and L2 columns: enter the first number, press $\boxed{\text{ENTER}}$, and use the arrow keys to move to the L2 column. Continue until all the data pairs have been entered. For example, you might enter the following data pairs:

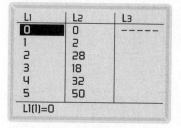

Plotting Points

To plot the data you have entered, use the STAT PLOT menu. Use the arrow keys and ENTER to move around in the screen and to highlight the elements (ON, ■, L1, L2, and ▣).

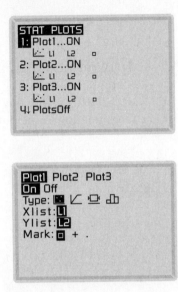

Next, press WINDOW, which will display a screen similar to that shown below. To accommodate the data you input, adjust the window settings by entering values and pressing ENTER, allowing some margin beyond for data points if possible. Then, press GRAPH.

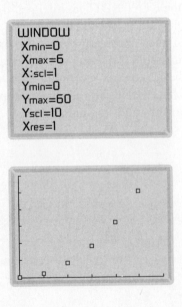

Student Activity CD-ROM

Includes interactive activities to enhance the learning in the Problems within Investigations.

PHSchool.com

For Students Multiple-choice practice with instant feedback, updated data sources, data sets for Tinkerplots data software.

For Teachers Professional development, curriculum support, downloadable forms, and more.

ExamView® CD-ROM

Create multiple versions of practice sheets and tests for course objectives and standardized tests. Includes dynamic questions, online testing, student reports, and all test and practice items in Spanish. Also includes all items in the *Assessment Resources* and *Additional Practice*.

Teacher Express™ CD-ROM

Includes a lesson planning tool, the Teacher's Guide pages, and all the teaching resources.

LessonLab Online Courses

LessonLab offers comprehensive, facilitated professional development designed to help teachers implement CMP2 and improve student achievement. To learn more, please visit PHSchool.com/cmp2.

Assessment Summary

Ongoing Informal Assessment

Embedded in the Student Unit

Problems Use students' work from the Problems to check student understanding.

ACE exercises Use ACE exercises for homework assignments to assess student understanding.

Mathematical Reflections Have students summarize their learning at the end of each Investigation.

Looking Back and Looking Ahead At the end of the unit, use the first two sections to allow students to show what they know about the unit.

Additional Resources

Teacher's Guide Use the Check for Understanding feature of some Summaries and the probing questions that appear in the *Launch, Explore,* or *Summarize* sections of all Investigations to check student understanding.

Self Assessment

Notebook Check Students use this tool to organize and check their notebooks before giving them to their teacher. Located in *Assessment Resources*.

Self Assessment At the end of the unit, students reflect on and provide examples of what they learned. Located in *Assessment Resources*.

Formal Assessment

Choose the assessment materials that are appropriate for your students.

Assessment	For Use After	Focus	Student Work
Check Up 1	Invest. 1	Skills	Individual
Check Up 2	Invest. 2	Skills	Individual
Partner Quiz	Invest. 3	Rich problems	Pair
Unit Test	The Unit	Skills, rich problems	Individual

Additional Resources

Multiple-Choice Items Use these items for homework, review, a quiz, or add them to the Unit Test.

Question Bank Choose from these questions for homework, review, or replacements for Quiz, Check Up, or Unit Test questions.

Additional Practice Choose practice exercises for each investigation for homework, review, or formal assessments.

***ExamView* CD-ROM** Create practice sheets, review quizzes, and tests with this dynamic software. Give online tests and receive student progress reports. (All test items available in Spanish.)

Spanish Assessment Resources

Includes Partner Quizzes, Check Ups, Unit Test, Multiple-Choice Items, Question Bank, Notebook Check, and Self Assessment. Plus, the *ExamView* CD-ROM has all test items in Spanish.

Correlation to Standardized Tests

Investigation	NAEP	Terra Nova CAT6	Terra Nova CTBS	ITBS	SAT10	Local Test
1 Introduction to Quadratic Relationships	A1e, A3a				✔	
2 Quadratic Expressions	A2g, A2a				✔	
3 Quadratic Patterns of Change	A1b, A2g	✔	✔	✔	✔	
4 What is a Quadratic Function?	A2g, A1a				✔	

NAEP National Assessment of Educational Progress

CAT6/Terra Nova California Achievement Test, 6th Ed.
CTBS/Terra Nova Comprehensive Test of Basic Skills

ITBS Iowa Test of Basic Skills, Form M
SAT10 Stanford Achievement Test, 10th Ed.

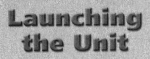

Introducing Your Students to Frogs, Fleas, and Painted Cubes

Students may remember something about the maximum area of a rectangle with a fixed perimeter from the *Covering and Surrounding* unit. Draw a graph of a parabola or discuss the one given for the height of the ball in the second problem of the three introductory questions in the student edition. Ask the class to describe some other situations that might have a similar graph. Put the first three triangular numbers on the black board.

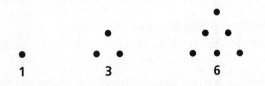

Ask the class to predict the next triangular number. Ask how they could determine the 10th or 50th triangular number.

You can also describe the coin jumping game that occurs in ACE 54 of Investigation 4. Tell the class to make up a game using pennies and nickels or two different colored chips, play the game, and keep track of the jumps that are needed. As you move through the unit, occasionally ask them if anyone has come up with a rule to predict the minimum number of moves to move *n* objects of one kind.

Using the Unit Opener

Discuss the questions posed on the opening page of the student edition, which are designed to start students thinking about the kinds of questions and mathematics in the unit. Don't look for "correct" answers at this time. Do, however, present an opportunity for the class to discuss the questions and to start to think about what is needed to answer them. You may want to revisit these questions as students learn the mathematical ideas and techniques necessary to find the answers.

Problems in contexts are used to help students informally reason about the mathematics of the unit. The problems are deliberately sequenced to provide scaffolding for more challenging problems. Contexts, models, estimation, and writing number sentences help students develop skills, strategies, and algorithms for fraction operations.

Using the Mathematical Highlights

The Mathematical Highlights page in the student edition provides information to students, parents, and other family members. It gives students a preview of the mathematics and some of the overarching questions that they should ask themselves while studying *Frogs, Fleas, and Painted Cubes*.

As they work through the unit, students can refer back to the Mathematical Highlights page to review what they have learned and to preview what is still to come. This page also tells students' families what mathematical ideas and activities will be covered as the class works through *Frogs, Fleas, and Painted Cubes*.

Investigation 1 — Introduction to Quadratic Relationships

Mathematical and Problem-Solving Goals

- Begin an introduction to quadratic relationships by looking at tables and graphs
- Make connections between the patterns in a table and graph of a quadratic relationship
- Use tables and graphs to predict the fixed perimeter and maximum area for a family of rectangles with a fixed perimeter
- Write an equation that describes the relationship between the length and area of rectangles with a fixed perimeter
- Use a quadratic equation to describe the graph and table of a quadratic relationship
- Use the equation, graph, and table to solve problems about quadratic relationship

Summary of Problems

Problem 1.1 Staking a Claim

Students begin their study of quadratic relationships by exploring the area of rectangles with a fixed perimeter. They find that within this family of rectangles, the square has the greatest (maximum) area. The focus is on the parabolic shape of quadratic function graphs and how the shape is reflected in the table of values.

Problem 1.2 Reading Graphs and Tables

Data on the area of a rectangle with a fixed area are given in a graph and then in a table of values. Students use the graph and table to find the information about the greatest area and the fixed perimeter. They also use the table and graph to describe some special features of the quadratic relationship such as intercepts and maximum points.

Problem 1.3 Writing an Equation

Students write an equation for the relationship between the area and length of rectangles with a fixed perimeter, P. The relationship is a quadratic function of the chosen length ℓ, or width w with the equation $A = \ell\left(\frac{P}{2} - \ell\right)$ or $A = w\left(\frac{P}{2} - w\right)$.

	Suggested Pacing	Materials for Students	Materials for Teachers	ACE Assignments
All	$3\frac{1}{2}$ days	Graphing calculators, student notebooks	Blank transparencies and transparency markers (optional), overhead graphing calculator	
1.1	1 day	20-cm lengths string (optional; 1 per group), square tiles (optional; 50 per group), poster paper (optional)	Transparency grid paper (optional)	1, 2, 14–16, 30
1.2	1 day		Transparencies 1.2 A–D	3–5, 17–27, 28
1.3	1 day	Grid paper (1 per student)	Transparency 1.3	6–13, 29
MR	$\frac{1}{2}$ day			

1.1 Staking a Claim

Goal

- Begin an introduction to quadratic relationships by looking at a table and graph

In this problem students explore the area of rectangles that have a fixed perimeter of 20 meters.

Launch 1.1

Suggested Questions You might begin this investigation by asking the following questions:

- *Name some situations in which your goal is to try to* maximize *something.* (profit or time on vacation)

- *Name some situations in which your goal is to try to* minimize *something.* (cost or time spent traveling)

- *Suppose you have 20 meters of fencing. That is not a lot of fencing. What shape would you enclose to give the most area?* (A circle—students may or may not remember this from *Covering and Surrounding.* Do not spend time developing this answer. It only serves as an introduction.)

- *Why are most fields and other pieces of property in the shape of rectangles?* (Most fields are rectangular because rectangles fit together well. Students explored this idea when they investigated tessellations in *Shapes and Designs.* Farmers in some parts of America have experimented with circular plantings, to facilitate irrigation from a central point, but those fields have the same problem as the pentagons: they do not fit together, so they leave unplanted space.)

Tell the story about prospecting on the planet Mars. You could launch the story as follows: To search for the rectangle with the greatest area for a fixed perimeter of 20 meters, you can begin with experiments using a scale model. Make a loop from a 20-centimeter length of string and use it to enclose various rectangular "claims" on a transparent centimeter grid. (Figure 1)

Students might recall a similar problem from *Covering and Surrounding.* Among the rectangular shapes, the square has the most area for a fixed perimeter. Among all shapes the circle has the most area for a fixed perimeter. If these answers occur, tell them that the challenge in this investigation is to look more closely at patterns in rectangles with a fixed perimeter.

Let students work in pairs.

Figure 1

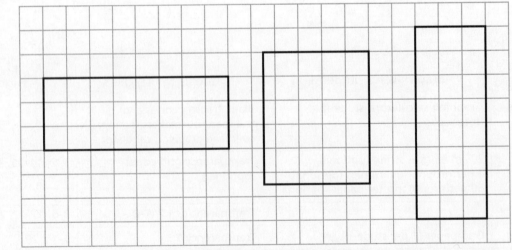

Explore 1.1

Each student should create his or her own table and graph.

If students are having trouble, encourage them to use string and grid paper, or square tiles, to visually explore the idea of a fixed perimeter. For many students the idea of a variable area with a fixed perimeter is so counter-intuitive that they have to see it to believe it. Another way to help students become comfortable with the idea is to encourage them to explain how they can increase or decrease the area enclosed by the rectangle.

You may want one group to put their table and graph on transparent paper or poster paper for the discussion.

Summarize 1.1

Help students to summarize their work in the problem. The following ideas should emerge in the discussion:

- The independent variable is the length of a side, and the dependent variable is the area.

- As the length of a side increases, the area increases to a certain point (the maximum point) and then decreases.

- As the length increases, the width decreases.

- The sum of the length and width is half of the perimeter.

- The graph is symmetric about a vertical line drawn through the maximum point. (Students may not use this language at this time. They might use ideas from *Shapes and Designs*, such as, "if you fold the graph in half through the point at the top, the two halves are identical—that is, the graph has a line of reflection.)

Suggested Questions The following questions can be used to assess students' understanding of the preceding ideas:

- *Describe patterns in the table.* (As the length increases, the width decreases. As the length increases, the area increases and then starts to decrease. The sum of the length and width is 10.)

At the end of the summary you may want to come back and look at the relationship between length and width.

- *Describe the shape of the graph.* (It is shaped like an "upside-down U." The area first starts to increase until it reaches a maximum point and then it starts to decrease.)

- *How can you predict the maximum area from the graph?* (At the top of the "U" shape is the point that represents the maximum greatest area. It is the *y*-value of the point.)

- *How can you predict the dimensions of the rectangle with greatest area from the graph?* (The first coordinate of the maximum point is the length of the base. The other dimension can be computed by using the fixed perimeter:

$$2\ell + 2w = P, \text{ so } \ell + w = \frac{P}{2} \text{ or } w = \frac{P}{2} - \ell.$$

Another method is to note that the second coordinate of the maximum point is the area. The other dimension can be computed from this area and the first dimension:

$$\ell \times w = A, \text{ so } w = \frac{A}{\ell}.)$$

- *What is the shape of the rectangle with the most area?* (square)

- *How can you find the maximum area from the table?* (It is the point where the area stops increasing and begins to decrease, or it is the greatest area in the table.)

- *What happens to values in the table after the maximum area has been reached? How does this show up in the graph?* (The length continues to increase, but the area starts to decrease. The graph increases until the maximum point has been reached and then it starts to decrease.)

- *If you folded the graph over a vertical line through the maximum point, what would happen to the two parts of the graph?* (The maximum point divides the graph into two identical halves, so the two halves would fold on top of one another.)

- *Do you remember a word we use to describe shapes that have this folding property?* (symmetry, mirror images)

- *In this unit, we will learn that this vertical line is called the* line of symmetry. *As the length of the rectangle gets closer and closer to 10, what happens to the area?* (It gets smaller and smaller.)

- *Could we make the area 0?* (Yes, if we choose $\ell = 10$ the rectangle will collapse and become a straight line.)

- *Suppose the dimensions of the rectangle were not restricted to whole numbers. Would this change your answer as to which rectangle has the greatest area?* (No, the dimensions of the maximum value would not change in this problem. For example, if the length of the base is 4.5, then the height would be 5.5. This rectangle will still have a perimeter of 20, but the area is $4.5 \times 5.5 = 24.8$, which is less than 25. Any other length you try will give an area of less than 25 square meters.)

- *If the length is 3.5, what is the area?* (The area is 22.75 square units.)

- *How many points on the graph show an area of 20 square meters?* (2)

- *If the area is 20 square meters, what is its length?* (The length is about 7.25 or 2.75. Students might say a bit more than 7 or a bit less than 3.)

- *What does each of these values mean in the problem situation?* (They are the dimensions of the rectangle whose area is 20 m².)

- *Describe the relationship between length and width of the rectangles in this problem.* (As the length increases by 1, the width decreases by 1. It is a linear relationship. The sum of the length and width is half the perimeter. That is, $\ell + w = 10$ or $\ell = 10 - w$. The slope of the line of this equation is -1 and the y-intercept is 10.)

- *Is the relationship between the length and area linear?* (No, as the length increases by 1, the area is increasing but not by a constant amount, and then it also starts to decrease.

These kinds of questions will reoccur throughout the unit.

1.1 Staking a Claim

Mathematical Goal

- Begin an introduction to quadratic relationships by looking at a table and graph

Launch

- *Name situations in which your goal is to try to maximize (minimize) something.*
- *Suppose you had 20 meters of fencing. What shape would you enclose to give the most area?*
- *Why are most fields and other pieces of property in the shape of rectangles?*

Tell the story about prospecting on the planet Mars. To search for the rectangle with the greatest area for a fixed perimeter of 20 meters, begin with experiments using a scale model. Make a loop from a 20-centimeter length of string and use it to enclose various rectangular "claims" on a transparent centimeter grid. Let students work in pairs.

Materials

- Transparency grid paper (optional)
- Graphing calculators
- 20-cm lengths string (optional; 1 per group)

Explore

Students should create their own table and graph.

Explain how you can increase or decrease the area enclosed by the rectangle. Have one group put their table and graph on poster paper.

Materials

- Square tiles (optional; 50 per group)
- Poster paper (optional)

Summarize

Ask students to describe patterns in the table and the shape of the graph.

- *How can you predict the maximum area from the graph?*
- *How can you find the maximum area from the table?*
- *What happens to values in the table after the maximum area has been reached? How does this show up in the graph?*
- *If you folded the graph over a vertical line through the maximum point, what would happen to the two parts of the graph?*
- *Suppose the dimensions of the rectangle were not restricted to whole numbers. Would this change your answer as to which rectangle has the greatest area?*
- *If the length is 3.5, what is the area?*
- *How many points on the graph show an area of 20 square meters?*
- *If the area is 20 square meters, what is its length?*
- *What does each of these values mean in the problem situation?*
- *Describe the relationship between length and width of the rectangles in this problem.*
- *Is the relationship between length and width linear? Between length and area?*

Materials

- Student notebooks

ACE Assignment Guide for Problem 1.1

Core 1, 2, 16
Other *Connections* 14, 15; *Extensions* 30;
unassigned choices from previous problems

Adapted For suggestions about adapting ACE exercises, see the CMP *Special Needs Handbook.*
Connecting to Prior Units 15, 16: *Accentuate the Negative*

Answers to Problem 1.1

A. Possible rectangles:

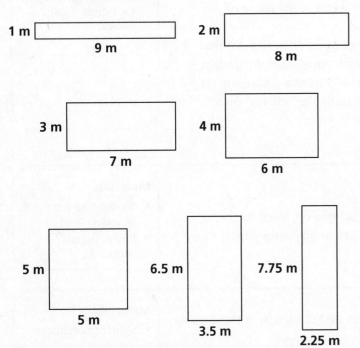

B. The area values increase up to 25, then decrease. The area values repeat, while the length of the base and the width switch values after they are the same at 5.

Rectangles With a Perimeter of 20 m

Length	Width	Area
0	10	0
1	9	9
2	8	16
3	7	21
4	6	24
5	5	25
6	4	24
7	3	21
8	2	16
9	1	9
10	0	0

C. The graph is a parabola that opens down. Students may describe it as an upside-down U. It has a maximum point where the area is the greatest.

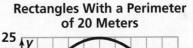
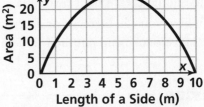

Rectangles With a Perimeter of 20 Meters

D. 1. The square has the maximum area. In this case, it is the 5-by-5 square and the area is 25 m². This can be shown on the graph since it is the maximum value.

2. No; the 5 × 5 square will still correspond to the maximum point on the graph (the maximum area). The bases with non-whole number side lengths will correspond to *x*-values, which are to the right and left of the *x*-value of 5 m. These *x*-values to the right and left of the *x*-value of 5 have corresponding *y*-values (areas), which are less than 25 m².

Reading Graphs and Tables

Goals

- Make connections between the patterns in a table and graph of a quadratic relationship

- Use tables and graphs to predict the fixed perimeter and maximum area for a family of rectangles with a fixed perimeter

The context for this problem is the same as Problem 1.1: looking at a family of rectangles with a fixed perimeter. The problem provides two situations. The data for the first one is presented in graphical form and the data for the second one is in tabular form.

This unit refers to maximum points and minimum points on parabolas. The point at which a graph turns around is also called a *vertex*, a term you may or may not want to introduce to your class.

Launch 1.2

Display or sketch the graph from Problem 1.1 (or draw it quickly) on the overhead. Tell the class that this kind of graph is called a *parabola*.

Parabolas describe quadratic relationships, which are also called quadratic functions. In this graph, the area depends on or is a function of, the length.

Next display the graph of the parabola from Problem 1.2. Explain that this graph represents the area of a family of rectangles with a certain fixed perimeter.

Suggested Question Ask:

- *How is this graph similar to the graph in the last problem?* (shape is similar; it has a maximum value)

Tell students that this graph contains clues about the greatest area for the fixed perimeter of another family of rectangles. They will use these clues to answer the questions in this problem.

Note: You could let students do Question A and then summarize it. Then let them explore Question B followed by a summary of Question B.

Students can work in groups of two or three.

Explore 1.2

As you move from group to group, make sure students note the symmetry of the graph in their answer. You may want to ask them where the line of symmetry is.

Suggested Questions If students are having trouble, especially with finding the fixed perimeter in A and B, ask the following:

- *What variables are shown in the graph?* (length and area)

- *How do you find the area of a rectangle?* (multiply length times width)

- *So what do you know about the point (10, 300) on this graph?* (For the rectangle represented by this point, the length of one side is 10 m and the area is 300 m^2.)

- *How can you find the length of the other side from what you know?* (Calculate it from the area and the known length: $300 \div 10 = 30$ m.)

Similar questions can be asked using the table in Question B.

Summarize 1.2

Ask students to talk about what they discovered in the problem, emphasizing the important ideas. Help them see that each area is associated with two side lengths, which are the dimensions of the rectangle with that area.

Suggested Questions Assess students' understanding of the graph in Question A.

- *If the area is 300 square meters, what is its length or width?* (The length is 10 or 30 meters. If the length is 10 m, then the width is 30 m and the other way around, if the length is 30 m, then the width is 10 m. Each point has a symmetric point or a twin. There are two points associated with a specific area except for the maximum point. The *x*-values or length values of the two points represent the length and/or width for a rectangle with the specific area.)

- *What are the lengths of the sides if the area is 200 square meters?* [The two points associated with the area of 200 are approximately (6, 200) and (34, 200). The two side lengths are 34 m and 6 m. Note that $6 \times 34 = 204$, which is approximately 200.]

- *What are the lengths of the sides if the area is 400 square meters?* (Both sides are 20 m.)

- *What would a table of values for this graph look like?* (As the length goes from 0 to 40 m, the area goes from 0 to 400 m², which is the maximum value, and then the area starts to decrease, reversing the values on the first half until the area reaches 0 m.)

Emphasize the symmetry of the graph.

- *If you fold the graph in half vertically through the top of the curve, what would happen?* (The graph has two identical halves—they fall on top of each other. Each point falls on its twin point.)

Help students see that each point on one side of the graph corresponds to a point on the other side and those two points are the dimensions of the rectangle with that area.

Students can find the fixed perimeter in several ways. Some may find the length and area for one of the points and then divide the area by the length to find the width and then use the dimensions to find the perimeter.

Go over the questions for Question B. The analysis for the table of data for rectangles with a fixed perimeter is similar to that for the graph.

Suggested Questions Ask:

- *Describe the pattern of change in the table. How does this pattern compare to the pattern of change in the graph?* (Students might recognize that the increase and decrease in the "area" column seems to fit a pattern. As the length of a side increases, the area increases until it reaches the maximum area. Each increase in the area is 2 less than the previous increase. After the maximum area is reached, the area decreases in a similar but opposite way. Each decrease is 2 greater than the previous decrease.)

- *How can you use the table to find the dimensions of a rectangle with a side length of 10 meters?* (From the table, the area of the rectangle is 20 square meters, so the other dimension is 2 meters because $2 \times 10 = 20$. Or since the perimeter is 24 meters, half the perimeter is 12 meters, so the other dimension is 2 meters because $2 + 10 = 12$.)

- *If you draw a graph using the data in the table, what would it look like?* [It would start at the point (0, 0) and increase until the point (6, 36), which corresponds to the maximum area; then it would decrease until it reached the point (12, 0).]

Comparing Graphs of Linear, Exponential, and Quadratic Relationships

This is a good time to ask students to compare the tables and graphs and growth patterns in linear, exponential, and quadratic relationships. Put the quadratic graph from this problem, a linear graph, and an exponential graph on the board or overhead. Transparency 1.2C contains the graphs shown below from *Thinking With Mathematical Models, Growing, Growing, Growing;* and Problem 1.2 Question A. If you do not use this transparency now, bring it back up later in the unit or post it in the room for reference.

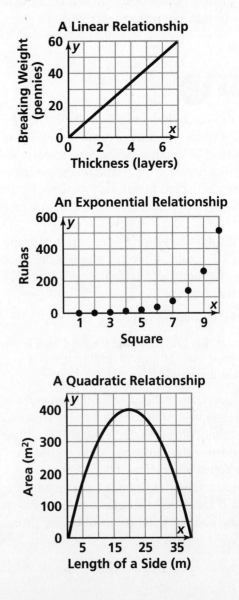

A Linear Relationship

An Exponential Relationship

A Quadratic Relationship

Suggested Questions Help students compare the patterns in the graphs. Ask:

- *Is there a maximum in the bridge-thickness problem?* (Theoretically, no. The graph goes on forever, rising at a constant rate. Practically speaking, however, there are limits to how thick a bridge would be made.)

- *Is there a maximum point for the Ruba problem?* (Theoretically, no. But practically, the king will run out of Rubas.)

- *Could you extend each graph to predict the y-value related to the next labeled value on the x-axis?* (Students should be familiar with the rate of changes in the linear and exponential graphs. It is a bit harder to accurately extend the quadratic graph, but you could get a good estimate.)

- *Describe the growth pattern of each situation.* (At this point they can claim that the growth pattern for quadratics is different. Students do not need to be able to describe it fully at this time, but they should notice that it is different. Make sure they realize that the graph is increasing on one portion, and decreasing on another. In the linear graph there is a constant rate of change, and in the exponential graph the rate of increase is by a constant factor.)

Comparing Tables of Linear, Exponential, and Quadratic Relationships

Transparency 1.2D shows an example of each type of table corresponding to the graphs on Transparency 1.2C.

Table For a Linear Relationship

Thickness (layers)	Breaking Weight (pennies)
0	0
1	8.4
2	16.8
3	25.2
4	33.6
5	42.06
6	50.4
7	58.8

Table For an Exponential Relationship

Square	Rubas
1	1
2	2
3	4
4	8
5	16
6	32
7	64
8	128
9	256
10	512

Table For a Quadratic Relationship

Length of a Side (m)	Area (m²)
0	0
5	175
10	300
15	375
20	400
25	375
30	300
35	175
40	0

Suggested Question Ask:

- *Describe the pattern of change between the variables in the table.* (Students should notice that the rate of change for quadratics is different than that for linear or exponential. Some might notice that the increase and decrease seem to fit a pattern. That is, as the length increases the area increases, until it reaches the maximum point. The amount of the increase in the area is two less than the previous increase until it reaches the maximum point and then the area decreases in a similar pattern. Each decrease is two more than the previous decrease.)

1.2 Reading Graphs and Tables

Mathematical Goals

- Make connections between the patterns in a table and graph of a quadratic relationship
- Use tables and graphs to predict the fixed perimeter and maximum area for a family of rectangles with a fixed perimeter

Launch

Sketch the Problem 1.1 graph on the overhead. Tell the class that this kind of graph is called a parabola and explain what that means. Explain that in this graph, the area depends on, or is a function of, the length.

Display Transparency 1.2A.

- *How is this graph similar to the graphs in the last problem?*

Students can work in groups of two or three.

Materials

- Transparency 1.2A
- Graphing calculators

Vocabulary

- quadratic relationship
- parabolas
- function

Explore

You might ask students where the line of symmetry is on their graphs.

- *What variables are shown in the graph?*
- *How do you find the area of a rectangle?*
- *So what do you know about the point (10, 300) on this graph?*
- *How can you find the length of the other side from what you know?*

Similar questions can be asked using the table in Question B.

Summarize

Help students see that each area is associated with two dimensions.

Ask questions about the graph in Question A.

- *If the area is 300 square meters, what is its length or width?*
- *What are the lengths of the sides if the area is 200?*
- *What are the lengths of the sides if the area is 400?*
- *What would a table of values for this graph look like?*
- *If you fold the graph in half vertically through the top of the curve, what would happen?*

Help students see that each point on one side of the graph corresponds to a point on the other side and those two points are the dimensions of the rectangle with that area.

- *Describe the pattern of change in the table. How does this pattern compare to the pattern of change in the graph?*
- *How can you use the table to find the dimensions of a rectangle with a side length of 10 meters?*

Materials

- Student notebooks
- Transparencies 1.2B–D

continued on next page

Use Transparency 1.2C to compare tables, graphs and growth patterns.

- *Is there a maximum in the bridge-thickness problem?*
- *Is there a maximum point for the Ruba problem?*
- *Could you extend each graph to predict the y-value related to next labeled value on the x-axis?*
- *Describe the growth pattern of each situation.*

Use Transparency 1.2D to compare tables of the graphs.

- *Describe the pattern of change between the variables in the table.*

ACE Assignment Guide for Problem 1.2

Differentiated Instruction
Solutions for All Learners

Core 3, 5, 17–25
Other *Applications* 4; *Connections* 26, 27, 28; unassigned choices from previous problems

Adapted For suggestions about adapting Exercise 4 and other ACE exercises, see the CMP *Special Needs Handbook*.
Connecting to Prior Units 17–23: *Accentuate the Negative*; 24–27, 28: *Moving Straight Ahead*

Answers to Problem 1.2

A. 1. The graph is shaped similarly to the graph in Problem 1.1, a parabola that opens down. The point at the top is a maximum point where the area is the greatest. As the length of a side increases, the area increases until it reaches the maximum area; then the area begins to decrease. The left and right sides of the graph are symmetrical about the line $\ell = 20$.

2. 400 m^2; it is a square with side length of 20 m.

3. 300 m^2; 300 m^2; these side lengths correspond to the same rectangle.

4. 5 m by 35 m

5. 80 m; possible explanations: The point (10, 300) represents a rectangle with a side length of 10 m and an area of 300 m^2; the second dimension is $300 \div 10 = 30$ m and the perimeter is $2(10 + 30) = 80$ m. Or, the rectangle with the greatest area is a square with a side length of 20 m; its fixed perimeter is $4 \times 20 = 80$ m. Or, the non-zero x-intercept is half of the perimeter, so the perimeter is $2 \times 40 = 80$ m.

B. 1. In the table, the maximum area, 36 m^2, is for a side length of 6 m. This point, (6, 36), is in the middle of the range of values in the table and is the highest point of the graph. As the length of a side increases from 6 to 12, area decreases from 36 to 0. This increase and then decrease can be seen in the "Area" column in the table and in the shape of the graph.

2. 24 units; possible explanation: The perimeter can be found from any pair in the table. For a rectangle with a side length of 2 m and area of 20 m^2, the other dimension is $20 \div 2$ or 10 m. So, the perimeter is $2(10 + 2)$ or 24 m.

3. 36 m^2; the rectangle has a length of 6 meters. This means that it is the 6-by-6 square.

4. For the table, an area of 16 m^2 is associated with a side length of about halfway between 1 m and 2 m, or about 1.5 m, and with a side length about halfway between 10 m and 11 m, or about 10.5 m. This gives a rectangle with area 10.5 m $\times$ 1.5 m = 15.75 m^2.

5. For the table, an area of 35.5 m^2 is associated with a side length of about halfway between 5 m and 6 m, or about 5.5 m, and with a side length about halfway between 6 m and 7 m, or about 6.5 m. Using 6.5 m $\times$ 5.5 m yields an area of 35.75 m^2. Students might use the pattern of change to say that the area is increasing more slowly as length increases from 0 to 6 m. So choosing a length of 5.5 m, to correspond to an area of 35.5 m^2, is likely to be an under-estimate.

Writing an Equation

Goals

- Write an equation that describes the relationship between the length and area of rectangles with a fixed perimeter

- Use a quadratic equation to describe the graph and table of a quadratic relationship

- Use the equation, graph, and table to solve problems about quadratic relationship

Launch 1.3

Do the Getting Ready as a whole-class discussion.
Draw a rectangle on the overhead or board and explain to the class that this rectangle represents rectangles with a perimeter of 20. Label one side ℓ.

Suggested Question Ask:

- *How can we write an equation for the relationship between area and length of a rectangle with a fixed perimeter of 20 meters?*

Give students time to offer suggestions for writing an equation. If they are having trouble, you can use some of the following questions:

Suggestion 1

Some students may reason about the relationship and then express their reasoning in symbols.

Suggested Question Ask:

- *If the length is ℓ, how can we express the lengths of the other sides?* (They might say that the sum of the length and the other dimension must be half the perimeter or 10. So $\ell + \blacksquare = 10$ or $\blacksquare = 10 - \ell$. If needed, you can remind students how to solve the linear equation of the form $\ell + \blacksquare = 10$. The width is $10 - \ell$.)

Suggestion 2

Some students may see the relationship between length and width from a table.

Suggested Questions Ask:

- *The perimeter is 20 meters. Suppose that ℓ is 6 meters. What is the width or the other dimension?* [2(length + width) = 20 or $\ell + w = 10$. If $\ell = 6$ then $w = 4$. Repeat if necessary for other values of the base.]

- *So, if you know the perimeter and length of a rectangle, what can you say about the width?* (The two dimensions add to half the perimeter. So take half the perimeter and then subtract the length from half the perimeter to get the width. For this rectangle, half of the perimeter is 10. So the width or the other dimension is $10 - \ell$.)

You can use a table that includes, length, width, and area to help students see the relationship between length and width.

Rectangles With a Perimeter of 20 m

Length	Width	Area
0	10	0
1	9	9
2	8	16
3	7	21
4	6	24
5	5	25
6	4	24
7	3	21
8	2	16
9	1	9
10	0	0

As they fill in the table, students should notice that $\ell + w = 10$ or $w = 10 - \ell$.
Finish labeling the rectangle and find the equation.

Suggested Questions Ask:

- *If we know the dimensions of the rectangle, how can we find the area? What is the equation that represents the area of this rectangle?* (The area is length times width. So the area = $\ell(10 - \ell)$. Students will need help in interpreting the parentheses. They may want to write $\ell \times 10 - \ell$. But tell them that the length must be multiplied by the entire expression for the width. We can use parentheses to make it clear what we mean for the entire expression.)

- *Use the equation to find the area if the length is 3.* [Area = $3(10 - 3) = 3(7) = 21$. Tell the students to think of this as finding the width using the expression in the parentheses and then multiply by the base. Alternately, have students explain the relationship expressed in the equation.]

Give the class time to use the graphing calculator to find the table and graph. Give them an interval of 0 to 10 for the *x*-values and 0 to 30 for the *y*-values.

- *Compare the table and graphs of this equation to those you found in Problem 1.1.* (They are similar in that they are parabolas opening down.)

Let the class work in pairs. Once they are finished they can work in larger groups of four to discuss their strategies.

Explore 1.3

If students are having difficulty, suggest they make a sketch to represent rectangles with a perimeter of 60 meters. Ask questions that focus students' attention on the relationship between the perimeter, P, and the sum of the dimensions of a rectangle, which is $\frac{P}{2}$. Since $\frac{P}{2} = 30$, the two dimensions must add to 30.

Perimeter = 60 m

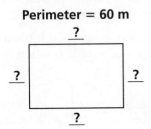

Suggested Questions Ask:

- *If $\ell = 2$, what is the other dimension?* (28)

- *If $\ell = 4$, what is the other dimension?* (26)

- *How are you finding the other dimension?* (Since $2\ell = 8$, then $2w = 52$ or $w = 26$; since $\ell + w$ = half the perimeter, subtract ℓ from 30.)

- *Write this procedure using symbols.* ($30 - \ell = w$)

Summarize 1.3

For Question A, ask questions to make sure students are able to write an equation. Then ask for specific information about the relationship.

Suggested Questions Ask:

- *What are the coordinates of the maximum point?* [(15, 225)]

Ask someone to draw a rectangle to represent the situation. Be sure they label the dimensions.

Perimeter = 60 m

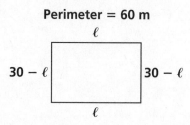

- *How do the patterns in the table and graph of this relationship compare to those you have seen in previous problems?* (All the graphs are shaped like upside-down U's. In the table, the area increases as the length increases until it reaches the maximum area; then the area decreases.)

In Question B, students use an equation to find the dimensions of a rectangle and from this information they can then find the perimeter. If needed, ask more questions that require the students to use the equation to find the area for specific lengths.

Suggested Questions Ask:

- *What is the area if the length is 10?* [Students can solve the following: $A = 10(35 - 10) = 10(25) = 250$ square units.]

Be sure to discuss the maximum point and its significance to the problem.

- *What are the coordinates of the maximum point?* [(17.5, 306.25)]

- *What does the maximum point represent in this context?* [Its coordinates represent the length and area of the rectangle with the greatest area. Both dimensions are equal so it is a square. Some might say it represents

the rectangle with the greatest area—it is a square whose side is $P \div 4$. For a fixed perimeter of 20, 80, or 60 the square had whole-number dimensions. But in Question B, for a perimeter of 70, the square has sides of length 17.5. On the graph this point is between the points (17, 306) and (18, 306).]

- *Where does this point fall?* (On the vertical line of symmetry for the parabola. This is discussed again in the next investigation.)

In Question D, ask:

- *In the labeling of the sides of the rectangle with perimeter 60 meters, you probably thought of the half perimeter, 30 meters, and used this to label the sides ℓ and $30 - \ell$. How does this "half perimeter" show up in the graph?* (It appears as one of the x-intercepts.)

Ask about the form of the equation in the Getting Ready:

- *For a perimeter of 20 units the equation for the area is the product of two factors, ℓ and $10 - \ell$. Is this reasonable?* (Yes, since the area of the rectangle is base times height or the product of its two dimensions.)

- *Why does it have this form?* (Students should begin to notice that the equation has 2 factors. Since it describes the area, then the two factors are the dimensions of the rectangle. But don't expect everyone to get this—this will be discussed again in the next investigation.)

- *Do the equations in Questions A and B have the same form? Explain.* [Students should be able to pick out the two factors (or expressions) that represent the dimensions of the rectangle.]

1.3 Writing an Equation

Mathematical Goals

- Write an equation that describes the relationship between the length and area of rectangles with a fixed perimeter
- Use a quadratic equation to describe the graph and table of a quadratic relationship
- Use the equation, graph, and table to solve problems about quadratic relationships

Launch

Do the Getting Ready as a whole class discussion.

- *How can we write an equation for the relationship between area and length of a rectangle with a fixed perimeter of 20 meters?*
- *If the length is ℓ, express the lengths of the other sides.*
- *The perimeter is 20 meters. Suppose that ℓ is 6 meters. What is the width or the other dimension?*
- *If you know the perimeter and length of a rectangle, what can you say about the width?*

Use a table that includes, length, width, perimeter and area. As they fill in the table, students should notice that $\ell + w = 10$ or $w = 10 - \ell$. Finish labeling the rectangle and find the equation.

- *If we know the dimensions of the rectangle, how can we find the area? What is the equation that represents the area of this rectangle? Use the equation to find the area if the length is 3.*

Have students use a graphing calculator to find the table and graph. Give them a range of 0 to 10 for *x*-values and 0 to 30 for *y*-values.

- *Compare the table and graphs of this equation to those you found in Problem 1.1.*

Let the class work in pairs and later work in larger groups of four.

Materials

- Transparency 1.3
- Graphing Calculators
- Grid paper (1 per student)

Explore

Suggest they make a sketch to represent rectangles with perimeters of 60 meters. Focus students' attention on the relationship between the perimeter, *P*, and the sum of the dimensions of a rectangle, or $\frac{P}{2}$.

- *If ℓ = 2, what is the other dimension?*
- *If ℓ = 4, what is the other dimension?*
- *How are you finding the other dimension? Write this procedure using symbols.*

For Question A, make sure students are able to write an equation. Ask:

- *What are the coordinates of the maximum point?*

Ask someone to draw a rectangle to represent the situation.

- *How do the patterns in the table and graph of this relationship compare to those you have seen in previous problems?*

In Question B, ask more questions that require students to use the equation.

- *What is the area if the base is 10?*
- *What are the coordinates of the maximum point?*
- *What does the maximum point represent in this context?*
- *Where does this point fall?*

In Question D, ask:

- *In the labeling of the sides of the rectangle with perimeter 60 meters, you probably thought of the half perimeter, 30 meters, and used this to label the sides ℓ and 30 − ℓ. How does this "half perimeter" appear in the graph?*

Ask about the equation's form in Getting Ready. See the extended Teacher's Guide.

Materials
- Student notebooks

ACE Assignment Guide for Problem 1.3

Differentiated Instruction
Solutions for All Learners

Core 6–8, 11–13
Other *Applications* 9, 10; *Connections* 29; unassigned choices from previous problems

Adapted For suggestions about adapting ACE exercises, see the CMP *Special Needs Handbook*.
Connecting to Prior Units 29: *Thinking With Mathematical Models*

Answers to Problem 1.3

A. 1.

The Perimeter = 60 m

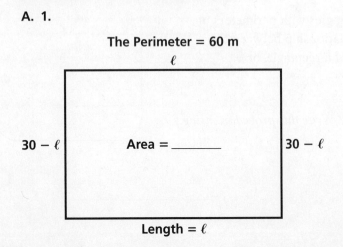

2. Area = Length × width = $\ell(30 - \ell)$

3. Maximum area is 225 m^2 and it happens when $x = 15$. It will be a square with side length 15.

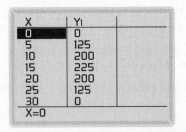

4–5. The maximum area occurs at the top of the graph. The coordinates of this point are (15, 225). Every other point has a *y*-value (area) that is less than 225. This can be seen on the graph since all other points have a smaller *y*-coordinate.

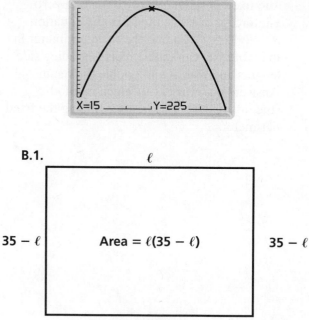

B.1.

ℓ

$35 - \ell$ Area = $\ell(35 - \ell)$ $35 - \ell$

Length = ℓ

2.

Length (m)	Width (m)	Area (m²)
0	35	0
5	30	150
10	25	250
15	20	300
20	15	300
25	10	250
30	5	150
35	0	0

Possible answer: The values for area increase as the side length increases until the side length is 15. The areas for side lengths of 15 m and 20 m are the same, 300, and then the values for area decrease from 300 m² to 0 m². Thus, the maximum for a length must occur between 15 and 20, probably halfway between, at 17.5. In fact, the maximum occurs when the length is exactly 17.5.

3. To describe the graph students may need to make a graph either by hand or on a graphing calculator. They should be able to say ahead of time that the shape is an upside down U, or a parabola opening down. They will probably need the actual graph to give more specific details about the shape and placement. Using the trace, or table function on the calculator they may find that the x-intercepts are at $(0, 0)$ and $(0, 35)$ and the maximum is $(17.5, 306.25)$.

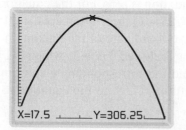

4. Explanations will vary. The maximum area is 306.25 m², which corresponds to a square with side lengths of 17.5 m. (NOTE: Students might find it helpful to use a calculator to make a table or a graph.)

5. Possible answer: The perimeter can be found from the dimensions of a particular rectangle. For example, 20 m and 15 m are a pair of dimensions, so the perimeter is $2(20 + 15) = 70$ m. Also, the perimeter is twice the constant that appears in the expression for the second dimension; in this case, that dimension is $(35 - \ell)$, so the perimeter is $2 \times 35 = 70$ m.

C. Possible answer: Call the length of one side l, and subtract l from half the perimeter to get an expression for the other dimension. Multiply the two expressions for the area. [NOTE: The description in words is acceptable at this time, although the area can also be expressed symbolically. Area is length times width, or $A = \ell \times w$. Length plus width equals half the perimeter, or $\ell + w = \frac{P}{2}$. Therefore, $w = \frac{P}{2} - \ell$ and $A = \ell(\frac{P}{2} - \ell)$. The perimeter is 70 m for this equation.]

D. The maximum area can be read fairly easily from the graph. It is the point with the greatest y-value, the point at which the graph is neither increasing nor decreasing. It is not always easy to read the maximum area directly from a table. The equation is the least useful representation for predicting the maximum area.

[**Note:** A few students may recognize that the x-coordinate of the maximum value lies halfway between the x-intercepts. The x-intercepts occur when one of the factors in the equation is zero. For the equation $A = \ell(35 - \ell)$ the x-intercepts are 0 and 35, so the x-coordinate of the maximum point is halfway between 0 and 35 which is 17.5. You can find the corresponding y-coordinate by substituting 17.5 into the equation for A.]

The fixed perimeter is twice the non-zero x-intercept or twice the 35 in the equation $A = \ell(35 - \ell)$. To find the fixed perimeter in the table you can look at corresponding side lengths and widths and double their sum. Answers may vary as to which method students believe is easiest for finding the fixed perimeter.

Investigation ❶

ACE Assignment Choices

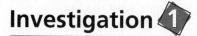
Differentiated Instruction
Solutions for All Learners

Problem 1.1
Core 1, 2, 16
Other *Connections* 14, 15; *Extensions* 30; unassigned choices from previous problems

Problem 1.2
Core 3, 5, 17–25
Other *Applications* 4, *Connections* 26, 27, 28; unassigned choices from previous problems

Problem 1.3
Core 6–8, 11–13
Other *Applications* 9, 10; *Connections* 29; unassigned choices from previous problems

Adapted For suggestions about adapting Exercise 4 and other ACE exercises, see the CMP *Special Needs Handbook*.
Connecting to Prior Units 15, 16: *Accentuate the Negative*; 17–23: *Accentuate the Negative*; 24–28: *Moving Straight Ahead*; 29: *Thinking With Mathematical Models*

Applications

1. Students may use various sketches. Here are some examples including the rectangle with the maximum area. In general, squares will have the maximum area for a given perimeter. Long and thin rectangles will have a smaller area. This is a principle that students have encountered in earlier units of CMP, but it may yet be a surprising result.

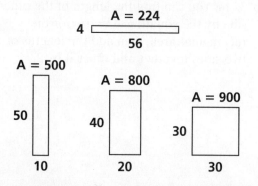

Students may put their sketches on graph paper to verify the areas. The rectangle with the greatest area for this fixed perimeter has sides all of which are 30. **Note:** At this point, students are probably not using graphing calculators, so their graphs will be sketched on paper.

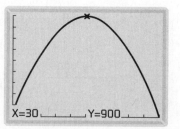

Students may use a table to verify that the maximum area of 900 is when the sides are each 30. Encourage students to take bigger increments for the base. For example, a table with increments of 5 is easy to generate. Then students can use this estimate where the maximum point occurs. The table can also be used to sketch a graph. Students may use the trace button on their graphing calculator to find the base.

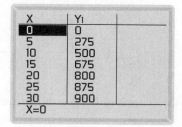

After Problem 1.3 you can come back to this problem and have the students find the equation and then connect the equation to the graph and table. The equation is:
$A = \ell(60 - \ell)$. The equation is helpful in generating tables and graphs.

2. Again, sketches of possible rectangles may vary. Students may choose to consider a table or graph to analyze the situation and find that the maximum area is 1,056.25 when the sides are both 32.5. Encourage students to take bigger increments for the base. For example a table with increments of 5 is easy to generate. Then students can use this estimate where the maximum point occurs. The table can also be used to sketch a graph.

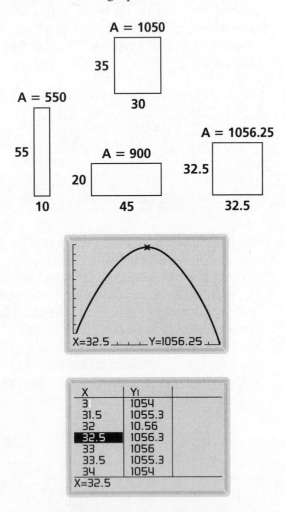

After Problem 1.3 you can come back to this problem and have the students find the equation and then connect the equation to the graph and table. The equation is: $A = \ell(65 - \ell)$. The equation is helpful in finding the table or graph.

3. **a.** Possible answer: The graph first increases and then decreases. It is symmetric about the line $\ell = 7.5$. It crosses the x-axis at $(0, 0)$ and $(15, 0)$.

   b. 56.25 units^2; the rectangle has a base and width length of about 7.5 units.

c. No such minimum area rectangle exists. If we find a rectangle with a given fixed perimeter and a small area, we can always find another rectangle with the same perimeter and an even smaller area. This process of finding smaller and smaller areas can continue indefinitely. **Note:** If we propose that one of the dimensions is zero, then the area becomes zero, but then this is not a rectangle.

d. about 36 units^2

e. The perimeter is 30 units. This can be found by using one set of dimensions and finding the perimeter. We can use the rectangle with dimensions of 7.5 units by 7.5 units. This gives us a perimeter of 30 units. The non-zero x-intercept is 15, which is half the perimeter.

4. **a.** Possible answer: The graph first increases and then decreases. It is symmetric about the line $\ell = 25$. It crosses the x-axis at $(0, 0)$ and $(50, 0)$. The maximum y-value is 625.

   b. 625 m^2; the length and width are both 25

   c. 400 m^2; 400 m^2; these two rectangles are related because they have the same dimensions and area, but the length and width are switched.

   d. 20 m by 30 m

   e. 100 m; if the length is 10 m, the area is 400 m^2, so the width is 40 m. So since $P = 2(\ell + w)$, the perimeter is $2(10 + 40) = 100$ m. Students might take advantage of the observation in part (c). For example, the area is 600 m^2 for both $\ell = 20$ and $\ell = 30$. These are the dimensions of the rectangle. Thus, the perimeter $= 2(20 + 30) = 100$ m.

5. **a.** As the length of a side increases by 1, the area increases first, and then it decreases after the length of a side is more than 8.

   b. 32 m. You can find the length of the other side by the equation $A = \ell w$ for the rectangular area, then add the lengths of two sides together and times it by 2.

c. The shape of the graph is a parabola that opens down.

Rectangles With a Perimeter of 32

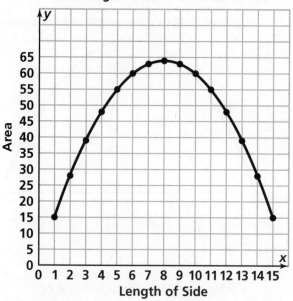

d. Possible approximate dimensions: 0.75 by 15.25

e. 8 by 8. From a table, students can find the largest value in the column of area, and then get the length of one side. From a graph, students can trace the graph to get the length of one side from the highest point with respect to area. To get the length of the other side, use the equation for rectangular area.

6. a. The perimeter of any figure is the distance around it. The perimeter of a rectangle: $P = \ell + \ell + w + w$, or $P = 2\ell + 2w$. If the perimeter of a rectangle is 30 m, and the length of one side is ℓ, then $30 = 2\ell + 2w$ or $15 = \ell + w$. So, $w = 15 - \ell$.

b. With the values given above $A = \ell(15 - \ell)$.

c. The graph is a parabola that opens down. It is symmetric about $x = 7.5$.

$y = x(15 - x)$

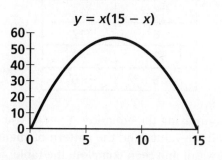

d. $A = \ell(15 - \ell)$
$A = 10(15 - 10)$
$A = 10(5) = 50 \text{ m}^2$

e. First look for the length on the x-axis, and then go up until you hit the curve. Go across to the y-axis values. This will tell you your y value or area of 50 m^2.

$y = x(15 - x)$

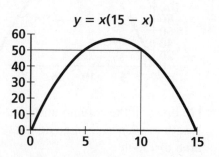

f. Go down in the column until you get to a length of 10, and then go across to find the area of 50 m^2.

g. To find the maximum area, students can either use a table, graph, or a trace on their calculator. The maximum value is when the length of one side is 7.5 m. This gives an area of 56.25 m^2.

7. a. If the perimeter of a rectangle is 50 m, and the length is ℓ, then $50 = 2\ell + 2w$ or $25 = \ell + w$, so $w = 25 - \ell$.

b. Area is the length times width, or $A = \ell w$. With the values given above $A = \ell(25 - \ell)$

c. The graph goes up and then down, like an upside-down U, or a parabola. It is symmetric about the line $x = 12.5$.

$y = x(25 - x)$

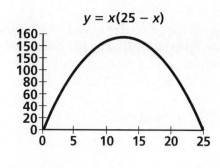

d. $A = \ell(25 - \ell)$
$A = 10(25 - 10)$
$A = 10(15) = 150 \text{ m}^2$

e. First look for the length on the *x*-axis, and then go up until you hit the curve. From there, go across to the *y*-axis. This will tell you your *y*-value or area of 150 m².

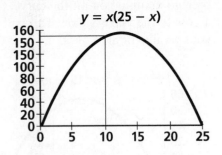

$$y = x(25 - x)$$

f. Go down in the column until you get to a length of 10, and then go across to find the area of 150 m².

g. To find the maximum area, students can either use a table, graph, or a trace on their calculator. The maximum value is when the length of one side is 12.5 m. This gives an area of 156.25 m².

8. a. Students may choose to use their graphing calculators to sketch this graph and either the trace function or table function to obtain various characteristics from the graph. The graph is a parabola that crosses the *x*-axis at $(0, 0)$ and $(20, 0)$. It has a greatest point at the point $(10, 100)$.

b. The dimensions of the rectangle with the greatest area is at the maximum value on the graph. These dimensions are 10 m by 10 m. The area would be 100 m².

c. A rectangle with length of 15 m would have an area of: $A = 15(20 - 15)$, $A = 15(5)$, or $A = 75$ m².

d. The fixed perimeter would be 40 units. You can find this by finding the perimeter of the maximum area rectangle, 10 units by 10 units, or you can find this from the equation, where 20 is the sum of two sides of the rectangles.

9. a. Students may use symmetry to complete their graphs with the additional points and then fill in the curve.

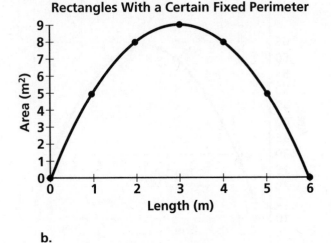

Rectangles With a Certain Fixed Perimeter

b.

Rectangles With Perimeter of 6 m

Length (m)	0	1	2	3	4	5	6
Area (m²)	0	5	8	9	8	5	0

c. The rectangle with the greatest area has dimensions of 3 m by 3 m. Students may look for the maximum point on the graph and find that the maximum occurs when the length is 3 m.

10. C

11. a.

Rectangles With Lengths Greater Than 4

Length (m)	Area (m²)
0	0
1	7
2	12
3	15
4	16
5	15
6	12
7	7
8	0

By applying the equation $A = \ell w$, you can find the values and the pattern of changes in width and then complete the table.

b.

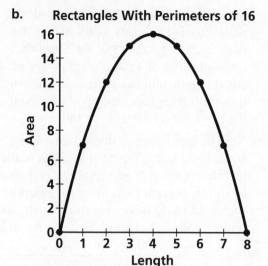

Rectangles With Perimeters of 16

c. The greatest area rectangle has dimensions 4 m by 4 m.

12. F; $A = \ell(8 - \ell)$

13. a.

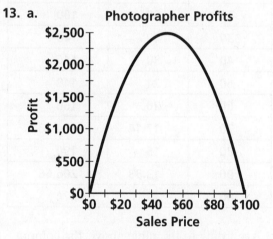

Photographer Profits

Profits of a Photographer

Sales Price	Profit
$0	$0
$10	$900
$20	$1,600
$30	$2,100
$40	$2,400
$50	$2,500
$60	$2,400
$70	$2,100
$80	$1,600
$90	$900
$100	$0

b. You can either get this from the table or graph. The price with the most profit is $50.

c. The shape of the graph seems to be the same. As the x-value increases, the y-value increases at first and then decreases in both the table and the graph.

The equation seems to be taking the same form. The only thing that seems to change is the number in the equation. In Problem 1.1 the equation was $A = \ell(10 - \ell)$, while in this problem, the equation had a 100 instead of a 10.

Connections

14. The rectangle with sides of length 4 and 5 has the smallest perimeter of 18 centimeters. You can use a table like the one below with ℓ, w, and P to find the smallest perimeter.

Rectangles With an Area of 20

Length	Width	Perimeter
1	20	42
2	10	24
4	5	18
5	4	18
10	2	24
20	1	42

15. D

16. a. 4,125 square meters; The area is 55(50 + 25) or 55(50) + 55(25) = 2,750 + 1,375 = 4,125 square meters.

b. The Distributive Property states that if two numbers are multiplied together and one is a sum, then the other factor can be distributed over the sum. That is, the factor is multiplied by each number in the sum. If a, b, and c are numbers, then the Distributive Property states that: $a(b + c) = ab + ac$. The Distributive Property also states that if each number in a sum has a common factor, then the common factor can be factored out from each number and the sum can be written as a product. The area of a rectangle that has been subdivided into two rectangles can be calculated by multiplying the length and width of the original rectangle or by calculating the area of the smaller rectangles and adding them.

Note that Exercises 15–32 are a review of the Distributive Property from *Accentuate the Negative*. The Distributive Property will be extended in the next investigation to quadratic expressions.

17. $21(5 + 6) = 21(5) + 21(6) = 105 + 126 = 231$

18. $2(35 + 1) = 2(35) + 2(1) = 70 + 2 = 72$

19. $12(10 - 2) = 12(10) - 12(2) = 120 - 24 = 96$

20. $9(3 + 5) = 9(3) + 9(5) = 27 + 45 = 72$

21. $15 + 6 = 3(5 + 2)$

22. $42 + 27 = 3(14 + 9)$

23. $12 + 120 = 12(1 + 10)$ or $6(2 + 20)$ or $3(4 + 40)$ or $2(6 + 60)$

24. $x = 25$

25. $x = 10$

26. As x increases by one unit, y increases by 5 units; the graph of the equation is a straight line with a slope of 5 and a y-intercept of 12. In the table as x increases by one unit, y increases by 5 units.

27. As x increases by one unit, y decreases by 3 units; the graph of the equation is a straight line with a slope of -3 and y-intercept of 10. In the table as x increases by one unit, the y-values are decreasing by 3 each time.

28. a. If w represents the width of the field and if the length is $\ell = 150 - w$ then the perimeter of the fields is $P = (150 - w) + (150 - w) + w + w = 300$ yards which is the perimeter given. So the equation of length works.

b. This is a linear relation with negative slope. As the width increases the length decreases.

c. Yes. The fact that the lengths of opposite sides of a parallelogram are equal guarantees the correctness of that equation.

Since the perimeter is 300 yards, half the perimeter is 150 yards. You can find the perimeter by taking $2\ell + 2w$. Since the opposite sides of a parallelogram are of equal length, half the perimeter is $\ell + w$. If the width is represented by w, the length is the rest of the 150 yards or $150 - w$.

d. No. The quadrilateral doesn't guarantee equal length of opposite sides. That is, the length of each side of a quadrilateral could be different from each other for example a trapezoid could have at least one pair of opposite sides that aren't equal in length.

29. a, b.

Rectangles With an Area of 1,200 (ft²)

Length (ft)	Width (ft)	Perimeter (ft)
10	120	260
20	60	160
30	40	140
40	30	140
50	24	148
60	20	160
70	17.14	174.28
80	15	190
90	13.33	206.66
100	12	224

c. According to the table above, the column of perimeter decreases first, and then increases after the length of one side is greater than 40. The rectangles with smaller difference between length and width have small perimeters. The rectangles with larger difference between length and width have large perimeters.

d. $\ell = \dfrac{1{,}200}{w}$

Extensions

30. a. The maximum area is 50 square meters with two sides of length 5 and 10 meters. You can use a table with Length, Width, and Area to find the maximum area. Be careful: 20 meters is only for three sides of a rectangle. That is, $\ell + 2w = 20$ (or $2\ell + w = 20$). (See table below.)

Rectangles With a Three-sided Perimeter of 20 (m)

Length	Width	Area
0	10	0
2	9	18
4	8	32
6	7	42
8	6	48
10	5	50
12	4	48
14	3	42
16	2	32
18	1	18
20	0	0

b. The shape and area of both rectangles that have the maximum areas are different from each other. One has dimensions 5 by 10 with 50 square meters, while the other has dimensions 5 by 5 with 25 square meters.

c. Both graphs have the same shape of upside down U with a maximum point, where the area is the greatest. However, both graphs have different maximum points.

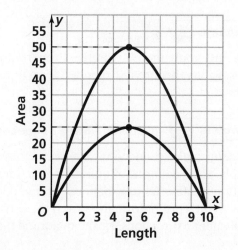

Possible Answers to Mathematical Reflections

1. a. There are several patterns students may recognize:

- The area increases fast at the beginning and then slows down at the maximum point and then decreases—slowly at first and then larger decreases occur as the length approaches half the perimeter.

- The x-coordinate of the maximum point occurs halfway between the x-intercepts. This value is also one-fourth of the perimeter.

- The x-intercepts occur at 0 and when $x =$ half the perimeter.

- The graph is symmetric about a line that passes through the maximum point and is perpendicular to the x-axis.

b. In the table, the growth pattern is similar to that described for the graph. The length increases at a steady rate from 0 to a point which is half the perimeter. The area increases until it reaches a maximum point and then it decreases. The area reaches its maximum value when the length is halfway between 0 and half the perimeter, or just one-fourth of the perimeter.

2. To find the maximum area for rectangles with a fixed perimeter, you could generate a table or a graph for the situation and find the greatest entry in the "Area" column of the table or find the y-coordinate of the maximum point on the graph. Or, since a square will have the greatest area, you could just find the area for the square with this perimeter.

3. The tables of quadratic functions cannot be generated by adding or multiplying the previous entry by a constant amount. The graphs of quadratic functions are not straight lines nor do they have the shape of an exponential function. Quadratic equations differ from exponential equations in that they don't contain a variable exponent, and they differ from linear equations in that they contain two linear factors multiplied together.

Investigation 2 Quadratic Expressions

Mathematical and Problem-Solving Goals

- Develop understanding of equivalent quadratic expressions, that is, of two expressions that model exactly the same relationship

- Continue the exploration of equivalent quadratic expressions of the form $ax^2 + bx$

- Represent a quadratic relationship in expanded and factored forms as two equivalent ways to write an expression for the area of a rectangle that has been subdivided into two rectangles

- Expand the context of area of rectangles to write equivalent quadratic expressions for the area of a rectangle $x^2 + bx + c$

- Use the area model to introduce the distributive property

- Use the area model and Distributive Property to multiply two binomials

- Use the area model and Distributive Property to re-write an expression that is in expanded form into an equivalent expression in factored form

- Make connections between a quadratic equation in factored/expanded form and its graph

- Predict the shape and features of a graph from the expanded and factored form of a quadratic equation

This investigation explores the context of area of rectangles as a means to develop understanding of the distributive property and to study equivalent expressions of quadratic functions.

Transforming squares into rectangles by increasing or decreasing the dimensions of a square leads to two equivalent expressions for the area of the rectangle. Students learn that quadratic expressions can be written in *expanded* or *factored* form—which are either formed by multiplying or factoring.

Summary of Problems

Problem 2.1 Trading Land

Students investigate how increasing one dimension of a square with sides of length *n* by 2 and decreasing the other dimension by 2 affects the area. The area of the new rectangle is $(x + 2)(x - 2)$. From a table, students discover that the area of the square is always 4 greater than the area of the rectangle, so the area of the rectangle is also $x^2 - 4$.

Problem 2.2 Changing One Dimension

Students use diagrams to help write equivalent expressions for the area of a rectangle created by increasing one of the dimensions.

Problem 2.3 Changing Both Dimensions

Students explore what happens when both dimensions of a square are increased. For example, if one dimension of a square of length *x* is increased by 2 and the other dimension is increased by 3, then the area of the rectangle can be written as $(x + 2)(x + 3)$ or as $x^2 + 5x + 6$. Students discover that quadratic expressions can be represented as the product of two linear expressions called the *factored form* or as the sum of one or more terms called the *expanded form*. These algebraic forms are interpreted geometrically as areas of rectangles and are written in two equivalent forms. This is an example of the Distributive Property, which was discussed in earlier units.

Problem 2.4 Factoring Quadratic Expressions

Students apply the Distributive Property to write expressions that are in expanded form in factored form.

Problem 2.5 A Closer Look at Parabolas

Students make connections among the tables, graphs and equations of quadratic functions written in factored or expanded form and learn how to interpret information from these two equivalent expressions for the quadratic function.

	Suggested Pacing	Materials for Students	Materials for Teachers	ACE Assignments
All	$7\frac{1}{2}$ days	Graphing calculators, student notebooks	Blank transparencies and transparency markers (optional), overhead graphing calculator, transparent grid paper	
2.1	1 day		Transparencies 2.1A and 2.1B	1, 50, 51
2.2	1 day		Transparency 2.2	2–16, 52, 53
2.3	2 days		Transparencies 2.3A and 2.3B	17–28, 54, 55
2.4	2 days	Poster paper (optional)		29–39, 56, 62–64
2.5	1 day	Waxed paper or transparent paper (optional)	Transparencies 2.5A, 2.5B, Labsheet 2.5	40–49, 57–61, 65
MR	$\frac{1}{2}$ day			

INVESTIGATION 2

Goals

- Introduce the concept of equivalent quadratic expressions

Students explore the area of a rectangle that has been created from a square by altering its dimensions. One dimension is increased by 2, the other is decreased by 2, then the areas are compared. By comparing the area of the new rectangle to the area of the square students discover the area of the new rectangle can be expressed as both $n^2 - 4$ and $(n - 2)(n + 2)$. In the rest of this investigation, students will continue to compare equivalent expressions, one in factored form and one in expanded form.

Launch 2.1

You might want to use Shel Silverstein's poem, "Smart" to introduce the idea of a fair trade. Then switch to the context of area and use the Getting Ready 2.1 to launch the problem.

Tell the story of the U.S. Malls. Ask the class to give their instinctive reaction to the question—not computations.

Suggested Questions

- *Does this seem like a fair trade?* (Some students will respond yes because adding 100 and subtracting 100 appears to equal 0. Some students may calculate the areas of the two pieces of land and find that the area of the rectangular piece of land is 10,000 square meters less than the area of the square piece of land and say that it is not a fair trade.)

Now let the class work on the problem. If you think students need a bit more help before they explore the problem, draw a square on the overhead or board. Explain that the square is to be traded for a rectangular piece of land. Describe how the "trade off" is to occur and then draw a rectangle.

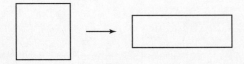

Suggested Questions

- *How could you find the areas of these two plots of land?* (In both cases, you can multiply the length by the width.)

In this problem, you will test several cases and record your data in a table. Your table will help you to see patterns that will tell you more about situations like these.

Let the class work in pairs.

Explore 2.1

Students may have trouble generalizing each column. Encourage them to first express the pattern for each column in words and then help them generalize their verbal expressions into symbols. For example, students may say that the length of the rectangle is always two more than the side length of the square. From this observation, you could ask the following questions:

Suggested Questions

- *If the side length of the square is n, then what is the length of the rectangle?* ($n + 2$)

- *What is the width of the rectangle?* (Similarly, the width of the rectangle is $n - 2$.)

- *What is the area of rectangle?* [The area is the product of the length and width or $(n + 2)$ $(n - 2)$. Some students may write this as $n + 2 \times n - 2$. If this occurs, try some values for n or say the entire expression for width must be multiplied by the entire expression for length or you could say the following:

"If you write $n + 2 \times n - 2$, it looks like n is added to $2 \times n$ and then 2 is subtracted. This is not the same as finding the two numbers $n + 2$ and $n - 2$ and then multiplying. The parentheses make this clear."]

As students finish, ask them to test their patterns on a different case:

- *What happens if one side length is increased by 5 and the other side length is decreased by 5?*

- *Suppose the two numbers are different. What happens if one side length is increased by 5 and the other side length is decreased by 1?*

Does your pattern still hold? (No; the pattern will not hold since the difference in the areas will no longer be a constant value.)

Summarize 2.1

Ask the class to discuss their answers. They should note that the area of the rectangle is 4 less than the area of the square. Use the table to look for patterns.

Put the table on the overhead or board. Solicit answers from the class for the first three squares. (Figure 1)

Suggested Questions

- *Why does the table start at 2 rather than 0 or 1?*

- *What patterns do you see in the table?* (Several patterns should emerge in the discussion:

   The area of each square is the square of the side length.

   The area of the square increases in the pattern 5, 7, 9, 11, 13, and so on.

The length and width of the rectangle each increase by 1 from one entry to the next.

The area of the rectangle increases in the pattern 5, 7, 9, 11, 13, and so on. This is the same as for the area of the square.)

The area of the rectangle is always 4 less than the area of the square.

- *How can we use these patterns to predict the numbers in the next row?* [The pattern in the area of the square is that they are consecutive square numbers 25, 36, 49, 64, etc. Note to teacher: The nature of quadratics is that there is a pattern in the second differences. Students will explore this further in Investigations 3 and 4. In this case, the differences in the difference between successive area values for the square are 2. The area of the rectangle has the same pattern in the differences of the differences, so when the sides are 10 and 6, the area will increase by 2 more than 13 (the difference between the areas of 45 and 32), or 15, so the new area is $45 + 15 = 60$. The difference between the areas of the square and the rectangle is always 4.] (Figure 2)

Figure 1 **Areas of Squares and Rectangles**

Square		Rectangle			Difference in Area
Length Side	Area	Length	Width	Area	
2	4	4	0	0	4
3	9	5	1	5	4
4	16	6	2	12	4
5	25	7	3	21	4
6	36	8	4	32	4

Figure 2 **Areas of Squares and Rectangles**

Square		Rectangle			Difference in Area
Length Side	Area	Length	Width	Area	
2	4	4	0	0	4
3	9	5	1	5	4
4	16	6	2	12	4
5	25	7	3	21	4
6	36	8	4	32	4
7	49	9	5	45	4
8	64	10	6	60	4

Suggested Questions

- *Can we find a general expression for each column?* (Enter their answers into the last row of the table—see table. The generalizations may be difficult for some students. See the comments in the Explore on how to help students write symbolic statements.) (Figure 3)

Use these generalizations to find the values corresponding to a square of length 100. (Figure 4)

- *Express the area of the rectangle in symbols.* [It is the product—$(n + 2)(n - 2)$.]

- *How else can we express the area of the rectangle?* (If the class does not see that $n^2 - 4$ is an expression for the area of the rectangle, ask more questions to guide them in this direction. The pattern in the table can help.)

- *What is the expression for the area of the square?* (n^2)

- *In general, how does the area of the rectangle compare to the area of the square?* (It will be 4 less than the area of the square.)

- *How could you write this as a symbolic expression?* ($n^2 - 4$)

- *What are the two expressions that represent the area of the new rectangle?* [($n^2 - 4$) or $(n + 2)(n - 2)$]

- *What must be true about these two expressions for the area of the new rectangle? [They are equivalent. That is, $n^2 - 4 = (n + 2)(n - 2)$ because both expressions describe the same area.]*

- *How can we check whether they are equivalent?* (We can try some values of n to see whether the two expressions predict the same area.)

- *Let's try some values for n.* [If $n = 10$, $n^2 - 4 = 10^2 - 4 = 100 - 4 = 96$ m^2 and $(10 + 2)(10 - 2) = (12)(8) = 96$ m^2. Try two more values.

- *Can we try all possible values for n?* [No. **Note:** Trying some examples of values of n is not a definitive proof that any 2 expressions are equivalent. However, if we know that 2 expressions are quadratic, then checking that they have equal values for 3 substitute values of the variable will suffice to show that they are equivalent. More on this in *Say It With Symbols*.]

- *Could we check whether the two expressions are equivalent by graphing A = $n^2 - 4$ and A = $(n + 2)(n - 2)$?* (Yes. They should give the same graph. Use a graphing calculator to get the graphs.)

- *In the expression for the area, $(n + 2)(n - 2)$, the term n + 2 represents the length, ℓ and the term n − 2 represents the width, w. What would the graph of each of these equations, ℓ = n + 2 and w = n − 2, look like?* (The graphs would both be straight lines. Each represents a linear relationship.)

Figure 3   **Expressions For Areas of Squares and Rectangles**

Square		Rectangle			Difference
Length Side	Area	Length	Width	Area	in Area
n	n^2	$(n + 2)$	$(n - 2)$	$(n + 2)(n - 2)$	4

Figure 4   **Areas of Squares and Rectangles**

Square		Rectangle			Difference
Length Side	Area	Length	Width	Area	in Area
100	10000	102	98	9996	4

Because each of these is a linear relationship, each factor of the expression for the area must be linear. In this case we call them *linear factors*.

Suggested Questions

- *Compare the two graphs of the areas and lengths of the square and the new rectangle.* (Both graphs are parabolas. Each has a minimum point and each is symmetric about a vertical line through the minimum point. The graph of $A = n^2 - 4$ seems to be shifted down 4 units from the graph of $A = n^2$.)

To illustrate this transformation, draw the two graphs on the same coordinate axis on the overhead. Put a blank transparency on top of the graphs. Draw an outline of the graph of $n^2 - 4$ and then move this graph 4 units up along the *x*-axis. It fits exactly on top of the graph of n^2.

- *Which part of the graph makes sense in this problem?* (The negative values for area do not make sense, so only the values for $x \geq 2$ make sense—that is, give areas with positive values or 0. Indicate these values on the graph by using a colored marker.)

When we model real situations with equations, graphs, or tables showing relationships, it is often possible to extend the table, or graph, or values for *x* in the equation beyond what makes sense in the real situation. Sometimes this helps us to see patterns that we miss if we look only at the values that make sense in the situation. For example, it is hard to tell whether a graph is a parabola by looking at only part of the graph.

Suggested Questions

- *How do the graphs in this problem compare to those you made in Investigation 1?* (The shapes of the graphs are similar to the graphs in Investigation 1, except in this problem the parabolas are upright rather than upside down and have a minimum point rather than a maximum point. Both types of parabolas

have symmetry about a vertical line through the minimum point or maximum point. In Investigation 1, the area increases to a certain point and then decreases. In this problem the area is increasing. But if one looks at the extended graph, then the graphs will be decreasing until it gets to the minimum point and then it starts to increase.)

- *How do the tables in this problem compare to those you made in Investigation 1?* (If one looks at the table generated by the equation on the calculator, then the table in this problem will be decreasing until it gets to the minimum point and then it starts to increase. The tables in Investigation 1 had an increase-decrease pattern in the dependent variable.)

- *How do the equations in this problem compare to those you made in Investigation 1?* (The equations in Investigation 1 are written as the product of two linear factors, which is similar to this problem. In Investigation 1 the equation is the product of two linear expressions, ℓ and $\frac{P}{2} - \ell$. In this problem the two linear expressions are $n + 2$ and $n - 2$. In both cases the two factors are multiplied together to get the area.)

Check for Understanding

- *Suppose one dimension of a square is increased by 3 and the other dimension is decreased by 3. How does the area of the square compare to the area of the new rectangle?* [The area of the rectangle will be 9 less than the area of the square. The generalizations are shown in Figure 5. Some students may need a table to write the expression or see the comparisons. Some will be able to write the area of the rectangle as $(n + 3)(n - 3)$. Some will be able to apply the pattern from Problem 2.1 to write the area as $n^2 - 9$. Thus, $n^2 - 9 = (n + 3)(n - 3)$.]

Figure 5   **Areas of Squares and Rectangles**

Square		Rectangle			Difference
Length Side	Area	Length	Width	Area	in Area
n	n^2	$(n + 3)$	$(n - 3)$	$(n + 3)(n - 3)$	9

- *Suppose one dimension of a square is increased by 3 and the other dimension is decreased by 1. How does the area of the square compare to the area of the new rectangle?* [Students might think that the generalization is the same as if the two numbers are the same—that is, it is the product of the two changes— 3×1 and that the difference is 3. But the expression $(x + 3)(x - 1)$ is equal to $x^2 + 2x - 3$, so the difference in area is the difference between x^2 and $x^2 + 2x - 3$, which is $2x - 3$. The pattern only holds if the increase and decrease are the same.]

- *What is the value of $(n + 3)(n - 2)$ when $n = 1$? What is the value of $(n^2 - 5)$ when $n = 1$? Are $(n + 3)(n - 2)$ and $n^2 - 5$ equivalent?* (No. To be equivalent, the expressions have to have the same value for *all* values of n.)

You could also go back to the question posed in the mall trade and instead of the square whose length is 125 meters, ask the class to generalize the problem for any square with side length n, being traded for a rectangular piece of land whose length is 100 meters longer and whose width is 100 meters shorter than the square.

2.1 Trading Land

Mathematical Goal

- Introduce the concept of equivalent quadratic expressions

Launch

Use the Getting Ready to launch the problem.

Have students give instinctive reactions—not computations:

- *Does this seem like a fair trade? Introduce the situation in the problem and make sure students understand how the land is traded.*

- *How could you find the areas of these two plots of land?*

You will use a table to record data for different cases in order to see patterns for situations like these. Let the class work in pairs.

Materials
- Graphing calculator
- Transparencies 2.1A, 2.1B

Explore

If students say that the length of the rectangle is always two more than the side length of the square, ask the following:

- *If the side length of the square is n, then what is the length of the rectangle?*

- *What is the width of the rectangle?*

- *What is the area of the rectangle?*

If students pick an incorrect expression have them try some values for *n*. Make sure students are using parentheses correctly.

- *What happens if one side length is increased by 5 and the other side length is decreased by 5?*

- *What happens if one side length is increased by 5 and the other side length is decreased by 1? Does your pattern still hold?*

Summarize

Put the table on the overhead or board.

- *Why does the table start at 2 rather than 0 or 1?*

- *What patterns do you see in the table? How can we use these patterns to predict the numbers in the next row?*

- *Can we find a general expression for each column?*

- *Use these generalizations to find the values corresponding to a square of length 100. Express the area of the rectangle in symbols.*

- *How else can we express the area of the rectangle?*

If students are having trouble, ask:

- *What is the expression for the area of the square?*

- *In general, how does the area of the rectangle compare to the area of the square?*

Materials
- Student notebooks

continued on next page

Summarize
continued

- *So how could you write this as a symbolic expression?*
- *Using the expression* n^2, *how could we write an expression for the area of the rectangle?*
- *What must be true about these two expressions for the area of the rectangle?*
- *How can we check whether they are equivalent?*
- *Could we check whether the two expressions are equivalent by graphing* $A = n^2 - 4$ *and* $A = (n + 2)(n - 2)$?
- *How do the graphs(tables)(equations) in this problem compare to those you made in Investigation 1?*
- *Suppose one dimension of a square is increased by 3 and the other dimension is decreased by 3. How does the area of the square compare to the area of the new rectangle?*
- *Repeat by increasing one dimension by 3 and decreasing the other by 1.*

Refer back to the question posed in the mall trade.

- *For any square with length* n, *being traded for a rectangular piece of land whose length is 100 m longer and whose width is 100 m shorter than the square.*

Materials
- Student notebooks

ACE Assignment Guide for Problem 2.1

Differentiated Instruction Solutions for All Learners

Core 1, 50, 51

Adapted For suggestions about adapting Exercise 1 and other ACE exercises, see the CMP *Special Needs Handbook*.
Connecting to Prior Units 50: *Moving Straight Ahead*; 51: *Thinking with Mathematical Models*

Answers to Problem 2.1

A. 1. (Figure 6)

2. The table starts at side length 2 because for any side length less than 2, the width of the new rectangle, $n - 2$, will be negative, which does not make sense for a length measurement. Students may argue that a side length of 2 doesn't work because area can't be zero. In this context, what that means is that you are traded no land in exchange for your original square plot, which is definitely not a fair trade.

Figure 6

Original Square		New Rectangle			Difference in Area (m²)
Side Length (m)	Area (m²)	Length (m)	Width (m)	Area (m²)	
2	4	4	0	0	4
3	9	5	1	5	4
4	16	6	2	12	4
5	25	7	3	21	4
6	36	8	4	32	4
...	...	...	...	...	...
n	n^2	$(n + 2)$	$(n - 2)$	$(n + 2)(n - 2)$	4

3. The area of the rectangular lot is always 4 m^2 less than the area of the square lot. The trade is not fair for any side length. Students may also generalize that the difference in areas is $n^2 - (n + 2)(n - 2)$ which is correct. This is equivalent to 4 using the Distributive Property since
$n^2 - (n + 2)(n - 2) =$
$n^2 - [(n + 2)n + (n + 2)(-2)] =$
$n^2 - (n^2 + 2n - 2n - 4) = 4.$
You may want to come back to this after Problem 2.3 or wait until students explore the unit *Say It With Symbols*, which explains distributing a negative over the parentheses.

B. 1. $A_1 = n^2$

2. $A_2 = n^2 - 4$ or $A_2 = (n - 2)(n + 2)$

3. Yes; The area of the new lot can be expressed as $(n + 2)(n - 2)$ as shown in the table above, and since the area of the new lot is 4 less than the area of the square lot another expression for the area of the new lot is $n^2 - 4$.

C. 1.

Areas of Original Lot and New Lot

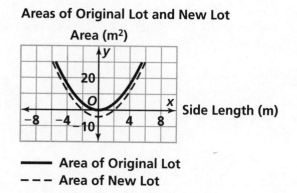

2. Since area and lengths are positive, representing the area of the original lot is only valid for $A > 0$ (or $n > 0$). For the area of the new rectangular lot, only the graph for $A > 0$ (or $n > 2$) is valid. See the bold part of the graphs above for possible values.

3. Both graphs are parabolas with a minimum point and are symmetric about the *y*-axis. The graph of the original square lot has a minimum point at $(0, 0)$ and the graph of the new lot has a minimum point at $(0, -4)$. The graph of the new lot looks like the graph of the original lot if it was moved down 4 units.

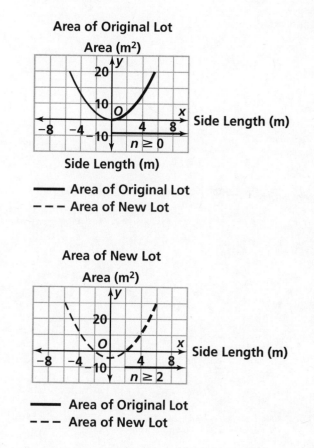

D. Both relationships are quadratic; the graphs are both parabolas with lines of symmetry. Students may note the expressions for the area contain a variable raised to the second power indicating a quadratic.

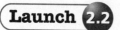

Changing One Dimension

2.2

Goals

- Continue the exploration of equivalent quadratic expressions of the form $ax^2 + bx$

- Represent a quadratic relationship in expanded and factored forms as two equivalent ways to write an expression for the area of a rectangle that has been subdivided into two rectangles

Students examine three cases in which a square is transformed into a rectangle. In the first case, in the Getting Ready for Problem 2.2, one of the dimensions of a square is increased by 3. In a second case, one of the dimensions is increased by 6. In the third case, one of the dimensions is decreased by 6. Diagrams of the area of the rectangle help to illustrate that the two quadratic expressions, the expanded form and the factored form, for the area in each case are equivalent.

A note on terminology In this first introduction to quadratic expressions, we prefer the term, *expanded form* to *standard form*, which is used in some texts. It provides intuition that this form represents the sum of the areas of the smaller rectangles that compose the large rectangle. Also, the word "standard" implies that standard is the preferred form. In the summary of this problem, students should be able to identify factored and expanded forms as examples of the distributive property which was discussed in earlier units: *Accentuate the Negative, Moving Straight Ahead,* and *Thinking with Mathematical Models.*

Launch 2.2

Refer to Problem 2.1 and how the area of the square changed when one side was increased by 2 and the other side was decreased by 2.

Suggested Questions Pose the following challenge.

- *Suppose we change just one dimension of a square. How do the areas of the square and new rectangle compare?* (Some students may quickly see that if the change to the dimension is positive, then the area of the new rectangle will be greater than the area of

the square and smaller if the dimension of the square is decreased.)

The goal in this problem is to get students to represent the areas geometrically in terms of a square and rectangle that will provide them with some intuition about the meaning of each term or factor in the expression for the area. This will also help them develop deeper understanding of the distributive property that is the focus of the next problem.

Discuss the Getting Ready:

- *How do the areas of the square and the rectangle compare?* (The area of the new rectangle is greater than that of the square by the amount of area in the narrow rectangle that was added to the square, which is $3x$.)

- *Write two expressions for the area of the new rectangle. How do you know that these two expressions are equivalent?* [Two expressions that represent the area of the new rectangle are $x^2 + 3x$ or $x(x + 3)$. These expressions are equivalent because they represent the area of the same figure. The area of the new rectangle is $x(x + 3)$ and $x^2 + 3x$.]

- *What is the area of each small rectangle? Write it on the rectangle.*

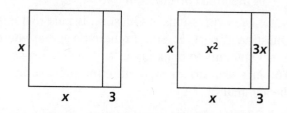

length times width = sum of the area of the sub parts

Now tell the class they will work on similar questions in the problem. You could summarize after Question A and then launch Questions B and C.

Let the class work in groups of two or three.

Explore 2.2

Some students may need assistance with finding the equivalent expression for area in Question A,

parts (1) and (2). You may need to point out that the rectangle consists of the original square and an additional rectangular area or the original square minus a rectangular area.

Suggested Questions

Question A, part (1)

- *What is the area of the original square?*
- *What are the dimensions of the added rectangle?*
- *What is the area of the added rectangle?*
- *So how can you find the area of the new rectangle?*

Question A, part (2)

- *What are the dimensions of the large rectangle? What is its area?*
- *What is the area of the unshaded rectangle? How can you use this area to find the area of the shaded part of the large rectangle?*

Question B and C

Some students may need hints on how to represent the expressions in equivalent forms.

- *What are the dimensions of the non-square rectangle in Question B, part (2)?* (x and $x - 4$)
- *What does the dimension $x - 4$ mean?* (We started with a square with side lengths x and then we decreased one side by 4.)
- *How can we represent this decrease?* (Shade in the area corresponding to $4x$.)

Note: The expressions in Question B, part (3), and Question C, part (3), aren't quadratic and are here to get students to think about adding like terms. You may want to ask students either here or in the summary:

- *Which expressions in Questions B and C do you think are quadratic? Why?*

Summarize 2.2

Be sure the class explains how they got their answers.

Suggested Questions Here are some questions to probe at students' understanding:

- *You have two expressions, $x(x + 6)$ and $x^2 + 6x$ for the area of the new rectangle. x and $(x + 6)$ are each factors of the expression $x^2 + 6x$. What do the two factors in the first*

expression say about what happened to the original square? [Each factor is one of the dimensions, length or width of the new rectangle. The factor x means one of the dimensions of the square was not changed and the factor $(x + 6)$ means one of the dimensions was increased by 6. The area of a rectangle is length times width, so the product is the area.]

- *What does the expression, $x^2 + 6x$, mean in terms of the area?* (The new rectangle has two parts—the original square whose area is represented by x^2, and a rectangular piece whose area is represented by $6x$.)

For Question A, part (2), you might pose a similar situation to test for understanding:
Suppose one dimension of a square is decreased by 2 units to create a new rectangle.

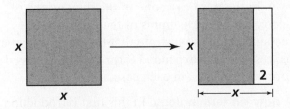

Make sure the class understands what the new rectangle is and how it was formed.

- *What does the unshaded part represent?* (It is the amount of area that is taken away from the square to form the new rectangle.)
- *How do the areas of the square and the new rectangle compare?* (They should be able to say that the area of the rectangle is smaller, because it consists of only part of the original square—a rectangular shape with area $2x$ has been taken away.)

Discuss the two equivalent forms for the area of the rectangle. The two factors are x and $x - 2$. They represent the dimensions of the new rectangle. The product, $x(x - 2)$ represents the area of the new rectangle. The expression $x^2 - 2x$ also represents the area of the new rectangle. The subtracted term, $2x$, says that a rectangle with dimensions x and 2 and an area of $2x$ has been subtracted from the area of the original square, which was x^2.

Introducing the terms
expanded form and *factored form*

Put the following pairs of equivalent expressions on the overhead or board to summarize

Question A and to introduce the terminology of *expanded form* and *factored form*.

$$x^2 - 4 = (x - 2)(x + 2)$$

$$x^2 + 3x = x(x + 3)$$

$$x^2 - 3x = x(x - 3)$$

In each equation look closely at the expressions on each side of the equal sign. One of the expressions in each pair is written as a product of two factors. Such expressions are said to be in *factored form*. (You may have to help students identify how we know this is a product of two factors. Where is the multiplication? What are the factors?)

The other expression is written as a sum or difference of terms. This form is called the *expanded form*.

Explain that in this context a term is an expression that consists of variables and/or numbers multiplied together, such as $3, x, 3x, \pi x, 3x^2$, and $3x$. (The definition of *term* will be expanded in high school and college. It was first used in *Moving Straight Ahead*.)

Suggested Question

- *Why does it make sense to express the area of a rectangle as a product and as a sum?* (In the factored form the dimensions—length and width— are used to compute the area. Area = length × width. In the expanded form the rectangle has been divided into rectangular parts. The area of the rectangle is the sum of the area of each of these parts.)

Now summarize Questions B and C using the terminology of expanded and factored forms.

Connecting to the Distributive Property

You can use the examples in this problem to remind students of the distributive property and to launch the next problem.

The equation $x(x + 3) = x^2 + 3x$ involving the two expressions $x(x + 3)$ and $x^2 + 3x$ is an example of the distributive property.

Draw a rectangle to show that $x(x + 3) = x^2 + 3x$.

The general form of the distributive property is: if a, b, and c are any three numbers, then

$$a(b + c) = ab + ac$$

factored form   expanded form

We multiply to expand the form $a(b + c)$ to $ab + ac$.

Writing $ab + ac$ as $a(b + c)$ is *called* factoring the expression.

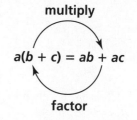

multiply

$$a(b + c) = ab + ac$$

factor

If needed, you might give the class a couple of numerical sentences that illustrate the distributive property. For example, the numerical sentence $3(4 + 5) = 3 \times 4 + 3 \times 5$ illustrates the distributive property. Since both expressions represent the same number 27, (i.e., $3 \times 4 + 3 \times 5 = 12 + 15 = 27$ and $3(4 + 5) = 3(9) = 27$), they are equal.

Check for Understanding

Put the following expressions on the board.

$$x(x + 8) \quad x(x - 8) \quad x^2 + 7x \quad x^2 - 9x$$

Suggested Question

- *These four expressions represent the area of a rectangle that was created from a square. What would a sketch of the rectangle look like? What is an equivalent expression for the area of the rectangle?* (Give the students a few minutes to try these and then have someone from the class come up and make a sketch. Ask for an equivalent expression that represents the area. Write the expressions for the area of each part of the rectangle.)

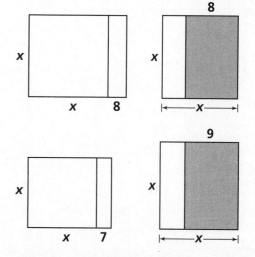

Describe how the two equivalent expressions for the area of each rectangle are an example of the Distributive Property.

2.2 Changing One Dimension

Mathematical Goals

- Continue the exploration of equivalent quadratic expressions of the form $ax^2 + bx$
- Represent a quadratic relationship in expanded and factored forms as two equivalent ways to write the area of a rectangle that has been subdivided into two rectangles

Launch

Refer back to Problem 2.1.

- *Suppose we change just one dimension of a square. How do the areas of the square and new rectangle compare?*

You could summarize after Question A and then launch Questions B and C. Let the class work in groups of two or three.

Materials
- Graphing calculators
- Transparency 2.2

Explore

Some students may need assistance with finding the equivalent expression for area in Question A, part (1).

- *What is the area of the original square?*
- *What are the dimensions of the added rectangle?*
- *What is the area of the added rectangle?*
- *So how can you find the area of the new rectangle?*

For Question A, part (2):

- *What is the area of the original square?*
- *What are the dimensions of the unshaded rectangle?*
- *What is the area of the unshaded rectangle?*
- *So how can you find the area of the shaded part of the square?*

Vocabulary
- equivalent
- factored form
- expanded form
- term

Summarize

Be sure students explain how they got their answers.

- *You have two expressions, $x(x + 6)$ and $x^2 + 6x$ for the area of the new rectangle. x and $(x + 6)$ are each factors of the expression $x^2 + 6x$. What do the two factors in the first expression say about what happened to the original square?*
- *What does the expression, $x^2 + 6x$, mean in terms of the area?*

After Question A, part (2), you might pose a similar situation:

- *Suppose one dimension of a square is decreased by 2 units to create a new rectangle. What does the unshaded part represent?*
- *How do the areas of the square and new rectangle compare?*

Discuss the two equivalent forms for the area and what the factors and terms in the expressions represent in terms of the rectangles.

Materials
- Student notebooks

continued on next page

- *Why does it make sense to express the area of the rectangle as both a product and as a sum?*

Use the examples in this problem to remind students of the Distributive Property.

Show pairs of equivalent expressions to summarize Question A and to introduce the terminology of *expanded form* and *factored form*. (See extended Teacher's Guide.) Summarize Questions B and C using the terminology of expanded and factored forms.

ACE Assignment Guide for Problem 2.2

Differentiated Instruction
Solutions for All Learners

Core 2–4, 8–16
Other *Applications* 5–7, *Connections* 52, 53; unassigned choices from previous problems

Adapted For suggestions about adapting ACE exercises, see the CMP *Special Needs Handbook*.
Connecting to Prior Units 52: *Covering and Surrounding*; 53: *Comparing and Scaling*

Answers to Problem 2.2

A. 1. $x(x + 6)$ and $x^2 + 6x$
  2. $x(x - 6)$ and $x^2 - 6x$

B. 1.

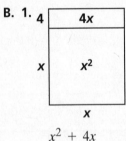

$x^2 + 4x$

2.

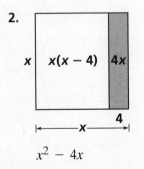

$x^2 - 4x$

3.

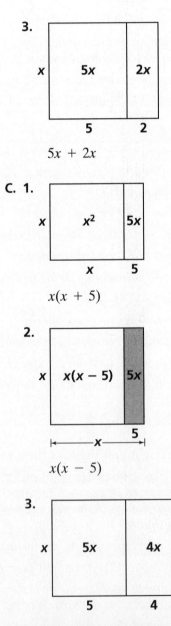

$5x + 2x$

C. 1.

$x(x + 5)$

2.

$x(x - 5)$

3.

$x(5 + 4) = 9x$; In the expanded form we can think of each term as a rectangular area which forms part of the divided rectangle.

Changing Both Dimensions

Goals

- Expand the context of area of rectangles to write equivalent quadratic expressions for the area of a rectangle $x^2 + bx + c$

- Use the area model to review the Distributive Property

- Use the area model and Distributive Property to multiply two binomials

In the last problem, only one dimension of a square was changed leading to the equivalent forms of $x(x + b)$ and $x^2 + bx$. In this problem both dimensions of a square are increased to form a new rectangle. The area of the rectangle can be expressed in factored and expanded form—$(x + a)(x + b)$ and $x^2 + (a + b)x + ab$. The Distributive Property can be used to multiply $(x + a)(x + b)$ to get the expanded form $x^2 + (a + b)x + c$.

Some caution on using the area models

Area models are used in this unit only for situations involving expressions of the form $x^2 + bx + c$ where b and c are both positive. An area model can be made to represent an expression such as $(x + 3)(x - 4)$. To find the expanded form for $(x + 3)(x - 4)$ we are looking at the unshaded region in the diagram below. The dimensions of this region are $(x + 3)$ and $(x - 4)$.

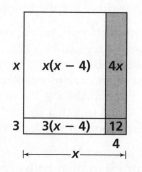

One sub-rectangle of the unshaded region has dimensions 3 and $(x - 4)$ and an area of $3x - 12$. The other sub-rectangle has dimensions x and $x - 4$, giving an area of $x^2 - 4x$. This is why the area of the total unshaded region is $(x^2 - 4x) + (3x - 12) = x^2 - x - 12$.

An area model can also be used for situations like $(x - 3)(x - 2)$. However, the logic involved requires students to be already comfortable using the Distributive Property.

At this point, the area model becomes too complex to be useful. The area model works best and is more intuitive in situations where the numbers are all positive. The goal of Problem 2.3 is to have students use area models to suggest a more general strategy that can be applied to the multiplication of all expressions of the form $(ax + b)(cx + d)$—the strategy is called the distributive property.

Once students are comfortable with the distributive property, examples such as $(x + 2)(x - 4)$ and $(x - 3)(x - 2)$ can be expanded by using the Distributive Property. But the point is not to dwell on the area model situations involving negative numbers. Help the students see the power of the distributive model.

Launch 2.3

If you did not review the Distributive Property in the summary of Problem 2.2, you should do so now. You can also review adding *like terms* using the Distributive Property. An effective way to develop understanding of like terms is to use the area of rectangles as follows.

Put the following picture on the overhead or board.

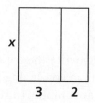

Suggested Questions Ask:

- *Find two equivalent expressions for the area of the large rectangle that is made up of the two smaller rectangles.* [$(3x + 2x)$ or $x(3 + 2)$ or $5x$]

- *Sketch a rectangle to show that the following two expressions for the area of the rectangle are equivalent:* $5x + 3x$ *and* $8x$. [This is an example of the Distributive Property: $5x + 3x = x(5 + 3) = 8x$]

- *Optional: Compare the graphs of each expression:* $y = 5x + 3x$ *and* $y = 8x$. (The graphs are the same. It is a straight line with a slope of 8, passing through origin.)

- *Write the expression,* $2x + 4x$, *as one term.* ($6x$)

- *Write the expression,* $10x$, *as the sum of two terms.* (There are many possibilities. Some are $10x = 5x + 5x = 1x + 9x = 2x + 8x = ...$ etc.)

Use the Getting Ready to launch the problem. Draw a square with side lengths equal to x units.

- *One dimension of the square is increased by 2 and the other dimension is increased by 3. What will the new rectangle look like?*

- *Compare the areas of the two rectangles.*

- *How can we represent the area of each rectangle?*

Give the students time to make suggestions for subdividing the rectangle, writing the dimensions and writing expressions for the areas. Write their suggestions for subdividing and labeling the new rectangle on the overhead. Some may use the dimensions to write it in factored form: $(x + 2)(x + 3)$. Some may add up the areas of the smaller rectangles to write it in expanded form: $x^2 + 2x + 3x + 6$ or $x^2 + 5x + 6$. These two expressions are equivalent because they represent the same area.

In this problem, you will work to express the area of the new rectangle in both factored form and expanded form.

Let the class work in groups of two to four.

Explore 2.3

Some students may write the expanded form in four parts rather than combining the like terms. If necessary, use an area model to remind students that $3x + 5x = 8x$. Some students may need help with Question B that doubles a side and then extends it by 2. If so, refer them back to rectangle 4 in Question A, which doubles a side.

Suggested Questions Some questions you may want to ask while students are working on Questions A and B include:

- *What are the dimensions of the large rectangle?*

- *How can you use these dimensions to find the area of the large rectangle?*

- *Is there another way to find the area of the large rectangle?*

In Question C, if students are struggling, suggest that they label the dimensions and areas of the subregions on the rectangle.

Summarize 2.3

Call on various groups to present their answers to the parts of the problem and to explain their reasoning. For each Question, ask questions to help them generalize their strategies. For example,

Suggested Questions If students are having trouble writing the expanded form, point to each smaller rectangle in Question A and ask:

- *What are the dimensions of this larger rectangle? What is its area? How can the area of each of the smaller rectangles be used to find the expression for the area of the whole rectangle?*

- *In Question B, how did you find the expression for the area in factored form?* [The dimensions of the new rectangle are $x + x + 2$ or $2x + 2$ and $x + 3$, so the area in factored form is $(2x + 2)(x + 3)$.]

- *How did you find the expression in factored form?* [(The area of the rectangle is equal to the sum of the areas of the smaller rectangles. So, the area is $2x^2 + 6x + 2x + 6$ or $(2x^2 + 8x + 6.)$]

To help develop deeper understanding of equivalent expressions, ask the following:

- *Describe two different ways to write quadratic expressions.* (They can be written in factored or expanded form. Factored form is when there are two linear expressions multiplied together. Expanded form is when everything is just all added together or subtracted and the highest exponent for the variable is two.)

- *How can you decide if two expressions are equivalent?* (Show that both expressions represent the same area for a given rectangle. Properties of numbers like the Distributive Property can be used. For example, $2(x + 3)$ and $2x + 6$ are equivalent using the Distributive Property. The Distributive Property can also be used to show that expressions such as $(x + 3)(x - 2)$ and $x^2 + x - 6$ are equivalent and you may want to begin to discuss how to use the Distributive Property on an expression like this in the summary of this problem. Problem 2.4 discusses this issue further.)

In Question C, most students will use an area model. Some may begin to see the connection to the Distributive Property.

Use Question D to begin to connect the methods of multiplying two binomials using an area model and the Distributive Property.

Ask the following:

• *Use the Distributive Property to write the expression $x(x + 2)$ in an equivalent form.* $[x(x + 2)] = x(x) + x(2) = x^2 + 2x$ which connects the area model below:

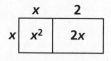

• *Use the Distributive Property to write the expression $(x + 2)(x + 4)$ in an equivalent form.*

$$[(x + 2)(x + 4) = (x + 2)(x) + (x + 2)(4)$$
$$= x(x) + 2(x) + 4x + 8$$
$$= x^2 + 6x + 8$$

(In the area model below, this is the area of the left two rectangles plus the right two.)]

	x	4
x	x^2	$4x$
2	$2x$	8

If students need more time with the rectangular model, let them use it. Multiplying binomials and factoring are revisited in *Say It With Symbols*.

Go over Question E, to check if students are using the Distributive Property correctly. If needed you can use the Check for Understanding.

Check for Understanding

Any part(s) of the following set can be used.

1. Put the following picture on the blackboard.

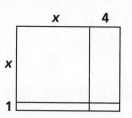

Find two equivalent expressions for the area of the rectangle.

2. Use the Distributive Property to multiply: $(x - 4)(x + 5)$.

2.3 Changing Both Dimensions

Mathematical Goals

- Expand the context of area of rectangles to write equivalent quadratic expressions for the area of a rectangle $x^2 + bx + c$
- Use the area model to introduce the Distributive Property
- Use the area model and Distributive Property to multiply two binomials

Launch

- *Sketch a rectangle that shows 5x + 3x and 8x are equivalent area expressions. This is an example of the Distributive Property: 5x + 3x = x(5 + 3) = 8x.*
- *Write the expression, 2x + 4x, as one term. Write the expression, 10x, as the sum of two terms.*

Use the Getting Ready to launch the problem.

Record student suggestions for subdividing and labeling the new rectangle on the overhead.

Let the class work in groups of two to four.

Materials
- Transparency 2.3A

Vocabulary
- Distributive Property
- like terms

Explore

Use an area model to remind students that $3x + 5x = 8x$. While students are working on Questions A and B ask:

- *What are the dimensions of the large rectangle?*
- *How can you use them to find the area of the large rectangle? Is there another way to find the area?*

Materials
- Transparency 2.3B

Summarize

Call on various groups to present their answers.

If students are having trouble writing the expanded form, point to each smaller rectangle in Question A and ask:

- *What are the dimensions of this larger rectangle? What is its area?*
- *How can the area of each of the smaller rectangles be used to find the expression for the area of the whole rectangle?*
- *In Question B, how did you find the expression for the area in factored form?*
- *Describe two ways to write different quadratic expressions for the area of a rectangle.*

Use Question D to begin to connect the methods of multiplying two binomials using an area model and the Distributive Property. Ask:

- *Use the distributive property to write the expression x(x + 2) in an equivalent form. Repeat for (x + 2)(x + 4).*

Materials
- Student notebooks

ACE Assignment Guide
for Problem 2.3

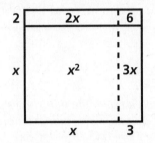

Differentiated Instruction
Solutions for All Learners

Core 17–28
Other *Connections* 54, 55: and unassigned choices from previous problems

Adapted For suggestions about adapting ACE exercises, see the CMP *Special Needs Handbook*
Connecting to Prior Units 54: *Comparing and Scaling*; 55: *Covering and Surrounding*

Answers to Problem 2.3

A. 1. $(x + 2)(x + 5)$; $x^2 + 2x + 5x + 10$ or $x^2 + 7x + 10$

2. $(x + 3)(x + 3)$; $x^2 + 3x + 3x + 9$ or $x^2 + 6x + 9$

3. $(x + 2)(x + 4)$; $x^2 + 2x + 4x + 8$ or $x^2 + 6x + 8$

4. $(x + 1)(x + x)$ or $2x(x + 1)$; $x^2 + x + x^2 + x$ or $2x^2 + 2x$

B. 1. Possible area model:

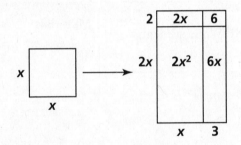

2. $(2x + 2)(x + 3)$; $2x^2 + 2x + 6x + 6$ or $2x^2 + 8x + 6$

C. 1. $x^2 + 3x + 5x + 15$ or $x^2 + 8x + 15$

2. $16 + 4x + 4x + x^2$ or $16 + 8x + x^2$

3. $3x^2 + 3x$

D. 1. Yes; at step 1, she used the Distributive Property to distribute the $(x + 3)$ to both the x and the 2 in the factor $(x + 2)$. In step 2, she carried out the multiplications $(x + 3)x$ and $(x + 3)2$ using the Distributive Property and then used the Commutative Property to write $(x)2$ as $2x$. At step 3, she combined like terms $3x + 2x = 5x$ since $3x + 2x = (3 + 2)x$.

2. Step 2 gives the same 4 terms as the area model: $x^2, 3x, 2x,$ and 6. The bottom rectangle below has dimensions $(x + 3)$ and x and area $(x + 3)x$ and the top rectangle has area $(x + 3)2$ giving a total area of $(x + 3)x + (x + 3)2$ which corresponds to step 1.

E. 1. $(x + 5)(x + 5) = (x + 5)x + (x + 5)(5) = x^2 + 5x + 5x + 25 = x^2 + 10x + 25$

2. Possible answers:

Method 1: $(x + 3)(x - 4) =$
$(x + 3)[x + (-4)] =$
$(x + 3)(x) + (x + 3)(-4) =$
$x^2 + 3x + (-4x) + (-12) =$
$x^2 + (-1x) + (-12)$.

Method 2: $(x + 3)(x - 4) =$
$(x + 3)(x) - (x + 3)(4) =$
$(x^2 + 3x) - (x + 3)(4) =$
$(x^2 + 3x) - (4x + 12) =$
$x^2 + 3x - 4x - 12 =$
$x^2 + (-1x) + (-12)$

Note: Method 2 involves a difficult concept of distributing a negative, which will be discussed in *Say It With Symbols*.

3. $2x(5 - x) = 2x(5) - 2x(x) = 10x - 2x^2$

4. $(x - 3)(x - 4) = (x - 3)x - (x - 3)(4)$
$= x^2 - 3x - 4x + 12$
$= x^2 - 7x + 12$

5. $(x + 2)(x - 2) = (x + 2)x - (x + 2)2$
$= x^2 + 2x - 2x - 4$
$= x^2 - 4$

Factoring Quadratic Expressions

Goal

- Use the area model and Distributive Property to rewrite an expression that is in expanded form into an equivalent expression in factored form

The area of a rectangle is used to write the factored form for the quadratic expression. Students use the expanded form of quadratic expressions to subdivide a rectangle into parts and to label each part with an appropriate expression for its area. These expressions provide clues on how to split the middle term, bx, of the expression $x^2 + bx + c$ to find the dimensions of the rectangle or the two linear factors for the factored form using the Distributive Property. We do not expect students to be experts in factoring. More factoring will be done in *Say It With Symbols*. We do want students to develop understanding of the Distributive Property and its connection to the area of a rectangle.

Launch 2.4

You can use the example in the student book to talk about combining like terms if you did not do it in the summary of the last problem.

In the last problem, Carminda claimed she did not need the rectangular model to multiply $(x + 3)$ by $(x + 2)$. You may want to review these steps with the students.

Suggested Question

- *Could you reverse Carminda's method to write the expression $x^2 + 8x + 12$ in factored form?* (This is more difficult, but some students may notice that you have to split the 8x to get the first step in reversing Carminda's method. Some may notice that you have to split the 8x to get the area of two of the smaller rectangles in a rectangle whose area is represented by $x^2 + 8x + 12$. Also, the product of the coefficients of x must be 12. Therefore, $8x = 2x + 6x$ and $x^2 + 8x + 12 = x^2 + 2x + 8x + 12$.)

Let the class work in pairs.

Explore 2.4

Look for interesting strategies for Questions A, B, and C. The purpose of these questions is to help students see that given the first and last terms of the expanded form $x^2 + bx + c$, such as $x^2 + bx + 9$, there are many possible factorings of $x^2 + bx + c$ which all depend on which factors of c you choose. The factors of c one chooses then determine the value of b.

Starting with the factors of c might be a good strategy for splitting bx into two parts. Students can put their work on large poster paper to use during the summary. If students find one pair of factors that work, ask them if other pairs might work. For Question A, whole-number factors that will work are: 1 and 9 and 3 and 3. Students can also use rational number factor pairs such as $\frac{1}{2}$ and 18. There are many factor pairs. Here it suffices to focus on whole-number pairs.

Some students may need more guidance on how to factor the expressions. The area model can be used to help students recall the steps needed to multiply two binomials like $(x + 1)(x + 4)$ or students can use the Distributive Property. This is true with factoring. Students can use the area model to factor; this method is illustrated with the expression $x^2 + 4x + 2x + 8$. However, the distributive property is a more useful tool when factoring expression like $ax^2 + bx + c$ especially when negative coefficients for a, b, and/or c are involved.

To factor an expression like $x^2 + 4x + 2x + 8$, you can use the metaphor of subparts of the rectangle to get the four expressions needed: $x^2 + 4x + 2x + 8$. This then becomes the first step in factoring a quadratic expression in expanded form. We are reversing the process of multiplying two binomials. Do an example, $x^2 + 8x + 15$, to help students see how to use the area model to do the factoring.

Sketch a rectangle whose area is represented by the expression $x^2 + 8x + 15$.

Subdivide it into four parts.

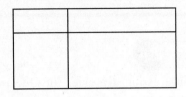

Suggested Questions

- *Which part has an area represented by x^2? By 15?*

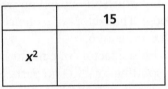

- *How can you split 8x into two pieces so that the pieces represent the remaining two subparts? What clues can you use to split 8x?* (The sum of the coefficients of each part must equal 8 and their product must equal 15.)

- *So what two numbers have a sum of 8 and a product of 15?* (3 and 5. So the areas of the two sub parts are $3x$ and $5x$. Students may try several different pairs.)

- *What are the dimensions of the rectangle?* ($x + 3$ and $x + 5$)

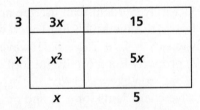

- *How can you use the Distributive Property to show that $(x + 3)(x + 5)$ is equal to $x^2 + 8x + 15$?*

Have some groups put their work on large sheets of paper. Make sure you get all of the different strategies that might occur in A–C. In Question D, ask:

- *Is Alyse correct? How do you know?*

- *What did she do in step 1? Step 2? Step 3?*

Summarize students' work in Question D before you have students do Question E.

Summarize 2.4

Call on different students to discuss their strategies for factoring expressions. Refer to the large posters of the student work. Many will have drawn diagrams. Have the class ask questions about the work. Be sure to relate the sub areas of the rectangle to the parts of the expanded expression and then relate the factored form to the dimensions and area of the whole rectangle. Collect several different rectangles for Question A.

Ask the students to show:

- A sketch of their rectangle with the area of its subparts appropriately labeled.

- The dimensions of the rectangle.

- The two equivalent expressions for the area of the rectangle.

You can tell the students that writing an expanded form in factored form is called factoring.

In Questions D and E, ask students to explain their method and why it is correct. For example, $x^2 + 7x + 12 = x^2 + 3x + 4x + 12 = x(x + 3) + 4(x + 3) = (x + 3)(x + 4)$.

Check for Understanding

Describe the steps you used to factor the expanded form of a quadratic.

Use the following expressions as examples: $x^2 + 7x + 8$ $x^2 - 3x + 2$ $4x^2 + 8x$ (Students should start by looking for factors of the constant term. Then they choose the pair whose sum is equal to the coefficient of the middle term or to b in bx. Some may start with finding various sums for b and then choosing the two whose product is equal to the constant term, c. **Note:** If the coefficient of x^2 is not 1, then finding the coefficient of x is more complicated.)

Suggested Question

- *How can you check that your answers are equivalent to the original expressions?* (Multiply the two factors to see if you get the original expanded form or use a rectangular model to check your work or check the graphs of each equation $y = $ factored form and $y = $ expanded form for each expression. The graphs should be identical.)

2.4 Factoring Quadratic Expressions

Mathematical Goal

- Use the area model and Distributive Property to rewrite an expression that is in expanded form into an equivalent expression in factored form

Launch

In the last problem, Carminda claimed she did not need the rectangular model to multiply $(x + 3)$ by $(x + 2)$.

You may want to review these steps with the students.

- *Could you reverse Carminda's method to write the expression $x^2 + 8x + 15$ in factored form?*

Let the class work in pairs.

Explore

Look for interesting strategies for Questions A, B, and C. Students could put their work on large poster paper to use during the summary.

If students find one pair of factors that works, ask them if other factor pairs might work. Some students may need more guidance on how to factor the expressions.

We are reversing the process of multiplying two binomials.

Do an example, $x^2 + 8x + 15$, to help students see how to use the area model to do the factoring.

Sketch a rectangle whose area is represented by the expression $x^2 + 8x + 15$. Subdivide it into four parts.

- *Which part has an area represented by x^2? By 15?*

- *How can you split 8x into two pieces so that the pieces represent the remaining two subparts? What clues can you use to split 8x? What two numbers have a sum of 8 and a product of 15? What are the dimensions of the rectangle?*

- *How can you use the Distributive Property to show that $(x + 3)(x + 5)$ is equal to $x^2 + 8x + 15$?*

Have some groups put their work on large sheets of paper. Make sure you get all of the different strategies that might occur in Questions A, B, and C. In Question D, ask:

- *Is Alyse correct? How do you know?*

- *What did she do in step 1? Step 2? Step 3?*

Summarize Question D before you have students do Question E.

Materials

- Poster Paper (optional)

Summarize

Call on different students to discuss their strategies for factoring expressions. Refer to the large posters of the student work. Relate the sub areas of the rectangle to the parts of the expanded expression and then relate the factored form to the dimensions and area of the whole rectangle.

In Questions D and E, ask students to explain their method and why it is correct. For example, $x^2 + 7x + 12 = x^2 + 3x + 4x + 12 = x(x + 3) + 4(x + 3) = (x + 3)(x + 4)$.

Describe the steps you used to factor the expanded form of a quadratic.

- *How can you check that your answers are equivalent to the original expressions?*

Materials
- Student notebooks

ACE Assignment Guide for Problem 2.4

Differentiated Instruction
Solutions for All Learners

Core 29–39
Other *Connections* 56, *Extensions* 62–64; unassigned choices from previous problems

Adapted For suggestions about adapting ACE exercises, see the CMP *Special Needs Handbook*.
Connecting to Prior Units 56: *Moving Straight Ahead*

Answers to Problem 2.4

A. 1. Possible drawing:

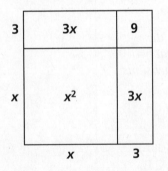

Since the lengths of the two segments marked with question marks seem to be the same length, students may argue that 3 and 3 are the only factors of 9 that will work, while others will claim that 1 and 9 are possibilities as well. Either case is acceptable.

2. Possible answers:
Factored form: $(x + 3)(x + 3)$;
Expanded: $x^2 + 3x + 3x + 9$ or
$x^2 + 6x + 9$;

Factored form: $(x + 1)(x + 9)$;
Expanded: $x^2 + x + 9x + 9$ or
$x^2 + 10x + 9$.

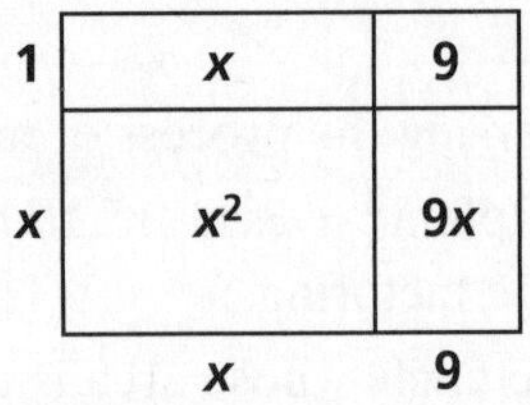

	x	9
x	x^2	$9x$
	x	9

(with 1 labeling the top-left, x labeling the bottom-left)

Note: There are infinitely more factor pairs that will work for 9 such as $\frac{1}{2}$ and 18 or $\frac{1}{4}$ and 36. For this problem we can focus on the whole-number factors.

B. 1. If $b = 9$, then $x^2 + 9x + 8$ in factored form is $(x + 1)(x + 8)$.

If $b = 6$, then $x^2 + 6x + 8$ in factored form is $(x + 2)(x + 4)$.

If $b = -9$, then $x^2 - 9x + 8$ in factored form is $(x - 1)(x - 8)$.

If $b = -6$, then $x^2 - 6x + 8$ in factored form is $(x - 2)(x - 4)$.

Note: Not every b value that students pick will result in a quadratic expression that is factorable at this time by students. For example a b value of 10 gives an expression of $x^2 + 10x + 8$. This expression cannot be factored by students unless they know the quadratic formula which they may not learn until high school.

In this problem, we want students to realize that they are looking at the factor pairs of 8 and finding a pair whose sum is the value for b that will make $x^2 + bx + 8$ an expression that can be factored. Restricting the factor pairs of 8 to integers, we have (1 and 8), (−1 and −8), (−2 and −4), and (2 and 4). So the values for b are 9, −9, −6 and 6, respectively, as illustrated above.

For the case where $b = 6$, a possible student explanation may include the use of an area model such as the one shown below:

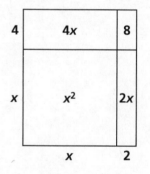

The factor pair consisting of 2 and 4 yields a b value of 6 and the factored form of $(x + 2)(x + 4)$ for $x^2 + 6x + 8$.

2. Students will probably find that not all of their classmates found the same expressions. However the expressions that students will have will be either $(x + 2)(x + 4)$, $(x + 1)(x + 8)$, $(x - 1)(x - 8)$ or $(x - 2)(x - 4)$.

C. 1. $r = 4$

2. $r = 3, s = 8$ (or $r = 8, s = 3$)

3. $r = 1$ and $s = 24$ or $r = 24$ and $s = 1$

4. A common strategy is to compare the "c" term of the $x^2 + bx + c$ form to the constant terms in the factors; r and s must be factors of c. Meanwhile, the sum of r and s must make b.

D. Yes; Students can make an area model to check that $x^2 + 10x + 16 = (x + 2)(x + 8)$. They may also reason that Alyse applied the Distributive Property. In step 1, she separated $10x$ into $2x + 8x$ and in step 2 she used the Distributive Property to rewrite $x^2 + 2x$ as $x(x + 2)$ and $8x + 16$ as $8(x + 2)$. In step 3, she used the Distributive Property to see that $(x + 2)$ is multiplied by both x and 8 so she can factor the $(x + 2)$ term out and multiply it by the remaining $(x + 8)$.

E. 1. Using the Distributive Property:
$x^2 + 5x + 2x + 10 =$
$x(x + 5) + 2(x + 5) =$
$(x + 5)(x + 2)$.

Note: Students may also write this as $(x + 2)(x + 5)$ which is equivalent because of the Commutative Property of Multiplication. In the answers for Question E, parts (1) and (4) the common factor has been pulled out in front since it seems the most natural. For part (1), the factor of $x + 5$ was pulled out in front to obtain $(x + 5)(x + 2)$.

2. Using the Distributive Property:
$x^2 + 11x + 10 = x^2 + 10x + x + 10 =$
$x(x + 10) + 1(x + 10) = (x + 10)(x + 1)$.

3. Using the Distributive Property:
$x^2 + 3x - 10 = x^2 + 5x - 2x - 10 =$
$x(x + 5) - 2(x + 5) = (x + 5)(x - 2)$.

4. Using the Distributive Property:
$x^2 + 16x + 15 = x^2 + 15x + 1x + 15 =$
$x(x + 15) + 1(x + 15) = (x + 15)(x + 1)$.

5. Using the Distributive Property:
$x^2 - 8x + 15 = x^2 - 3x - 5x + 15 =$
$x(x - 3) - 5(x - 3) = (x - 5)(x - 3)$.

6. Using the Distributive Property:
$x^2 - 12x + 36 = x^2 - 6x + -6x + 36 =$
$x(x - 6) + -6(x - 6) = (x - 6)(x - 6)$.

Note: Students may need help seeing that −5 is a factor of −5x and 15 in part (5) or that −2 is a factor of −2x and −10 in part (3). Factoring out a negative quantity is represented somewhat differently in the part (6) solution.

A Closer Look at Parabolas

Goals

- Make a connection between a quadratic equation in factored/expanded form and its graph
- Predict the shape and features of a graph from the expanded and factored form of a quadratic equation

Launch 2.5

Discuss the Getting Ready for Problem 2.5. Discuss as a class how to sketch the graph of $y = (x + 3)(x - 2)$ and make the graph on the overhead either with a graphic calculator or manually.

Suggested Questions

- *What are the x-intercepts?* $[(-3, 0)$ and $(2, 0)]$
- *What is the y-intercept?* $[(0, -6)]$
- *Is there a maximum or minimum point?* (Yes, there is a minimum point.)
- *What is the maximum or minimum point?* $[(-0.5, -6.25)]$
- *Sketch the graph of $y = x^2 + x - 6$. How does this graph compare to the graph of $y = (x + 3)(x - 2)$?* (They are the same graph.)

To review the idea of the line of symmetry you might sketch the graph of $y = x^2$ on a piece of waxed paper or transparent paper. Show it to the class. Then fold the graph along the y-axis, and place it on the overhead.

- *What do you observe here?* (The two halves of the graph are identical.)
- *What is the fold line called?* (line of symmetry)
- *Where is the minimum point when I fold the graph in half?* (on the fold line or line of symmetry)
- *What happens to the x-intercepts when I fold the graph?* (The x-intercepts fall on each other. In this case they are both 0.)
- *What else can you say about the x-intercepts?* (The line of symmetry is halfway between the two intercepts. The x-intercepts occur when $y = 0$.)

- *Does this occur for any other pairs of points?* (Except for the minimum point, each point in the graph matches up, or is the reflection, with a point on the other half of the graph.)

In the graph of $y = x^2$, the x- and y-intercepts and the minimum point all occur at the point $(0, 0)$. You can repeat these questions for another graph that has distinct features such as $y = x^2 + 6x + 8$. In addition to the preceding questions, include the following questions:

- *Write the equation $y = x^2 + 6x + 8$ in factored form.*
- *What is the y-intercept? How can you predict this from the equation?*
- *What are the x-intercepts? How can you predict these from the equation?* (Students may say that it is the x-values when $y = 0$. Some might be able to use the factored form to predict these. This idea is more fully developed in the problem.)

Describe the problem to the class. Pick one of the equations and write it on the board or overhead.

- *What can you tell about the graph by looking at this equation?* (Some students may recognize the similarity to the graphs in previous problems and predict whether the graph has a maximum or minimum point. It is not necessary at this time to be able to predict the max/min point. Some students may be able to predict the x-intercepts from the factored form of the equation.)

Suggest that they work on Question A without using a graphing calculator. They can use a calculator to check their answers.

Pass out Labsheet 2.5.

The class can work in groups of two or three.

Explore 2.5

Suggested Questions

- *How do you know your equation matches the graph you chose?*
- *What is the y-intercept of the graph? How can you predict this from the equation?*

- *What are the x-intercepts of the graph? How can you predict these from the equation?*

- *Can you predict what the graph for $y = (x + 3)(x + 7)$ would look like? Explain.*

Summarize 2.5

Collect answers from the class to Question A. Be sure to label the relevant pieces of the graph such as the intercepts, maximum/minimum and line of symmetry. It would be helpful to have a transparency of the labsheet of the graphs.

Suggested Questions Focus the class's attention on the symmetry in the graph.

- *What is the line of symmetry? How can you describe its location?* (It is a vertical line that passes through the maximum or minimum point. It intersects the x-axis at a point halfway between the x-intercepts, if they exist. You can use the x coordinate of the point where the line of symmetry crosses the x-axis to make an equation describing the line.)

Focus the class's attention on predicting intercepts and maximum/minimum points from the equation. Use one of the equations, say $y = (x + 3)(x + 3)$.

- *How can you predict the x-intercepts from the equation?* [To find the x-intercepts means that $y = 0$. So in the case of $y = (x + 3)(x + 3)$, the area equals zero when $(x + 3)(x + 3) = 0$. So $x + 3 = 0$ or $x + 3 = 0$. Thus in the first factor $x = -3$ and in the second factor $x = -3$. In the case of $y = (3x + 3)(x + 3)$, the first factor is 0 if $3x + 3 = 0$ or $x = -1$ and the second factor is 0 if $x = -3$. In other words the x-intercepts can be read from the factored form of a quadratic equation.] **Note:** Finding the x-intercepts is the same as solving the equation $y = (x + 3)(x + 3)$ when $y = 0$. In this unit, students rely more on tables and graphs to find x-intercepts. In *Say it with Symbols*, students will continue to explore solving equations like $0 = ax^2 + bx + c$, using factoring, which is started in this unit.

- *How can you predict the y-intercept from the equation?* [The y-intercept can be read from the expanded form of a quadratic equation. It is the constant term, c, in the equation, $y = x^2 + bx + c$. The coordinates of the y-intercept are $(0, c)$.]

- *How can you predict the location of the line of symmetry from the equation?* (The line of symmetry is halfway between the two intercepts of the graph. So the factored form of a quadratic equation is most useful for predicting the line of symmetry. Find the x-intercepts and then find the point halfway between them. The vertical line that passes through this point is the line of symmetry.)

- *How can you predict whether the graph has a maximum or a minimum from the equation?* (If the coefficient of x^2 is negative, then the graph has a maximum and the shape of the graph is an upside down U, or parabola. If the coefficient of x^2 is positive, then the graph has a minimum and the shape of the graph is an upright U.

- *How can you predict the maximum or minimum point from the equation?* (It lies on the line of symmetry. Its x-coordinate is the value halfway between the x-intercepts. Its y-coordinate can be found by substituting its x-coordinate into the equation and solving for y. If the coefficient of x^2 is negative, then the graph has a maximum point. If the coefficient of x^2 is positive, then the graph has a minimum point.)

For many of the graphs in this problem one of its x-intercepts is $(0, 0)$. Use some other equations for final summary.

Check for Understanding

- *For each equation below, use an appropriate form of the equation to predict the following features of the graph:*

  y-intercept

  x-intercepts

  line of symmetry

  the coordinates of the maximum or minimum point.

Indicate which form of the equation you used. Then use your graphing calculator to check your answers.

1. $y = x^2 + 9x + 20$

2. $y = (x - 4)(x - 4)$

3. $y = -2x(x - 5)$

4. $y = -x^2 - 4x$

2.5 Looking Back at Parabolas

Mathematical Goals

- Make a connection between a quadratic equation in factored/expanded form and its graph
- Predict the shape and features of a graph from the expanded and factored form of a quadratic equation

Launch

Use Transparency 2.5A for the Getting Ready.

Sketch the graph of $y = x^2$. Then fold the graph along the y-axis and place on the overhead.

- *What do you observe here? What is the fold line called?*
- *Where is the minimum point when I fold the graph in half?*
- *What happens to the x-intercepts when I fold the graph?*
- *What else can you say about the x-intercepts?*
- *Does this occur for any other pairs of points?*

Repeat the above questions for the equation $y = x^2 + 6x + 8$. Then ask:

- *Write the equation in factored form. What is the y-intercept? How can you predict this from the equation?*
- *What are the x-intercepts? How might you predict these from the equation?*

Pass out Labsheet 2.5. The class can work in groups of two or three.

Materials
- Transparency 2.5A
- Labsheet 2.5
- Waxed paper or transparent paper (optional)

Vocabulary
- line of symmetry

Explore

- *How do you know your equation matches the graph you chose? What is the y-intercept? How can you predict this from the equation? What are the x-intercepts? How can you predict these from the equation?*
- *What would the graph for* $y = (x + 3)(x + 7)$ *look like?*

Materials
- Transparency 2.5B

Summarize

Label the relevant pieces of the graph such as the intercepts, maximum/minimum and line of symmetry. It would be helpful to have a transparency of the labsheet of the graphs.

- *What is the line of symmetry? How can you describe its location?*

Use one of the equations, say $y = (x + 3)(x + 3)$.

- *How can you predict the x-intercepts from the equation? The y-intercept? The line of symmetry? Whether the graph has a maximum or a minimum? How can you find the maximum or minimum point from the equation?*

Materials
- Student notebooks

ACE Assignment Guide for Problem 2.5

Differentiated Instruction
Solutions for All Learners

Core 40–42, 44–47, 57–60
Other *Applications* 43, 48, 49; *Connections* 61;

Extensions 65; unassigned choices from previous problems

Adapted For suggestions about adapting ACE exercises, see the CMP *Special Needs Handbook*.

Answers to Problem 2.5

A. 1–4. (Figure 7)

2. You can predict the x-intercepts by finding the value for x that makes each factor 0. You can predict the y-intercepts by setting x equal to zero.

3. You can predict a value midway between the x-intercepts. For example, if the x-intercepts are -2 and -3, then the line of symmetry passes through the point $(-2.5, 0)$. Its equation is $x = -2.5$. **Note:** Students are very familiar with equations of lines in the $y = mx + b$ format. They are less familiar with equations of vertical lines, which are always $x = a$.

4. The maximum or minimum point is on the line of symmetry, so its x-coordinate is halfway between the x-intercepts. Once you know the x-coordinate, you can substitute in the equation to find the y-coordinate.

5. Descriptions of the graphs will vary.

B. 1.

Equation	Expanded Form
$y_1 = x^2$	$y_1 = x^2$
$y_2 = 2x(x + 4)$	$y_2 = 2x^2 + 8x$
$y_3 = (x + 2)(x + 3)$	$y_3 = x^2 + 5x + 6$
$y_4 = (x + 3)(x + 3)$	$y_4 = x^2 + 6x + 9$
$y_5 = x(4 - x)$	$y_5 = 4x - x^2$
$y_6 = x(x - 4)$	$y_6 = x^2 - 4x$
$y_7 = x(x + 4)$	$y_7 = x^2 + 4x$
$y_8 = (x + 3)(x - 3)$	$y_8 = x^2 - 9$

2. Expanded form: The constant term is the y-intercept. If there is no constant term, there is an assumed constant value of 0.

So the equation $y = x^2 + 5x + 6$ has a y-intercept of $(0, 6)$ or 6. The y-intercept has an x-coordinate of 0 so if you substitute 0 for x in a quadratic equation the value of y is the same as the constant term. Factored form: The x-intercept is the value for x that makes each factor equal to 0. The axis of symmetry is a line $x = a$ where the value of a is in the middle of the two x-intercept values.

C. 1. The y-intercept is 5. The x-intercepts are -1 and -5. The line of symmetry is half way between the x-intercepts at $x = -3$. The graph has a minimum point whose x-coordinate is -3. The y-coordinate is -4.

2. The y-intercept is 0. The x-intercepts are 0 and 4. The line of symmetry is halfway between the x-intercepts at $x = 2$. The graph has a maximum point whose x-coordinate is 2 and the y-coordinate is 4.

3. The y-intercept is -6. The x-intercepts are 2 and -3. The line of symmetry is halfway between the x-intercepts at $x = -0.5$. The graph has a minimum point whose x-coordinate is -0.5 and y-coordinate is -6.25.

D. Expanded form is $ax^2 + bx + c$ (where $a \neq 0$) and 2 is the greatest exponent to which the variable in the expression is raised. Factored form is the product of two linear factors, each containing an x term.

Figure 7

Equation	Graph	x-intercept	y-intercept	Line of Symmetry	Maximum or Minimum
$y_1 = x^2$	C	$x = 0$	$y = 0$	$x = 0$	$(0, 0)$ min
$y_2 = 2x(x + 4)$	E	$x = 0, x = -4$	$y = 8$	$x = -2$	$(-2, -8)$ min
$y_3 = (x + 2)(x + 3)$	D	$x = -2, x = -3$	$y = 6$	$x = -2.5$	$(-2.5, -0.25)$ min
$y_4 = (x + 3)(x + 3)$	F	$x = -3$	$y = 9$	$x = -3$	$(-3, 0)$ min
$y_5 = x(4 - x)$	B	$x = 0, x = 4$	$y = 0$	$x = 2$	$(2, 4)$ max
$y_6 = x(x - 4)$	H	$x = 0, x = 4$	$y = 0$	$x = 2$	$(2, -4)$ min
$y_7 = x(x + 4)$	A	$x = 0, x = -4$	$y = 0$	$x = -2$	$(-2, -4)$ min
$y_8 = (x + 3)(x - 3)$	G	$x = -3, x = 3$	$y = -9$	$x = 0$	$(0, -9)$ min

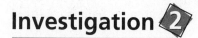

Investigation 2

ACE Assignment Choices

Differentiated Instruction
Solutions for All Learners

Problem 2.1
Core 1, 50–51

Problem 2.2
Core 2–4, 8–16
Other *Applications* 5–7; *Connections* 52, 53; unassigned choices from previous problems

Problem 2.3
Core 17–28
Other *Connections* 54, 55; unassigned choices from previous problems

Problem 2.4
Core 29–39
Other *Connections* 56, *Extensions* 62–64; unassigned choices from previous problems

Problem 2.5
Core 40–42, 44–47, 57–60
Other *Applications* 43, 48, 49; *Connections* 61; *Extensions* 65; unassigned choices from previous problems

Adapted For suggestions about adapting Exercise 1 and other ACE exercises, see the CMP *Special Needs Handbook*.
Connecting to Prior Units 50, 56: *Moving Straight Ahead*; 51: *Thinking with Mathematical Models*; 52, 55: *Covering and Surrounding*; 53, 54: *Comparing and Scaling*; 57, 59, 60: *Accentuate the Negative*; 58: *Bits and Pieces II*

Applications

1. a. (Figure 8)

   b.

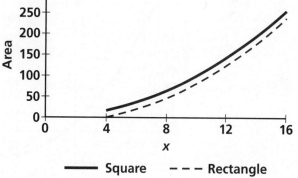

Rectangles and Squares With Equal Perimeters

Figure 8

Square		Rectangle		
Side	Area	Length	Width	Area
4	16	8	0	0
5	25	9	1	9
6	36	10	2	20
7	49	11	3	33
8	64	12	4	48
9	81	13	5	65
10	100	14	6	84
11	121	15	7	105
12	144	16	8	128
13	169	17	9	153
14	196	18	10	180
15	225	19	11	209
16	256	20	12	240

c. The graph and the table both show that the area of the rectangle increases as the area of the square increases. The area of the square is always 16 cm² greater than the area of the rectangle; this constant difference between the two can be seen on the graph, but the table shows the exact value of the difference.

d. Area of the square is $A = x^2$ where x is the side length and the area of the new rectangle is $(x + 4)(x - 4)$ or $x^2 - 16$.

e. (Figures 9 and 10)

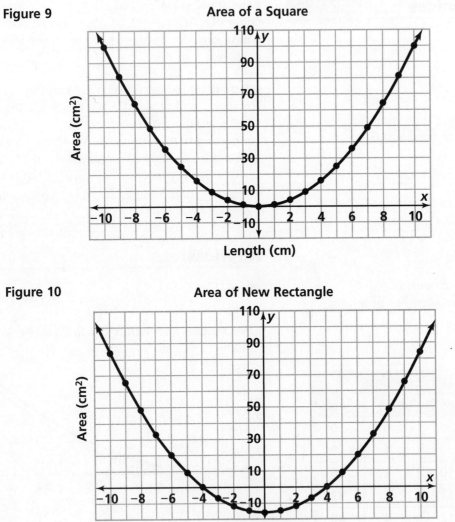

Figure 9

Area of a Square

Length (cm)

Figure 10

Area of New Rectangle

Length (cm)

2. a.

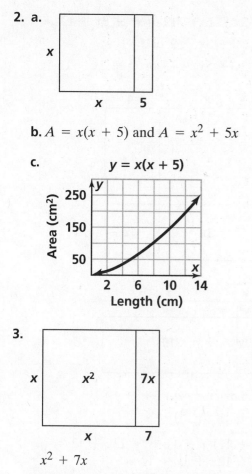

b. $A = x(x + 5)$ and $A = x^2 + 5x$

c.

$y = x(x + 5)$

3.

$x^2 + 7x$

Note: In Exercises 4, 6, and 7, students may reverse the shaded/unshaded portions of the square.

4.

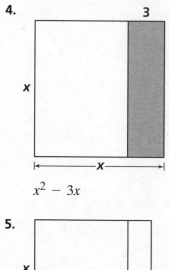

$x^2 - 3x$

5.

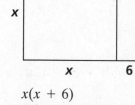

$x(x + 6)$

6.

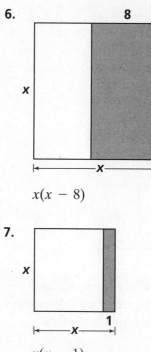

$x(x - 8)$

7.

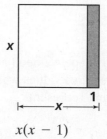

$x(x - 1)$

8. $x(x + 10)$ **9.** $x(x - 6)$

10. $x(x + 11)$ **11.** $x(x - 2)$

12. $x^2 + x$ **13.** $x^2 - 10x$

14. $x^2 + 6x$ **15.** $x^2 - 15x$

16. $(x + 5)x$ and $x^2 + 5x$

17. $x^2 + 5x + 5x + 25$ and $(x + 5)(x + 5)$

18. $x(x - 4)$ and $x^2 - 4x$

19. $(x)(2x + 3)$ and $x^2 + x^2 + 3x$

20. $(x + 5)(x + 6)$ and $x^2 + 5x + 6x + 30$

21. a.

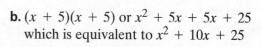

b. $(x + 5)(x + 5)$ or $x^2 + 5x + 5x + 25$
which is equivalent to $x^2 + 10x + 25$

c. $A = x^2 + 10x + 25$

$y = x^2 + 10x + 25$

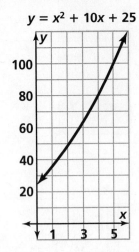

Note: To see the parabola shape we need a window which includes negative values which could not, in practical terms, represent lengths.

22. a.

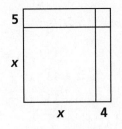

b. $A = (x + 5)(x + 4)$ and
$A = x^2 + 5x + 4x + 20$

$y = (x + 4)(x + 5)$

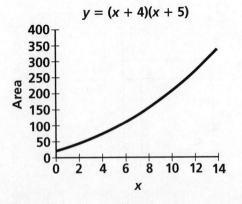

Note: To see the parabola shape we need a window which includes negative values which could not, in practical terms, represent lengths.

23. $x^2 - 3x + 4x - 12$ or $x^2 + x - 12$

24. $x^2 + 3x + 5x + 15$ or $x^2 + 8x + 15$

25. $x^2 + 5x$

26. $x^2 - 2x - 6x + 12$ or $x^2 - 8x + 12$

27. $x^2 - 3x + 3x - 9$, or $x^2 - 9$

28. $x^2 - 3x + 5x - 15$, or $x^2 + 2x - 15$

29. a.

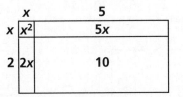

b. $(x + 3)(x + 4)$

$(x + 2)(x + 5)$

30. a. $(x + 12)(x + 1); x^2 + 13x + 12 =$
$x^2 + 12x + 1x + 12 =$
$x(x + 12) + 1(x + 12) =$
$(x + 12)(x + 1)$

b. $(x - 12)(x - 1); x^2 - 13x + 12 =$
$x^2 - 12x - 1x + 12 =$
$x(x - 12) + -1(x - 12) = (x - 12)(x - 1)$

c. $(x + 6)(x + 2); x^2 + 8x + 12 =$
$x^2 + 6x + 2x + 12 =$
$x(x + 6) + 2(x + 6) = (x + 6)(x + 2)$

d. $(x - 6)(x - 2); x^2 - 8x + 12 =$
$x^2 - 6x - 2x + 12 = x(x - 6) +$
$-2(x - 6) = (x - 6)(x - 2)$

e. $(x + 3)(x + 4); x^2 + 7x + 12 =$
$x^2 + 3x + 4x + 12 =$
$x(x + 3) + 4(x + 3) = (x + 3)(x + 4)$

f. $(x - 3)(x - 4); x^2 - 7x + 12 =$
$x^2 - 3x - 4x + 12 =$
$x(x - 3) + -4(x - 3) = (x - 3)(x - 4)$

g. $(x + 12)(x - 1); x^2 + 11x - 12 =$
$x^2 + 12x - 1x - 12 =$
$x(x + 12) + -1(x + 12) = (x + 12)(x - 1)$

h. $(x - 12)(x + 1)$; $x^2 - 11x - 12 =$
$x^2 - 12x + 1x - 12 =$
$x(x - 12) + 1(x - 12) = (x - 12)(x + 1)$

i. $(x + 6)(x - 2)$; $x^2 + 4x - 12 =$
$x^2 + 6x - 2x - 12 =$
$x(x + 6) + -2(x + 6) = (x + 6)(x - 2)$

j. $(x - 6)(x + 2)$; $x^2 - 4x - 12 =$
$x^2 - 6x + 2x - 12 = x(x - 6)$
$+ 2(x - 6) = (x - 6)(x + 2)$

k. $(x + 4)(x - 3)$; $x^2 + x - 12 =$
$x^2 + 4x - 3x - 12 =$
$x(x + 4) + -3(x + 4) = (x + 4)(x - 3)$

l. $(x - 4)(x + 3)$; $x^2 - x - 12 =$
$x^2 - 4x + 3x - 12 = x(x - 4)$
$+ 3(x - 4) = (x - 4)(x + 3)$

31. Quadratic since it has an x^2 term and this is the highest power of x.

32. Not quadratic, it is linear.

33. Quadratic; it is quadratic because it is the product of two linear factors, neither of which is constant.

34. Quadratic; it is the product of two linear factors, neither of which is constant.

35. Not quadratic, it is exponential.

36. Quadratic since it has an x^2 term and this is the highest power of x.

37. Quadratic; it is the product of two linear factors, neither of which is constant.

38. Not quadratic, it is linear.

39. Quadratic since it has an x^2 term and this is the highest power of x.

40. a. Line of symmetry: $x = 0$;
x-intercepts: 3 and -3; y-intercept: -9;
Minimum: $(0, -9)$

b. Line of symmetry: $x = -\frac{5}{2}$;
x-intercepts: 0 and -5; y-intercept: 0;
Minimum: $(-\frac{5}{2}, -\frac{25}{4})$

c. Line of symmetry: $x = -4$;
x-intercepts: -3 and -5; y-intercept: 15;
Minimum: $(-4, -1)$

d. Line of symmetry: $x = -1$;
x-intercepts: 3 and -5; y-intercept: -15;
Minimum: $(-1, -16)$

e. Line of symmetry: $x = 1$;
x-intercepts: -3 and 5; y-intercept: -15;
Minimum: $(1, -16)$

41. a. $y = (x + 3)(x + 2)$

b. y-intercept: $(0, 6)$;
x-intercepts: -3 and -2

c. Minimum: $(-2.5, -0.25)$

d. $x = -2.5$

e. The factored form can be useful in predicting the x-intercepts and the axis of symmetry. The expanded form can be useful in predicting the y-intercept. Students may have different preferences in equation forms, however they should be able to justify their choices.

42. a. $y = (x + 5)(x - 5)$

b. y-intercept: $(0, -25)$;
x-intercepts: -5 and 5

c. Minimum: $(0, -25)$

d. $x = 0$

e. The factored form can be useful in predicting the x-intercepts and the axis of symmetry. The expanded form can be useful in predicting the y-intercept. Students may have different preferences in equation forms, however they should be able to justify their choices.

43. a. Students may choose to draw a rectangle to help them answer this problem. They can represent the area as $A = x(2x + 3)$

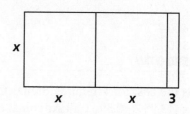

b.

$$y = 2x^2 + 3x$$

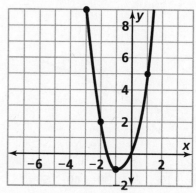

c. The x-intercepts are $(0, 0)$ and $(-\frac{3}{2}, 0)$. To find the x-intercept on a graph you find the point(s) where the parabola hits the x-axis. To determine the x-intercepts from the equation, find the values for x that make the factors $2x + 3$ and x equal to zero.

44–47. The line of symmetry can be found by finding the point on the x-axis that is halfway between the x-intercepts. If this point is a, then the line of symmetry is $x = a$. The x-intercepts can be read directly from the factored form or estimated from the graph of a quadratic equation.

44. a. B **b.** $x = -\frac{9}{2}$

45. a. D **b.** $x = -\frac{3}{2}$

46. a. C **b.** $x = -1$

47. a. A **b.** $x = 0$

48. a. Possible answer: They both have the same x-intercepts and they both have the same axis of symmetry.

b. Possible answer: One opens up and the other opens down.

c. $(5, 25)$; the x-intercepts are $(0, 0)$ and $(10, 0)$, so the vertex is on the line $x = 5$. Substituting $x = 5$ into $y = x(10 - x)$ produces $y = 25$.

d. $(5, -25)$; substituting $x = 5$ into $y = x(x - 10)$ produces $y = -25$.

49. D

Connections

50. a. C is the cost for t minutes. Stellar Cellular: $C = 13.95 + 0.39t$, Call Anytime: $C = 0.95t$

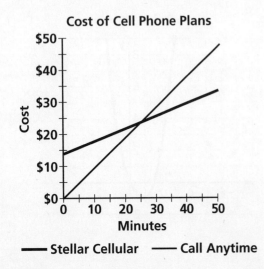

Cost of Cell Phone Plans

— Stellar Cellular — Call Anytime

Calls per Minute in Cell Phone Plans

Time in Minutes	Cost in Dollars	
	Stellar Cellular	Call Anytime
0	$13.95	-
5	$15.90	$4.70
10	$17.85	$9.50
15	$19.80	$14.25
20	$21.75	$19.00
25	$23.70	$23.75
30	$25.65	$28.50
35	$27.60	$33.25
40	$29.55	$38.00
45	$31.50	$42.75
50	$33.45	$47.50

b. Neither of these plans are quadratic. Both are linear. This can be seen in the rules since we do not multiply t by another factor of t. Both equations are in the linear form $y = mx + b$. In the table, you can see that both have a constant rate of change, which means they are linear. For the Stellar Cellular, the cost increases $1.95 for every 5 minutes. In the Call Anytime plan, the increase is $4.75 every 5 minutes. Both graphs look like straight lines, so they are not quadratic.

c. The plans are equal when the number of minutes is about 25 reading from the table. Solving the equation $13.95 + 0.39t = 0.95t$ for t gives an exact answer of about 24.91 minutes.

51. a. $P = \frac{\$500}{n}$

b. This is an inverse relationship: as the number of friends increases, the amount of money each person receives decreases, $n \neq 0$.

c. A graph would help you answer questions about how the amount of money each person receives changes with the number of people sharing the prize. A table would help answer questions about how much money each person would receive given a specific number of friends. An equation would help answer specific questions about any value of n.

d. This relationship is inverse, which can be seen from the graph or the equation. Students investigated inverse relationships in *Thinking With Mathematical Models*.

52. a. Recall, $C = \pi d$, where d is the diameter. So, $x = \pi d$. Or, we can say that $d = \frac{x}{\pi}$.

b. The radius is one half of the diameter, so radius $= \frac{1}{2}(\frac{x}{\pi})$ or $r = \frac{x}{2\pi}$.

c. $A = \pi r^2$, where r is the radius; $A = \pi(\frac{x}{2\pi})^2$.

d. This is a quadratic relation since the x-value is squared.

e. $C = 10$ ft, $d = \frac{10}{\pi} \approx 3.18$ feet, $r = \frac{10}{2\pi} = \frac{5}{\pi} \approx$ 1.59 feet and $A = \pi(\frac{10}{2\pi})^2 \approx 7.96$ feet.

53. a. $A = 2x(2x)$ or $4x^2$

b. The area of the new square is 4 times the area of the original square. Students may choose to make a drawing to help them see this relation between the areas.

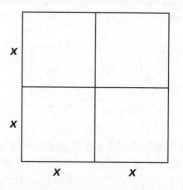

c. Yes; the angles are still 90° and the ratios of pairs of corresponding sides are 2:1.

54. a. $A = 2(x + 1)(2x)$ or $4x^2 + 4x$

b. The area of the new rectangle is 4 times the area of the original rectangle. It can be seen on the drawing below.

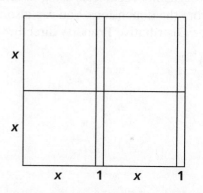

c. Yes; the angles are still 90° and the ratios of pairs of corresponding sides are 2:1.

55. Rectangle: $A = \ell(10 - \ell) = 10\ell - \ell^2$ and $P = \ell + \ell + (10 - \ell) + (10 - \ell) = 20$.

Parallelogram: Area cannot be determined since you are not given the height. $P = 20$.

Symmetric Kite: $P = 20$; Area cannot be determined. We can make two triangles by drawing diagonals, but we don't know the bases or heights, so comparing area is not possible.

Non-isosceles Trapezoid: Area and perimeter cannot be determined. Area cannot be determined because you are not given the length of one of the bases or the height. The perimeter cannot be determined because you are not given the length of the other two sides.

Isosceles Right Triangle: Since the triangle is isosceles right the base is $10 - \ell$ and the height is $10 - \ell$ so
$$A = \tfrac{1}{2}(10 - \ell)(10 - \ell) = 50 - 10\ell - \tfrac{1}{2}\ell^2$$
and
$$P = \ell + (10 - \ell) + (10 - \ell) = 20 - \ell.$$

56. a. $y = x$

b. No; given two points, there is only one line that you can draw through them.

57. If $x = 5$, then $x(x - 5) = 0$. If $x = -5$, then $x(x - 5) = 50$.

58. If $x = 1$, then $3x^2 - x = 2$. If $x = \frac{1}{3}$, then $3x^2 - x = 0$.

59. If $x = 2$, then $x^2 + 5x + 4 = 18$.
If $x = -4$, then $x^2 + 5x + 4 = 0$.

60. If $x = -2$, then $(x - 7)(x + 2) = 0$. If $x = 2$, then $(x - 7)(x + 2) = -20$.

61. a. The equation was $y = x(x + 4)$. The new graph would have x-intercepts at $x = -5$ and $x = -1$, and the equation would be $y = (x + 1)(x + 5)$.

b. The original equation was $y = 2x(x + 4)$. The new parabola would have x-intercepts at $x = 0$ and $x = 4$, and the equation would be $y = 2x(x - 4)$.

c. If you translate the vertex of Graph E right by 3 units it would coincide with the vertex of graph G. But the shapes of the parabolas are different. So we would need more than a translation to transform one parabola into the other.

Extensions

62. H

63. $(2x + 1)(x + 1)$

64. $(2x + 3)(2x + 2)$

65. a. The graphs are both parabolas, which open up.

$y = x^2 + 2x$

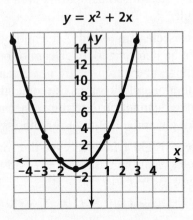

$y = x^2 + 2$

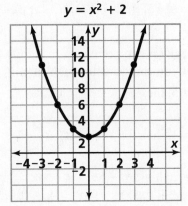

b. The graph of $y = x^2 + 2x$ has x-intercepts of 0 and -2 and the graph of $y = x^2 + 2$ has no x-intercepts. It doesn't pass through the x-axis.

c. The y-intercept for $y = x^2 + 2x$ is $(0, 0)$ and for $x^2 + 2$, it is $(0, 2)$.

d. The graph of $y = x^2 + 2x$ has x-intercepts of 0 and -2. It is not possible to find the x-intercepts for the equation $y = x^2 + 2$ because there is no value of x that that you could square and add 2 and get zero.

e. Yes; A parabola will always cross the y-axis since if you extend the end of the parabola out to the right and out to the left eventually it is going to cross the y-axis.

Possible Answers to Mathematical Reflections

1. Possible answer: The Distributive Property can be modeled using a rectangle. For example, if you are multiplying x and $x + 7$ you can make a rectangle model like the one below. The area of the rectangle can be represented by $x(x + 7)$ or $x^2 + 7x$. The Distributive Property states that $x(x + 7) = x^2 + 7x$ which is the same as saying that the expressions for the area of the rectangle, $x^2 + 7x$ and $x(x + 7)$, are equivalent.

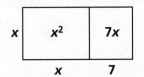

2. a. To find the expanded form, draw a rectangle whose dimensions are the given factors and then subdivide the rectangle as follows:

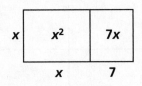

The expanded form is the sum of the area of the parts of the rectangle $x^2 + 7x$. So $x(x + 7) = x^2 + 7x$. Each of these expressions represents the area of the above rectangle. The factored form represents the method of finding the area of the rectangle by multiplying its width and length. The expanded form represents the method of subdividing the rectangle into smaller rectangles using information from the dimensions. You can also apply the Distributive Property directly.

b. In the expanded form, $x^2 + 7x + 12$, each term represents the area of a part of the rectangle. The middle term, $7x$, is the sum of two parts. To find the factored form, find a rectangle that can be subdivided into four smaller rectangles as follows:

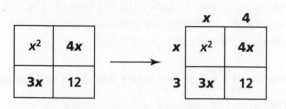

Trial and error must be used to find the areas that add to $7x$. Different combinations can be tried and then the dimensions of the large rectangle found. Then you must check to make sure that the area of each small rectangle can be found using these dimensions. The coefficients of x in each case must add to 7 and the product of the coefficients must be 12. The Distributive Property can also be applied directly. This also involves some trial and error to write the x term, $7x$, into two parts such that the product of their coefficients is equal to the constant term 12.

$x^2 + 7x + 12 =$
$x^2 + 3x + 4x + 12 =$
$x(x + 3) + 4(x + 3) = (x + 3)(x + 4)$.

3. An equation in factored form is quadratic if it has exactly two linear factors—each factor represents a linear relation that contains the variable x. An equation in expanded form is quadratic if the highest power of the variable is 2 or it contains an x^2 term and no other term with a higher exponent. It is of the form $y = ax^2 + bx + c, a \neq 0$.

4. The graph of a quadratic equation is a parabola with a minimum point or maximum point. Parabolas are U-shaped or shaped like an upside down U. The graph has zero, one, or two x-intercepts, and it has a vertical line of symmetry that separates the graph into two symmetric parts. Every quadratic will cross through the y-axis. The y-intercept can be predicted from the equation by looking for a constant term. For example, the y-intercept for the graph of the equation $y = x^2 + 3x + 2$ is $(0, 2)$ and if there is no constant term as in the equation $y = x^2 + 2x$, the y-intercept is $(0, 0)$. The x-intercepts can be predicted easily from the factored form of the equation. For the equation $y = (x + 3)(x + 3)$, the x-intercepts are the values for x that make each factor equal to 0, so here the x-intercept is $(-3, 0)$.

Mathematical and Problem-Solving Goals

- Write an equation for a quadratic relationship represented by triangular numbers
- Observe that one equation can model different contexts
- Examine the patterns of change in quadratic relationships
- Use the patterns of change to predict the next entry in a table for a quadratic relationship

The classic triangular number and handshake problems offer an interesting context in which to explore quadratic functions.

Summary of Problems

Problem 3.1 Exploring Triangular Numbers

In Exploring Triangular Numbers, each counting number from 1 to n is arranged as dots and students explore the questions: How many dots are in the 20th triangular number? What about the nth triangular number?

Problem 3.2 Counting Handshakes

In this problem, students explore the number of handshakes that occur between members of two teams or among members of the same team. The patterns that emerge are similar to those for the triangular numbers in Problem 3.1.

Problem 3.3 Examining Patterns of Change

Counting Handshakes and Examining Patterns of Change, involve the number of handshakes. Students explore the questions: How many handshakes take place when two athletic teams with n members line up to shake hands after a game? How many handshakes are exchanged among two teams with different numbers of members? How many "high fives" are exchanged among the players of a single team after a win?

The equations of the triangular number and handshake problems are similar to those in Investigation 2 and provide an opportunity for students to discuss that a single model can describe more than one context. They also offer the opportunity for students to look at the rate of change between the two variables in a quadratic function.

	Suggested Pacing	Materials for Students	Materials for Teachers	ACE Assignments
All	$3\frac{1}{2}$ days	Graphing calculators, student notebooks	Blank transparencies and transparency markers (optional)	
3.1	1 day	Poster paper (optional)	Transparency 3.1	1–8, 20–28, 47, 48
3.2	1 day	Poster paper (optional)		9–11, 29–37, 49
3.3	1 day	Labsheet 3.3		12–19, 38–46, 50, 51
MR	$\frac{1}{2}$ day			

Exploring Triangular Numbers

Goals

- Write an equation for a quadratic relationship represented by triangular numbers.

- Introduce the patterns of change for a quadratic relationship as observed in a table and graph.

As the *x*-values increase by 1, the pattern of change between consecutive *y*-values in the tables of quadratic patterns appears to have some additive characteristics. Students may note that the *y*-values are not increasing by a constant amount, but there seems to be some additive pattern to the change. Triangular numbers can be modeled by a quadratic function. Each triangular number can be represented by a triangular array of dots (or squares) and is the sum of consecutive whole numbers. For example, the fifth triangular number contains 15 dots—the sum of the whole numbers 1 through 5.

Launch 3.1

Suggested Questions You could launch this problem by putting the square numbers arranged as a set of dots.

- *Describe a rule for the number of dots in each square array.* ($1 \times 1, 2 \times 2, 3 \times 3, \ldots$ or $n \times n$.)

- *These numbers are called square numbers. Name some more square numbers.* (25, 36, 49, 64, etc.)

- *If n represents the number of the arrangement or figure and S represents the number of dots in the arrangement, write an equation that represents the relationship between n and S.* ($S = n^2$)

Put the first four triangular dot patterns on the overhead or blackboard. Label each set as first, second, third, etc. Tell the class that the number of dots in each triangular arrangement is called a triangular number.

- *How many dots are in each pattern?* (Put the number of dots below each figure: 1, 3, 6, 10, . . .)

- *Predict the number of dots for the 5th or 6th triangular number.* (15, 21)

Now show the class that these dot patterns can also be shown as arrangements of square tiles. Explain to the class that their first challenge is to find an equation for the *n*th triangular number.

Let students work in groups of two to three.

Explore 3.1

Some students will have difficulty with the variables. The independent variable is the position or location number in the configuration and the dependent variable is the number of dots or squares in the configuration.

In Question A, encourage students to write down the differences between each successive triangular number. They should begin to notice some patterns of change.

In Question B, give students time to find the equation. Keep track of the different ways that students use to find the equation. If students are having a difficult time finding an equation, ask the following questions:

Suggested Questions

- *If you put two copies of the same figure together to form a rectangle, what are the dimensions of the rectangle?* (*n* and $n + 1$)

- *How many square tiles are in the rectangular arrangement? Or what is the area of the rectangle?* [$n(n + 1)$]

- *How does this number of square tiles compare to the number of square tiles in the original figure?* (The number is twice as many square tiles.)

- *How can you use the total number of square tiles in the rectangle to find the number of square tiles in the original figure?* [divide the total by 2 or divide $n(n + 1)$ by 2]

Ask some groups to make a large sketch of their work for how they found the equation. Ask them to include the table and graph on poster paper or on transparencies to be used in the summary.

Summarize 3.1

In Question A discuss the change from one triangular number to the next. Students should notice that from the first to the second you add 2, to get the third you add 3, then add 4, then 5 etc. Add a column to the table to indicate the change as follows. Note: The table has a 0 triangular number. Some students may argue that this is impossible and others may say it makes sense, since it is the triangular number with no squares or dots. Its place in the table may help some students see the change pattern more easily.

Changes in Consecutive Triangular Numbers

Figure Number	Number of Squares	Change Between Consecutive Triangular Numbers
0	0	
		+1
1	1	
		+2
2	3	
		+3
3	6	
		+4
4	10	
		+5
5	15	
		+6
6	21	
		+7
7	28	
		+8
8	36	
		+9
9	45	
		+10
10	55	

Suggested Questions

- *What pattern do you see in the table?* (As the figure number increases, the number of squares is increasing and the increase is the next consecutive integer. Some may notice that the increase is not constant, but if you find the differences of the differences you get a constant number.)

- *Use the pattern of change to predict the next five entries in the table.*

Be sure students see that while the difference between consecutive y-values (triangular number) is not a constant value (as in a linear relationship), it is regular and predictable. Therefore, we can use the pattern to generate additional y-values. The second difference is constant. This is a characteristic of quadratic functions and will be discussed further in the next investigation. In this investigation the focus is using the pattern to predict the next entry and to relate the pattern of change to the shape of the graph.

Suggested Question In Question B, ask:

- *How did you find the equation?* Some students may have tried to complete a rectangle for each figure by making a duplicate copy of the figure as shown in the diagram below:

The area of the rectangle is $n \times (n + 1)$. But this is twice the number of square tiles so you divide by 2, so $t = \frac{n}{2}(n + 1)$.

Other students may try to make a square. The number of square tiles needed is equal to $n^2 -$ (the $n - 1$ triangular number) or $n^2 - (1 + 2 + 3 ... + n - 1)$.

Some students may complete a square and then divide by 2 since the square number is too large. In so doing, they have taken away too much and so they add $\frac{n}{2}$. This gives the equation, $T_n = \frac{n^2}{2} + \frac{n}{2}$.

Some students may have made a chart and used patterns they observed in the numbers to write an equation.

Some students may say that the nth triangular number is the sum of the first n whole numbers or $T_n = 1 + 2 + 3 + 4 \ldots + n$.

To show that these are equivalent it is sufficient to validate the contextual reasoning, or to use the Distributive Property. Comparing tables and graphs gives additional evidence.

As students put forth equations, have them explain their reasoning.

Suggested Questions

- *Use your equation to find the 10th triangular number.*

- *Is 120 a triangular number? Explain why.*

In Question C, ask some students to display their graphs.

- *Does this graph represent the triangular number relationship?* (only the part of the graph for $x > 0$)

- *Describe some features of the graph.* (The y-intercept is 0 and the x-intercepts are 0 and -1. The minimum point occurs at $(-\frac{1}{2}, -\frac{1}{8})$. The line of symmetry passes through the point $-\frac{1}{2}$ on the x-axis. The graph is increasing at an increasing rate.)

- *What information do these features represent in the context?* (Not much, since the data for this context is valid only for integers greater than zero.)

- *Compare these relationships to those we have studied in Investigations 1 and 2.* (For the most part, all of the equations that represent contextual situations such as fixed perimeter, trading land, or triangular numbers are of the form, $y = x(x + a)$ or $y = x(a + x)$. The graphs of these equations all pass through the origin. Some have maximum points and some have minimum points. A few equations in Investigation 2 had non-zero y-intercepts.)

- *Are there any other patterns that you observe?* (One of the patterns students should notice is that each triangular number is the sum of the first n consecutive numbers. This equation describes a rule for adding the first n whole numbers. See the Did You Know? in the ACE for this investigation on how Gauss discovered this fact. Another way to see this sum pattern is to duplicate the sum as follows:

$$\begin{array}{ccccccccc} 1 + & 2 + & 3 + & \ldots + & 98 + & 99 + & 100 \\ 100 + & 99 + & 98 + & \ldots + & 3 + & 2 + & 1 \\ \hline 101 + & 101 + & 101 + & \ldots + & 101 + & 101 + & 101 \end{array}$$

So the sum is $[100(101)] \div 2$ or $(\frac{100}{2})(101)$.

Some students have fun showing their family how quickly they can add the first n numbers. First they ask a family number to pick a large number and then they tell them that they will quickly give them the sum of the set of whole numbers from 1 to this number without a calculator.

3.1 Exploring Triangular Numbers

Mathematical Goals

- Write an equation for a quadratic relationship represented by triangular numbers
- Introduce the patterns of change for a quadratic relationship as observed in a table and graph

Launch

Launch by putting the square numbers arranged as a set of dots.

- *Describe a rule for the number of dots in each square array.*
- *These are called square numbers. Name some more square numbers.*
- *If n represents the number of the arrangement or figure and S represents the number of dots in the arrangement, write an equation that represents the relationship between n and S.*

Put the first 4 triangular dot patterns on the overhead.

- *The number of dots in each triangular arrangement is called a triangular number. How many dots are in each pattern?*
- *Predict the number of dots for the 5th or 6th triangular number.*

Show the class that these dot patterns can also be shown as arrangements of square tiles. Let students work in groups of 2 to 3.

Materials
- Transparency 3.1

Vocabulary
- triangular numbers

Explore

Keep track of the different ways that students use to find the equation.

- *If you put two copies of the same figure together to form a rectangle, what are the dimensions of the rectangle? What is the area of the rectangle?*
- *How many square tiles are in the rectangular arrangement? How does this number compare to the number of tiles in the original figure?*
- *How can you use the total number of square tiles in the rectangle to find the number of square tiles in the original figure?*

Encourage students to write down the differences between each successive triangular number. Ask some groups to sketch their work including the table and graph on poster paper or on transparencies.

Materials
- Poster paper (optional)
- Blank transparencies (optional)

Summarize

- *How did you find the equation?*
- *Use your equation to find the 10th triangular number. Is 120 a triangular number? Explain why. In Question A, discuss the change from one triangular number to the next. Add a column to the table to indicate the change.*
- *What pattern do you see in the table? Use the pattern of change to predict the next 5 entries in the table.*

Materials
- Student notebooks

continued on next page

Be sure students see that while the difference between consecutive *y*-values is not a constant value, it is regular and predictable. In Question C, ask students to display their graphs.

- *Does this graph represent the triangular number relationship?*
- *Describe some features of the graph. What information do these features represent in the context?*
- *Compare these relationships to those we have studied in Investigations 1 and 2. Are there any other patterns that you observe?*

ACE Assignment Guide for Problem 3.1

Differentiated Instruction
Solutions for All Learners

Core 1–3, 20, 21, 23–25
Other *Applications* 4–8; *Connections* 22, 26–28; *Extensions* 47, 48; unassigned choices from previous problems

Adapted For suggestions about adapting ACE exercises, see the CMP *Special Needs Handbook*.

Answers to Problem 3.1

A. **1.** 21 squares; 55 squares

   2. (Figure 1)

   3. The change from one triangular number to the next is increasing and it increases by the *n*th consecutive whole number—it is not a constant change. The number that gets added on is always one more than the number that was added on previously.

   4. To find the 11th triangular number you add 11 to the 10th triangular number. To get the 12th triangular number you add 12 to the 11th triangular number, and so on.

B. **1.** $T_n = \dfrac{n(n+1)}{2}$, T_n is the *n*th triangular number or

   $T_n = n^2 - (n - 1 \; triangular \; number)$ or

$T_n = \dfrac{n^2}{2} + \dfrac{n}{2}$ or

$T_n = 1 + 2 + 3 + \dots + n.$

There may be other equations equivalent to

$T_n = \dfrac{n(n+1)}{2}.$

2. $T_{11} = \dfrac{11(11+1)}{2} = \dfrac{11(12)}{2} = \dfrac{132}{2} = 66$

$T_{12} = \dfrac{12(12+1)}{2} = \dfrac{12(13)}{2} = \dfrac{156}{2} = 78$

C. **1.**

$$y = \frac{x^2}{2} + \frac{x}{2}$$

2. Yes; The graph has points that aren't in the table, but both represent the same pattern.

3. Yes, because it is a product of two linear factors.

4. This equation is similar to those in Investigations 1 and 2. They are composed of a product of two linear factors.

Figure 1

Triangular Numbers

Figure Number	1	2	3	4	5	6	7	8	9	10
Triangular Number	1	3	6	10	15	21	28	36	45	55

Counting Handshakes

Goals

- Continue to look at patterns of change in tables for quadratic relationships

- Observe that one equation can model different contexts

In this problem students continue their experience with quadratic functions by considering handshakes between members of one or two sport teams. The equation, $y = \frac{n}{2}(n + 1)$, represents the nth triangular number and $y = \frac{n}{2}(n - 1)$ represents the number of handshakes. It also represents the n–1st triangular number. These relationships are similar to many of the quadratic relationships in Investigation 2 in that the parabolas have a minimum point. By recording data in tables and graphs they are able to observe patterns of change in that data and to compare those to patterns that they have previously observed in linear and non-linear relations.

Launch 3.2

To introduce the context of this problem, you might ask eight students to model the handshakes of two teams with four members each. Have two groups of four students stand at the front of the classroom and act out the handshaking.

Suggested Questions

- *How many handshakes will occur if each person on one of the four-member teams shakes hands with each person on the other four-member team? What do you think? (Collect some answers.)*

- *How many handshakes occur if each team has seven members? Ten members? Or n members?*

You will find a generalization by gathering data for different size teams and looking for patterns.

You could now model the next two parts of the problem by having students act out the number of handshakes between a team of five with a team of four, a team of seven with a team of six, etc. giving students a chance to observe the variation in the two situations.

- *How many handshakes will occur if one team has five members and the other has four members? (Collect some answers.)*

- *How many handshakes will occur if the four members of one team all do a round of "high fives?"*

This problem asks you to consider each of these three situations and to write equations to generalize each of them.

Have students work in groups of two or three.

Explore 3.2

Some students may be able to reason about the problem without using tables. For example, they might reason as follows: "If there are five students then each of these five shakes hands with each member on the other five-person team, so there are 5×5 handshakes."

If some students have difficulties, suggest that they might find it helpful to make a sketch using points for players and line segments for handshakes to visually represent each situation they encounter. The sketch for the two 10-player basketball teams could begin as shown in Figure 2.

Figure 2

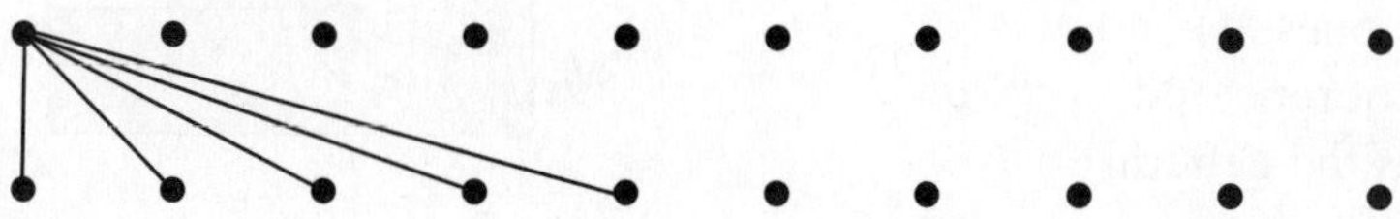

INVESTIGATION 3

If some students struggle with Case 3, a diagram of the players standing in a circle may help. The diagram below shows that player 1, P_1, is involved in four high fives or if the team has five members (or $n - 1$ high fives if the team has n members.). However, each of the other players in the five member team is also involved in four high fives, as shown below.

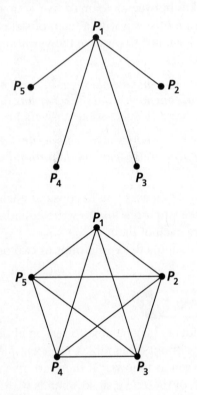

Suggested Question

• *If we just multiply 5 × 4, we are counting each high five twice. How can we correct for counting each twice?* (Divide by 2.)

Some students may make connections with triangular numbers to find an equation.

Strategy 1: Number of high fives among a team of 4 is $3 + 2 + 1$, which is the third triangular number. So, for a team of n players, the number of high fives is the $(n - 1)^{\text{th}}$ triangular number. This leads to the formula $0.5n(n - 1)$.

Strategy 2: The square area organizes the number of high fives for a team of 4. The dark area is half of 4^2 minus the diagonal (which is marked with X's and represents high fiving with oneself) and represents the high fives that are not repeated among members. This method gives the general formula: $0.5(n^2 - n)$.

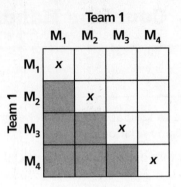

In relation to the strategy shown above, one student decided to move all the X's to the left and then found the number of high fives among a team of 4 is $\frac{1}{2}$ of the rectangle which has dimensions 3 by 4, so in general this leads to $\frac{1}{2}n(n - 1)$.

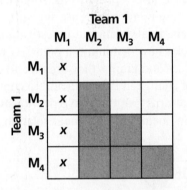

Strategy 3: Students may look at the square and say that $\frac{4^2}{2}$ gives you the shaded region below but then you still need to subtract the two squares on the diagonal where Member 3 (M_3) and M_4 high fived themselves. These two squares represent half the diagonal of 4. In general, this strategy leads to the expression $\frac{n^2}{2} - \frac{n}{2}$.

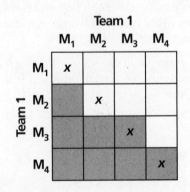

Look for interesting ways the students solve the problem. Discuss each of these different strategies in the summary. You might suggest that they put their work on large poster paper.

Summarize 3.2

Call on different groups to discuss Questions A, B, and C. Have each group explain how they got their answers. After each presentation, ask the class if they have any questions concerning the reasoning. Then ask the class if there are any other ways to solve the problem. See some of the suggestions discussed in the Explore.

There are several ways that students might think about each case. Several examples are given in the Explore. Here are some ways to reason about Case 2:

- Students might draw pictures using dots to represent the members on a team and lines to represent handshakes. From the sketches, it is evident that the increase in the number of handshakes follows in the pattern 2, 4, 6, ... Students can write an equation directly from this pattern. (Figure 3)

- Some students may use a table and find the handshakes are 0, 2, 6, 12, 20, etc. Some may notice that each of these numbers is the product of two consecutive integers: $2 = 1 \times 2, 6 = 2 \times 3, 12 = 3 \times 4$, etc. and write $n(n - 1) = h$.

- Some may notice that each of these numbers is twice a triangular number:
$2 = 2 \times 1, 6 = 2 \times 3, 12 = 2 \times 6$, etc. For teams with 4 and 5 members, for example, the number of handshakes is 2(10) or 2(4th triangular number). So, for teams with $n - 1$ and n members, the number of handshakes is 2($n - $1th triangular numbers). Thus $h = (n - 1)n$.

- Some may notice that the number of handshakes increases by 2, then 4, then 6, then 8 etc. They increase by the consecutive even whole numbers and this pattern of change can be used to continue the table. Some students may guess at a rule from the table. For example, to find the number of handshakes for teams with 10 and 9 members, add the first 9 even numbers or 10, if you count 0 as an even number: $0 + 2 + 4 + 6 + 8 + 10 + 12 + 14 + 16 + 18 = 10 \times 9 = 90$. Writing an equation from this pattern is not as easy as the other patterns.

- Others may reason that each of the n members on one team must shake hands with each of $n - 1$ members on the other team, which gives $n(n - 1)$ handshakes. You could also go over Exercise 33 with the class. This question suggests a pattern for adding a sequence of numbers such as the first n or $n - 1$ even numbers.

- Some students may use rectangular arrangements of squares similar to the method used for triangular numbers.

For Case 3: Similar strategies can be used to find the number of high fives.

- Students might make a drawing to help them find the high fives. From the sketches, it is evident that the number of "high fives" is 0, 1, 3, 6, 15, etc. These are the triangular numbers—or they are the first n − 1 triangular numbers. They can write $\frac{n(n - 1)}{2}$. (Figure 4, on next page)

- The increase in the number of high fives occurs in the pattern 1, 2, 3, 4, ..., and note that the number of high fives is the sum of the first $12 - 1 = 11$ whole numbers:
$1 + 2 + 3 + 4 + 5 + 6 + 7 + 8 + 9 + 10 + 11 = 66$. Students might use this pattern to write an equation.

Figure 3

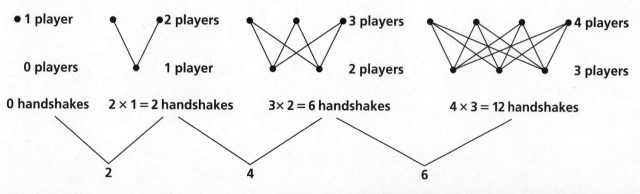

- Students might reason that each of the n people must high-five with $n - 1$ other people, giving $n(n - 1)$ high fives; as this counts each high five twice, the total is $\frac{n(n - 1)}{2}$.

- Students might make a table. This sometimes helps them to see a pattern. This will be discussed in Problem 3.3.

Students should be looking for similarities among the three situations.

Suggested Question

- *What are the three equations? How are they similar?* (If you write each in expanded form they each have an x^2 term. So they are quadratic equations. The last two are similar to the relationships in Problem 2.2.)

Call attention to the similarities between the table for the triangular numbers and the handshake problem in Case 3. The expression for the number of handshakes is $\frac{n(n - 1)}{2}$ and the expression for the nth triangular number is $\frac{n(n + 1)}{2}$. The graphs are similar. The expression for the $n - 1$ triangular number is $\frac{n(n - 1)}{2}$. There are other situations in the ACE that will have the same equations. This is important to point out that one equation can represent several different situations.

The following student strategy can also be discussed:

Here are two different ways students thought about Case 2:

Tyler expressed the number of handshakes between a team with n members and a team with $n - 1$ members as $n(n - 1)$.

Asuko wrote $n^2 - n$ to represent the same situation.

- *Describe how Tyler might have thought about the situation to formulate his expression.*

- *Describe how Asuko might have thought about the situation.*

Students might need a hint:

Draw and label a rectangle whose area can be represented by these expressions.

- *What information does each expression represent in this situation?*

Students will find more situations that can be represented by the triangular number relationship in the Connections section of the ACE.

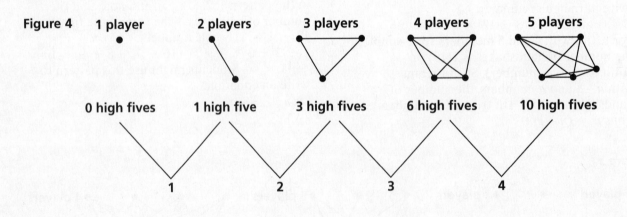

Figure 4

1 player 2 players 3 players 4 players 5 players

0 high fives 1 high five 3 high fives 6 high fives 10 high fives

1 2 3 4

Counting Handshakes

Mathematical Goals

- Continue to look at patterns of change in tables for quadratic relationships
- Observe that one equation can model different contexts

Launch

Have 8 students act out handshakes of 2 teams with 4 members.

One question you will be pursuing in this problem is:

- *How many handshakes will occur if each person on one of the five member teams shakes hands with each person on the other five member team? What do you think?*
- *How many handshakes occur if each team has 7 members? 10 members? n members?*

You will find a generalization by gathering data for different size teams and looking for patterns. Model the next two parts of the problem by having students act out the number of handshakes between a team of 5 and a team of 4, a team of 7 and one of 6, etc. giving students a chance to observe the variation in the situations.

- *How many handshakes will occur if one team has 5 members and the other has 4 members? How many handshakes will occur if the four members of one team all do a round of "high fives?"*

Have students work in groups of two or three.

Explore

Some students may be able to reason about the problem without using tables. For some, you may need to suggest that they make a sketch using points for players and line segments for handshakes to visually represent each situation they encounter or, for Case 3, a diagram of the players standing in a circle may help.

- *If we just multiply 5 × 4, we are counting each high five twice. How can we correct for counting each twice?*

Some students may use a rectangular array of squares like they did for triangular numbers to find an equation. Look for interesting ways the students are using to solve the problem. Suggest that they put their work on large poster paper.

Materials
- Poster paper (optional)

Summarize

Call on different groups to discuss Questions A, B, and C. There are several ways that students might think about each case. Students should be looking for similarities among the three situations.

Materials
- Student notebooks

continued on next page

- *What are the three equations? How are they similar?*

Call attention to the similarities between the table for the triangular numbers and the handshake problem in Case 3. The following student strategy can also be discussed:

Here are two different ways students thought about Case 2:

Tyler expressed the number of handshakes between a team with n members and a team with $n - 1$ members as $n(n - 1)$.

Asuko wrote $n^2 - n$ to represent the same situation.

- *Describe how Tyler might have thought about the situation to formulate his expression. How about Asuko?*

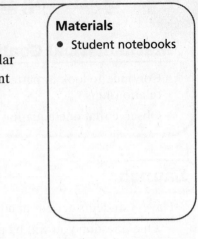

Materials
- Student notebooks

ACE Assignment Guide for Problem 3.2

Differentiated Instruction
Solutions for All Learners

Core 9–11, 29–31
Other Connections 32–37, Extensions 49; unassigned choices from previous problems

Adapted For suggestions about adapting Exercise 9 and other ACE exercises, see the CMP *Special Needs Handbook*.
Connecting to Prior Units 37: *Shapes and Designs*

Answers to Problem 3.2

A. 1. $h = 5^2 = 25$ and $h = 10^2 = 100$

2. For two squads with n players on each side, $h = n^2$.

B. 1. $h = 7(6) = 42$ and $h = 9(8) = 72$

2. $h = n(n - 1)$

C. 1. 6 and 28; for a 4-member team,
6 or $3 + 2 + 1 = 6$ or $4(3) \div 2 = 6$;
for an eight member team, 28 or
$7 + 6 + 5 + 4 + 3 + 2 + 1 = \frac{8(7)}{2} = 28$

2. $h = \frac{n(n - 1)}{2}$

Examining Patterns of Change

Goals

- Examine the patterns of change in quadratic relationships.
- Use the patterns of change to predict the next entry in a table for a quadratic relationship

In this problem students use the quadratic equations from Problem 3.2 to look at patterns of change and to compare them to the patterns of change in the handshake problem.

Launch 3.3

You could start this problem, by asking:

Suggested Questions

- *Do any of the three handshake (or high-five) equations represent quadratic relationships? Explain.*

- *How else can you determine whether a relationship is a quadratic relationship?* (Some may suggest that the shape of the graph is a parabola. Some might begin to describe patterns of change in the table.)

In this problem, we will look more closely at the patterns of change in a table for quadratic relationships and how these patterns affect the graph and equation of the relationship.

Pass out Labsheet 3.3. Have students work in pairs.

Explore 3.3

Be sure that students are making note of their reasoning. They may not use the language of second differences, but they should begin to notice that the differences of the (first) differences are constant.

Summarize 3.3

Go over the tables and graphs for each case. Help the students articulate the patterns of change and how the pattern of change affects the table, graph, and equation.

Suggested Questions

- *How can you tell whether or not a situation is modeled by a quadratic equation?* (In a table, there is no common "first" difference, but these differences seem to be changing by a constant amount. In a graph, the data points make a parabola shape. In an equation there should be a product of two linear factors.)

- *How does the pattern of change affect the equation and graph of a quadratic relationship?* (If as the x-values increase, the y-values increase to a certain point and then decrease, the coefficient of the x^2 term is negative, and the graph of the relationship will have a maximum point. If as the x-values increase, the y-values decrease to a certain point and then increase, the coefficient of the x^2 term is positive, and the graph will have a minimum point. The increasing/decreasing pattern is regular which produces a parabola with a line of symmetry.)

Put up a table, graph and equation from this problem and demonstrate the patterns of change in the table. Then show how this increasing/decreasing pattern shows up in the graph and then finally look at the coefficient of x^2. Note the increasing/decreasing pattern shows up in the graph in that there are two symmetric sides to a parabola—one side increasing and the other decreasing or vice versa. The sides are not straight lines because the increase/decrease is not constant. The two sides meet at the vertex. If the change pattern is increasing/decreasing, there is a maximum point. If the change pattern is decreasing/increasing, there is a minimum point.

Suggested Questions Put the three equations in factored form on the overhead or board.

- *Do you notice anything about the form of these equations that might be a clue that they are all quadratic equations?* (In each equation there are two linear factors, and each factor contains the variable x raised to the first power.)

- *How do these equations differ from linear equations?* (In linear equations, the variable appears only once and it has the exponent of 1.)

Check for Understanding

The following equations are similar to those found in Investigation 1 or 2.

$$y = x^2 - 4 \qquad y = x(4 - x)$$

Suggested Questions

- Make a table for each equation for x-values from -5 to 5 and describe the pattern of change in the table.

- Without sketching the graph, describe the shape of the graph of each equation.

- How can you tell from the equations that these are quadratic relationships?

- How can you tell from the equations which of these quadratic relationships will have a maximum and which will have a minimum?

Examining Patterns of Change

Mathematical Goals

- Examine the patterns of change in quadratic relationships
- Use the patterns of change to predict the next entry in a table for a quadratic relationship

Launch

- *Do any of the three handshake (or high-five) equations represent quadratic relationships? Explain.*
- *How else can you determine whether a relationship is a quadratic relationship?*

In this problem, we will look more closely at the patterns of change in a table for quadratic relationships and how these patterns affect the graph and equation of the relationship.

Have students work in pairs.

Materials
- Labsheet 3..3

Explore

Be sure that students are making note of their reasoning. They may not use the language of second differences, but they should begin to notice that the differences of the (first) differences are constant.

Summarize

Help the students articulate the patterns of change and how the pattern of change affects the table, graph, and equation.

- *How can you tell whether or not a situation is modeled by a quadratic equation?*
- *How does the pattern of change affect the equation and graph of a quadratic relationship?*

Put up a table, graph and equation from this problem and demonstrate the patterns of change in the table. Then show how this increasing/decreasing pattern shows up in the graph and then finally look at the coefficient of x^2. Note the increasing/decreasing pattern shows up in the graph in that there are two symmetric sides to a parabola—one side increasing and the other decreasing or vice versa. The sides are not straight lines because the increase/decrease is not constant.

Put the three equations in factored form on the overhead or board.

- *Do you notice anything about the form of these equations that might be a clue that they are all quadratic equations?*
- *How do these equations differ from linear equations?*

Materials
- Student notebooks

continued on next page

The following equations are similar to those found in Inv. 1 or 2.

$$y = x^2 - 4 \qquad y = x(4 - x)$$

- *Make a table for each equation for x-values from −5 to 5 and describe the pattern of change in the table.*

- *Without sketching the graph, describe the shape of the graph of each equation.*

- *How can you tell that these are quadratic relationships?*

ACE Assignment Guide for Problem 3.3

Differentiated Instruction
Solutions for All Learners

Core 12–16, 41–45
Other *Applications* 17–19; *Connections* 38–40, 46; *Extensions* 50, 51; unassigned choices from previous problems

Adapted For suggestions about adapting ACE exercises, see the CMP *Special Needs Handbook.*
Connecting to Prior Units 39, 40: *Filling and Wrapping*

Answers to Problem 3.3

A. 1. Table for Case 1: (Figure 5)
   Table for Case 2: (Figure 6)
   Table for Case 3: (Figure 7)

2. Patterns in table: a constant change in x does not lead to a constant change in y. Students might see the following patterns:

Case 1: As the number of people increases by one, the number of handshakes increases by 3, 5, 7, 9, etc. The increases are the consecutive odd integers. So for $n = 11$, add the 11th odd integer, that is 21, to 100. Or the number of handshakes increases steadily by odd numbers. Thus the number of handshakes is 121. Each time the increase is two more than the time before.

Case 2: As the number of people increases by one, the number of handshakes increases by 4, 6, 8, 10, etc. The increases are the consecutive even integers or the number of handshakes increases steadily by even numbers. So for $n = 11$, add the 10th even integer, which is 20, to 90. Thus the number of handshakes is 110. Each time the increase is two more than the time before.

Figure 5   Table for Case 1

# of Members	1	2	3	4	5	6	7	8	9	10	n
# of Handshakes	1	4	9	16	25	36	49	64	81	100	n^2

Figure 6   Table for Case 2

# of Members	2 & 1	3 & 2	4 & 3	5 & 4	6 & 5	7 & 6	8 & 7	9 & 8	10 & 9	$n \ \& \ n - 1$
# of Handshakes	2	6	12	20	30	42	56	72	90	$n(n - 1)$

Figure 7   Table for Case 3

# of Members	1	2	3	4	5	6	7	8	9	10	n
# of High Fives	0	1	3	6	10	15	21	28	36	45	$\frac{n}{2}(n - 1)$

Case 3: As the number of people increases by one, the number of high fives increases by 1, 2, 3, 4, 5, etc. The increases are the consecutive integers or the increases each increase by 1 each time. So for $n = 11$, add the 10th integer, which is 10, to 45. Thus the number of high fives is 55. Each time the increase is one more than the time before.

B. Similarity: The increases of the number of handshakes differ by 2.
Difference: In Case 1, the increases are consecutive odd integers. In Case 2, the increases are consecutive even integers. In Case 3, the increases are consecutive integers.

C. 1. graph of $y = x^2$ for $-5 \le x \le 5$ and $-2 \le y \le 10$

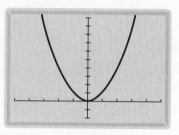

graph of $y = x(x - 1)$ for $-5 \le x \le 5$ and $-2 \le y \le 10$

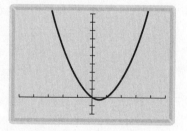

graph of $y = \dfrac{x(x - 1)}{2}$ for $-5 \le x \le 5$ and $-2 \le y \le 10$

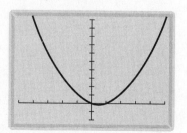

2. The three graphs are parabolas with minimum values. Graph A has only one x-intercept of 0. Graphs B and C have the same x-intercepts of 0 and 1. Note: If you use a graphing calculator to find the graphs, the graphing calculator gives y-value outputs for fractional as well as integer x-value inputs. You might want to point out that the calculator (in this mode) doesn't know that we have a situation in which only integers make sense. The equation is a model of the situation.

D. The table and the graph show the same pattern of increasing changes, however the graph shows more values than the table. As the table's x-values increase the y-values increase. Also the more spread out the y-values in the table are as x increases by 1, the faster the graph increases in that corresponding interval. For example, for the graph of Case 1: the graph increases faster between 9 and 10 member teams than 1- and 2-member team values and in the table the difference in handshakes among 9 and 10 members (19) is larger than that of the handshakes for 1 and 2 member teams (3).

E. All three relationships are quadratic. We can deduce this from the shape of the graph (a parabola), or from the format of the equations (each is a product of 2 linear factors). If we use the Distributive Property on the equations we see that each equation has an "n^2" term and no higher power than 2.

F. The differences in the table are changing by a constant amount. In Investigation 4, these differences are named "second differences." So that looking at the differences between successive y-values in an x, y table you see that these difference increase (or decrease) by a constant amount each time. Students can look back at the tables for quadratic relationships for Investigations 1 and 2 to check this. When looking at the graphs in this investigation, as the x-values increase, the y-values decrease to a certain point and then increase, the coefficient of the x^2 term is positive, and the graph will have a minimum point. In Investigation 1, the y-values increased to a certain point and then decreased with a negative coefficient associated with the x^2 term.

Investigation 3

ACE Assignment Choices

Differentiated Instruction
Solutions for All Learners

Problem 3.1
Core 1–3, 20, 21, 23–25
Other *Applications* 4–8; *Connections* 22, 26–28; *Extensions* 47, 48; unassigned choices from previous problems

Problem 3.2
Core 9–11, 29–31
Other *Connections* 32–37; *Extensions* 49; unassigned choices from previous problems

Problem 3.3
Core 12–16, 41–45
Other *Applications* 17–19; *Connections* 38–40, 46; *Extensions* 50, 51; unassigned choices from previous problems

Adapted For suggestions about adapting Exercise 9 and other ACE exercises, see the CMP *Special Needs Handbook*.
Connecting to Prior Units 37: *Shapes and Designs*; 39, 40: *Filling and Wrapping*

Applications

1. **a.** 25 and 36
   b. n^2
   c. The numbers seem to be getting bigger by a larger amount each time. The square number increases by consecutive odd integers, beginning with 3: 3, 5, 7,....

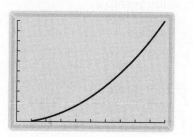

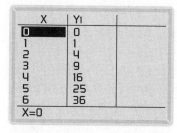

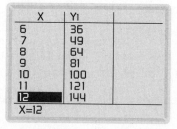

2. **a.** 2, 6, 12, 20, 30, 42
   b. The rectangular number increases by consecutive even integers beginning with 4: 4, 6, 8, 10, 12,....
   c. The seventh number is 14 greater than the sixth number, or 56. The eighth number is 16 greater than the seventh number, or 72.
   d. $r = n(n + 1)$, where r is the rectangular number.

3. **a.** $\frac{18(18 + 1)}{2} = \frac{18(19)}{2} = 171$

   b. yes; It is a triangular number because $\frac{20(20 + 1)}{2} = \frac{20(21)}{2} = 210$ (Note: students may substitute into the equation or continue the table to answer this.)

4. **a.** Sam is correct because if you look at the triangles in Problem 3.1, each row of a triangle represents a counting number: 1, 2, 3.... Therefore the equation for triangular numbers, $\frac{n(n + 1)}{2}$, represents the sum of the numbers 1 to n.
   b. 55   **c.** 120   **d.** $\frac{n(n + 1)}{2}$

5. Rectangular, because it satisfies the equation $r = n(n + 1)$, 110 is the tenth rectangular number. $110 = 10(11)$

6. Triangular, because it satisfies the equation $t = \dfrac{n(n + 1)}{2}$, 66 is the 11th triangular number: $66 = \dfrac{11(12)}{2}$.

7. Square, because it satisfies the equation $s = n^2$, 121 is the 11th square number: $121 = 11^2$.

8. None, because it does not satisfy any of the associated equations, 60 is none of these.

9. a. The eight people on each side shake hands with 8 others, so $8^2 = 64$ handshakes will be exchanged.

   b. 28. $7 + 6 + 5 + 4 + 3 + 2 + 1 = \dfrac{7(8)}{2} = 28$, or each of 8 people shake hands with the other 7, but as this counts each handshake twice, $\dfrac{8(7)}{2} = 28$ handshakes will be exchanged.

   c. 12. $6 \times 2 = 12$

10. a. 15. $5 \times 3 = 15$

    b. 10. $4 + 3 + 2 + 1 = \dfrac{4(5)}{2} = 10$, or each of 5 people high-five with the other 4, but as this counts each high five twice, $\dfrac{4(5)}{2} = 10$ high fives will be exchanged.

11. a. 10. $4 + 3 + 2 + 1 = \dfrac{4(5)}{2} = 10$, or each of 5 rooms connects with each other 4 by cables, but as this counts two cables between each two rooms, $\dfrac{4(5)}{2} = 10$ cables will be needed.

    b. 21. $6 + 5 + 4 + 3 + 2 + 1 = \dfrac{6(7)}{2} = 21$.

    c. They are the same situation mathematically, where the cables are associated with high fives and rooms are associated with people.

12. Possible answer: P represents the area of a rectangle formed from a square of a side length n in which one dimension is decreased by 1 unit, or P represents the number of handshakes between a team of n players and a team of $n - 1$ players.

13. Possible answer: P represents the area of a rectangle with sides of length 2 and n.

14. Possible answer: P represents the area of a rectangle formed from a square of a side length n in which one dimension is decreased by 2 units.

15. Possible answer: P represents the area of a rectangle with perimeter 32 units.

16. a. Graph ii; Possible explanation: The equation $h = \dfrac{n}{2}(n - 1)$, which represents the relationship between the number of high fives and the number of team players, tells us that the graph will have x-intercepts of 0 and 1.

    b. Graph iii; Possible explanation: The area of rectangles with a fixed perimeter grows and then declines as the length of a side increases. That means the graph has a maximum point.

    c. Graph i; possible explanation: Since the equation for the relationship described is $y = (x + 2)(x - 3)$, we know that $y = 0$ when $x = -2$ or 3. So, the x-intercepts must be -2 and 3.

    d. Graph iv; Possible explanation: The nth triangular number can be represented by the equation $T = \dfrac{n(n + 1)}{2}$. This equation that tells us the graph will have two x-intercepts of 0 and -1.

17. **Quadratic Relationship 1**

x	y
0	0
1	1
2	3
3	6
4	10
5	15
6	21

18. **Quadratic Relationship 2**

x	y
0	0
1	3
2	8
3	15
4	24
5	35
6	48

19. Quadratic Relationship 3

x	y
0	0
1	4
2	6
3	6
4	4
5	0
6	−6

Connections

20. a.

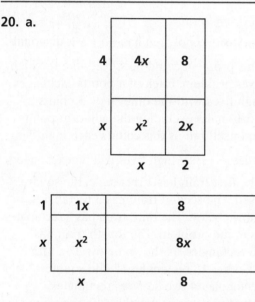

Expanded form: $x^2 + 6x + 8$; factored form: $(x + 2)(x + 4)$ and expanded form: $x^2 + 9x + 8$; Factored form: $(x + 8)(x + 1)$. We can't have negative values for sides given the area models in the student edition so factored forms like $(x − 2)(x − 4)$ aren't possible even though they give you the terms 8 and x^2.

b. No; expanded form: $x^2 + 6x + 5$; Factored form: $(x + 1)(x + 5)$ (excluding commutation of the factors of $x + 1$ and $(x + 5)$. Again there are more possibilities if we use non-whole-number factors of 5.

21. $2x^2 + 3x + 3x + 3x + 9 = 2x^2 + 9x + 9$ or $(2x + 3)(x + 3)$

22. a. $2x^2 + 7x + 6$

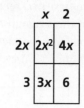

$x^2 + 6x + 8$

	x	4
x	x^2	$4x$
2	$2x$	8

b. $2x^2 + 7x + 6 = (2x + 3)(x + 2)$; $x^2 + 6x + 8 = (x + 4)(x + 2)$; $x^2 + 6x + 8$ is easier to do because x^2 has a coefficient of one.

23. $x(5 − x) = 5x − x^2$

24. $(x + 1)(x + 3) = x^2 + 4x + 3$

25. $(x − 1)(x + 3) = x^2 + 2x − 3$

26. $3x(x + 5) = 3x^2 + 15x$

27. $(2x + 1)(x + 3) = 2x^2 + 7x + 3$

28. $(2x − 1)(x + 3) = 2x^2 + 5x − 3$

29. $x^2 − 9x + 8 = (x − 8)(x − 1)$

30. $4x^2 − 6x = 2x(2x − 3)$

31. $x^2 − 2x − 3 = (x − 3)(x + 1)$

32. $3x^2 + 14x + 8 = (3x + 2)(x + 4)$

33. $4x^2 + 6x = 2x(2x + 3)$

34. $4x^2 − x − 3 = (4x + 3)(x − 1)$

35. $x^3 − 2x^2 − 3x = x(x + 1)(x − 3)$

36. a. Subdivide a rectangle into four parts. Label the area of one of the smaller rectangles as $3x^2$ and the one diagonal to it as 8. Use these areas to find the dimensions of these two smaller rectangles. (Note that there are several ways to do this.) Once you have picked the dimensions, use them to find the area of the remaining two rectangles. If the sum of the area of these two rectangles is $14x$, then you picked the right dimensions. And the dimensions that you picked for the first two rectangles are the dimensions of the original rectangle. These two dimensions are the factors in the factored form of $3x^2 + 14x + 8$.

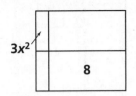

Let the dimensions of the rectangle whose area is $3x^2$ be $3x$ and x and the dimensions of the rectangle with area 8 be 4 and 2. The areas of the remaining two rectangles are $2x$ and $12x$ and their sum is $14x$.

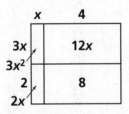

The dimensions of the original rectangle are $3x + 2$ and $x + 4$. Then write $14x$ as $12x + 2x$. Label the area of the two remaining rectangles as $12x$ and $2x$.

b. Look at the factors of the coefficient of x^2 and the factors of the constant term. Put these values in the factor pairs: $(\underline{\ ?\ }x + \underline{\ ?\ })(\underline{\ ?\ }x + \underline{\ ?\ })$. Use the distributive property to check if the coefficient of x is correct.

37. a. A pentagon has 5 diagonals, a hexagon has 9 diagonals, a heptagon has 14 diagonals and an octagon has 20 diagonals.

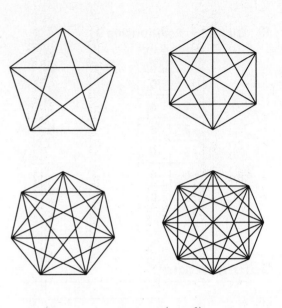

b. An n-sided polygon has $\dfrac{n(n-3)}{2}$ diagonals.

This problem could be solved like the high fives problem. Each of n points exchanges high fives with the other $n - 3$ points (diagonals) excluding the adjacent points and itself but as this counts each high five twice, $\dfrac{n(n-3)}{2}$ high fives will be exchanged.

38. a. The first train has 1 rectangle, the square itself. The second train has 3 rectangles, as shown below. The third train has 6 rectangles, as in the problem. The fourth train has 10 rectangles, as shown below. The fifth train has 15 rectangles (5 one-square rectangles, 4 two-squares rectangles, 3 three-square rectangles, 2 four-square rectangles and 1 five-square rectangle.)

(Figure 8)

Figure 8

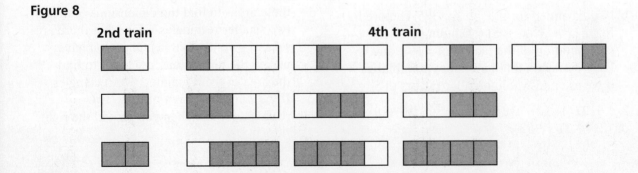

b.

Number of Rectangles in the First Ten Trains

Train	Number of Rectangles
1	1
2	3
3	6
4	10
5	15
6	21
7	28
8	36
9	45
10	55

c. The number of rectangles increases by a greater amount each time. The pattern of increase is 2, 3, 4, 5, 6, ... So, we could expect an increase of 15 from the 14th train to the 15th train. The table below shows that there are 120 rectangles in the 15th train.

Number of Rectangles in Trains 11 Through 15

Train	Number of Rectangles
11	66
12	78
13	91
14	105
15	120

d. $r = \dfrac{n(n + 1)}{2}$ where r is the number of rectangles (Note: The numbers are the same as the triangular numbers, an observation that students may use to solve this equation).

e. $r = \dfrac{15(15 + 1)}{2} = \dfrac{15(16)}{2} = \dfrac{240}{2} =$ 120 rectangles.

39 a. About 78.5 cm^2

b. About 78.5 centimeter cubes

c. 10 layers

d. $\approx$ 785 cm^3; this is the product of the number of cubes in one layer and the number of layers that fill the can.

e. $\approx$ 31.4 cm

f. $\approx$ 314 cm^2

g. $\approx$ 471 cm^2; this is the sum of twice the area of the base and the area of the paper label.

40. a. Possible net:

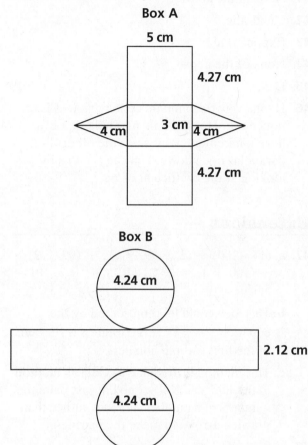

Box A

5 cm

4.27 cm

4 cm   3 cm   4 cm

4.27 cm

Box B

4.24 cm

2.12 cm

4.24 cm

b. Box A: 69.7 cm^2, Box B: 56.48 cm^2; To find the surface area of box A you would have to add the area of the base which is $3 \times 5 = 15$ cm^2, the area of the two triangles each of which has an area of $\frac{1}{2}(3 \times 4) = 6$ cm^2 and the areas for the side rectangles. The rectangles have dimensions 5 and about 4.27. To find the 4.27 you use the Pythagorean theorem on the right triangle on the front of the box with the side lengths of 3 and 4 to obtain the hypotenuse of $\sqrt{1.5^2 + 4^2} = 4.27$. So the surface area is $15 + 2(6) + 2(5 \times 4.27) = 69.7$ cm^2. To find the surface area of Box B, you would have to add the area of the top and bottom two circles, which each have an area of $\pi(2.12)^2 \approx 14.12$ cm^2, to the area of the

rectangle which has an area of
$2.12 \times \pi(4.24) \approx 28.24$ cm². So the surface
area is $14.12 \times 2 + 28.24 = 56.48$ cm².

c. Box A will require more cardboard to
construct, since it has a larger surface area.

41. None of the above.

42. Quadratic

43. Exponential

44. None of the above

45. D

46. H; one way to eliminate certain choices is to
notice that H is the only parabola that can
have a minimum point since the other three
parabolas open down. You can see this by
looking at the coefficient of x^2.

Extensions

47. a. $(1 + 100) + (2 + 99) + \ldots + (99 + 2)$
$+ (100 + 1) = \frac{100}{2} \times (101) = 50 \times 101 =$
$5,050$

b. This idea could be represented by the
equation $s = \frac{n}{2}(n + 1)$, where s is the sum
of the first s whole numbers.

c. This method is the same as Gauss's method
in the Did You Know? box. It just pairs the
numbers in a number sentence rather than
drawing arrows to make the pairings.

48. a. $8, 21, 40$

b. $65, 96, 133; 5 \times 5 + 10 \times 4 = 65;$
$6 \times 6 + 15 \times 4 = 96;$
$7 \times 7 + 21 \times 4 = 133.$

c. $s = (n + 1)^2 + \frac{4n(n + 1)}{2}$

For the Teacher: Students may not be able to find
this equation. You might help them to write an
equation by pointing out that each star has a
center square and four triangular points. Each star
number is thus composed of 4 times the triangular
number of the same number plus the next square
number. For example, the first star number has a
center of 4 (the second square number) and four
"points" of 1 (the first triangular number); the
second star number has a center of 9 (the third
square number) and four points of 3 (the second
triangular number).

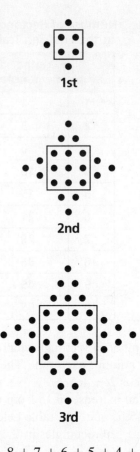

1st

2nd

3rd

49. a. $45.; 9 + 8 + 7 + 6 + 5 + 4 + 3 + 2 + 1 =$
$\frac{9(10)}{2} = 45$, or each of the 10 classmates
shakes hands with 9 others, but as this
counts each handshake twice, $\frac{10(9)}{2} = 45$
handshakes exchanged. Three diagrams
that express this are shown below.

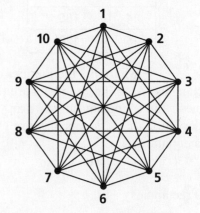

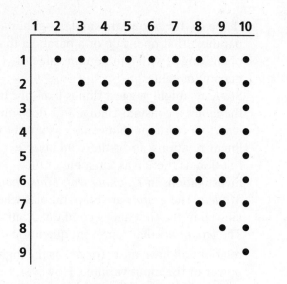

People: A, B, C, D, E, F, G, H, I, J
Handshakes: AB, AC, AD, AE, AF, AG, AH, AI, AJ
BC, BD, BE, BF, BG, BH, BI, BJ
CD, CE, CF, CG, CH, CI, CJ
DE, DF, DG, DH, DI, DJ
EF, EG, EH, EI, EJ
FG, FH, FI, FJ
GH, GI, GJ
HI, HJ
IJ

b. Each of the 2 friends shakes hands with 11 others, but as one handshake is counted twice (when they shake hands with each other), there are $2(11) - 1 = 21$ handshakes in all. Three diagrams that express this are shown here.

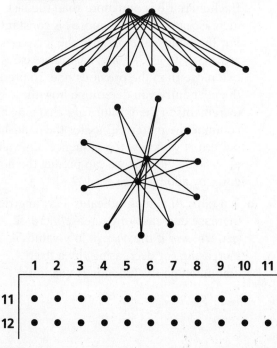

50. a. 1, 6, 15

b. 28, 45

c. $h = n(2n - 1)$.

For the teacher: Students may not be able to find this equation. You might help them write an equation by pointing out that there are four lines along which they can add $1 + 2 + 3 + \ldots + n$ dots. The equation for triangular numbers, $\frac{n(n + 1)}{2}$, is multiplied by 4 to get this sum. However, this counts the dots circled on the diagram an extra 3 times for each hexagon, for a total of $3n$ times for the whole figure. Thus, the complete equation for hexagonal numbers is as follows: $h = 4(\frac{n(n + 1)}{2}) - 3n = 2n^2 + 2n - 3n = 2n^2 - n = n(2n - 1)$

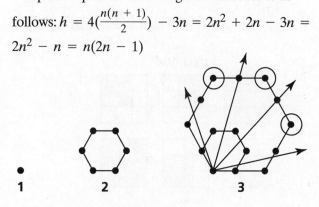

51. a. Of the 14 remaining squares, 9 are 2-by-2 squares, 4 are 3-by-3 squares, and 1 is a 4-by-4 square.

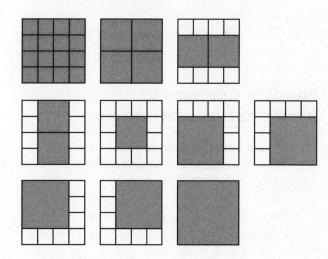

b. Possible answer: The squares found in a 1-by-1 grid, a 2-by-2 grid and a 3-by-3 grid are shown below. Each grid contains n^2 more squares than the previous grid, so an equation for the number of squares in an n-by-n grid is

$s = n^2 + (n - 1)^2 + \ldots + 1^2$, where s is the number of squares.

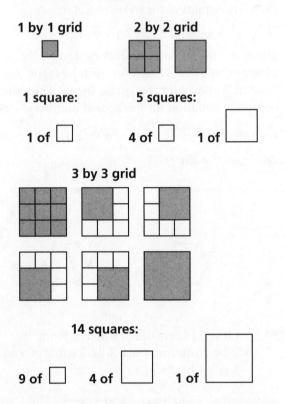

1 by 1 grid

2 by 2 grid

1 square:

5 squares:

1 of ☐

4 of ☐   1 of ☐

3 by 3 grid

14 squares:

9 of ☐   4 of ☐   1 of ☐

This shows that the pattern is a sum of squares.

Possible Answers to Mathematical Reflections

1. a. The relationships in the handshake and triangular number problems have similar graphs and tables in which y increases at an increasing rate. The high-five situation and the triangular number pattern are applications of the same formula. However, one formula is $\frac{n}{2}(n + 1)$ and the other is $\frac{n}{2}(n - 1)$.

b. These functions are the same as in Investigations 1 and 2, which also were expressed as the product of 2 factors. The shape of the graphs are similar—either a parabola that opens up or a parabola that opens down, with a minimum value or maximum value.

Students might suggest things like this: In the *tables* a constant change in x does not lead to a constant change in y as it did for linear relations, nor is there an inverse relation as there was for some of the investigations in *Thinking with Mathematical Models*. The *graphs* are all parabolas when viewed in the first and second quadrants. The *equations* that represent quadratic relations all have an x^2 (or n^2) as the highest power of the input variable. However, students will not always see them in this form. They have seen expressions such as $n(n + 1)$ or $n(n - 1)$ or $6(n - 2)^2$ or $\frac{n(n + 1)}{2}$ or $\frac{n(n - 1)}{2}$. At this point they should not be expected to discuss the degree of the equation, but they should begin to notice some similarities in all of the expressions such as "an expression with n is multiplied by another expression having n in it."

2. a. The rate of change for a sequence of numbers associated with a quadratic equation is not constant. However, the rate of change for each increment or increase seems to be constant. For example, in the triangular numbers, $1, 3, 6, 10, 15, 21, \ldots$, the increases are $+2, +3, +4, +5, +6, \ldots$. Each increase is one more than the last increase, and this "one more" is constant. For the handshake pattern, the increases are $3, 5, 7, 9, 11, \ldots$, and each increase is two more than the previous one. To predict the next entry you determine how the increments in the y-values are changing and continue the pattern. Thus, for the handshake pattern, if we know the sequence of y-values is $\ldots 56, 72, 90, 110$, we can predict the next entry by adding 22 to get 132.

b. If a table of values indicates a symmetric increase/decrease or decrease/increase pattern, *and* if the *change* in y-values is increasing (or decreasing) by a fixed amount, then the function is quadratic.

 **What Is a Quadratic Function?**

Mathematical and Problem-Solving Goals

- Examine patterns of change associated with quadratic situations that are represented by equations in expanded form such as the height of a ball over time that is thrown in air

- Predict the maximum or minimum point from an equation, graph, or table

- Predict the *y*-intercept from an equation, graph, or table

- Interpret the information that the *y*-intercept represents

- Identify the first and second differences for a quadratic relationship represented in a table

- Summarize the understandings about quadratic functions

- Explore the "Painted Cube" situation, which has linear, quadratic and cubic functions

- Compare linear, quadratic and exponential functions

The first two problems are examples of classic projectile motion problems, which are used here to extend understanding of quadratic polynomials and their graphs. These contexts provide a situation in which maximum or minimum points are important as well as the *y*-intercept.

Summary of Problems

Problem 4.1 Tracking a Ball

Students explore the pattern of change over time in the height of a ball thrown into the air.

Problem 4.2 Measuring Jumps

Students investigate quadratic equations describing the jumps of frogs, fleas, and basketball players. The equation describes the height of the jumpers as a function of time in the air.

Problem 4.3 Putting It All Together

Students investigate patterns of change more closely—particularly those for equations in expanded form that are not easy to factor. They discover that the differences between consecutive *y* values, called *first differences*, are constant for linear relationships and that *second differences* are constant for quadratic relationships.

Problem 4.4 Painted Cubes

Students observe linear, quadric, and cubic relationships in this classic exploration. A painted cube with edge length *n* is separated into n^3 small cubes. Students determine how many of the faces of the smaller cubes have three faces painted, two faces painted, one face painted or no faces painted. Rate of change, shape of the graph, form of the equation and tables all come together in this investigation to characterize a quadratic function.

	Suggested Pacing	Materials for Students	Materials for Teachers	ACE Assignments
All	$4\frac{1}{2}$ days	Graphing calculators, student notebooks	Blank transparencies and transparency markers, (optional), overhead graphing calculator (optional)	
4.1	1 day	Motion detector (optional), ball (optional), stopwatch (optional)	Transparency 4.1, motion detector (optional), ball (optional), stopwatch (optional)	1–4, 31, 32, 51–53
4.2	1 day		Transparency 4.2A, 4.2B	5–17, 33–35, 54
4.3	1 day	Poster paper (optional), Labsheets 4.3A and B	Transparency 4.3	18–26, 36–40, 55
4.4	1 day	Base ten thousands block (optional), Centimeter or other unit cubes	Transparency 4.4, Rubik's Cube or other large cube (optional)	27–30, 41–50, 56, 57
MR	$\frac{1}{2}$ day			

4.1 Tracking a Ball

Goals

- Examine patterns of change associated with quadratic situations that are represented by equations in expanded form, such as the height of a ball over time that is thrown in the air

- Predict the maximum or minimum point from an equation, graph or table

   In this classic problem students examine the data about the height of a ball thrown into the air. If you have access to a motion detector that can accurately read information directly into a calculator or computer, this problem could be conducted as an experiment.

Launch 4.1

If you have a motion detector, you could collect data on the height of a ball to introduce this problem or you could start by throwing a ball straight up into the air and asking the class to describe how the height of the object changes as it travels. Ask someone to time how long it takes for the object to hit the floor: a stopwatch is helpful for making a good approximation of the measurement. Throw another object into the air using a similar initial velocity (amount of force) asking the class to repeat their observations.

Suggested Questions

- *Name some situations that are similar to tossing a ball into the air.* (Launching rockets, kicking a soccer ball, pole vaulting, diving, etc. are all possibilities.)

- *Ask the class to examine the data in the table, which describes how the height of a ball might change as it travels through the air.*

- *How long does the ball stay in the air?* (4 seconds)

- *How long does it take the ball to reach its maximum height?* (2 seconds)

- *What is the maximum height?* (64 ft)

- *Are there two different times when the ball is at the same height?* (Yes, many, for example: at 0.5 sec. and 3.5 sec. the ball is 28 feet in the air.)

Then let them work in pairs on the rest of the problem.

Explore 4.1

In Question A, you could ask students about the patterns of change.

Suggested Questions

- *Compare the patterns of change to those in the last investigation.*

   Students may need help in describing the change in time, which is increasing by increments of 0.25 seconds, particularly as they describe the patterns of change.

   In Question B, you could ask the class to factor the equation.

- *What information does the factored form give about the situation?*

Summarize 4.1

You can start by asking:

Suggested Questions

- *What are some characteristics of quadratic functions?* [In a quadratic function, the values increase or decrease until they reach a maximum or a minimum value and then decrease or increase (turn back around) in an opposite way.]

- *Does this height-versus-time function satisfy those characteristics?* (Yes.)

Using students' descriptions of what a graph of the data would look like for Question A, sketch a graph at the overhead or board. Talk about the fact that it is possible to sketch a parabola when the maximum or minimum point and *x*-intercepts are known.

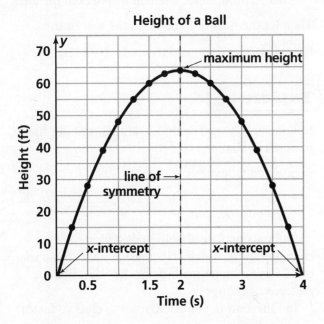

Height of a Ball

• *Approximately what is the maximum height and at what time does it occur?* (Students should be able to say that the maximum occurs around 2 seconds and the height is 64 feet.)

• *How can you be sure that this is the maximum?* (The time value occurs halfway between the *x*-intercepts. Since the *x*-intercepts are 0 and 4, the maximum time occurs at time = 2 seconds.)

As a review you can ask the class to write the equation in factored form and then predict the *x*-intercepts of the graph of the equation.

• *What is the factored form for the equation in Question B? What information does it give us?* [$h = -16t^2 + 64t = 16t(-t + 4)$. It is easy to read the *x*-intercepts from this form. They are $t = 0$ and $t = 4$. This means the ball is on the ground at 0 seconds and again at 4 seconds.]

• *What is the height of the ball after 3.5 seconds?* (28 ft)

• *At what time will the ball reach a height of 48 ft?* (1 second and 3 seconds)

A new equation with a constant term is introduced in the Getting Ready for Problem 4.2 in the next problem. It can be used a final summary to this problem and as a launch to Problem 4.2.

4.1 Tracking a Ball

Mathematical Goals

- Examine patterns of change associated with quadratic situations that are represented by equations in expanded form, such as the height of a ball over time that is thrown in the air
- Predict the maximum or minimum point from an equation, graph, or table

Launch

If you have a motion detector, you could collect data on the height of a ball to introduce this problem or you could start by throwing a ball straight up into the air and asking the class to describe how the height of the object changes as it travels. Ask someone to time how long it takes for the object to hit the floor: a stopwatch is helpful.

- *How long does the ball stay in the air?*
- *How long does it take the ball to reach its maximum height? What is the maximum height?*
- *Are there two different times when the ball is at the same height?*

Then let them work in pairs on the rest of the problem.

Materials

- Motion detector (optional)
- Ball (optional)
- Stopwatch (optional)
- Transparency 4.1

Explore

In Question A, you could ask students about the patterns of change.

- *Compare the patterns of change to those in the last investigation.*

Students may need help in describing the change in time, which increases by increments of 0.25 seconds, while they describe the patterns of change.

- *In Question B, you could ask students to factor $-16t^2 + 64t$. What information does the factored form give about the situation?*

Summarize

- *What are some characteristics of quadratic functions?*
- *Does this height-versus-time function satisfy those characteristics?*

Using students' description of what a graph of the data would look like for Question A, sketch a graph at the overhead or board. Talk about the fact that it is possible to sketch a parabola when the maximum or minimum point and x-intercepts are known.

- *Approximately what is the maximum height and at what time does it occur? How can you be sure that this is the maximum?*
- *What is the factored form for the equation in Question B? What information does it give us?*
- *What is the height of the ball after 3.5 seconds? At what time will the ball reach a height of 48 ft?*

Materials

- Student notebooks

continued on next page

A new equation with a constant term is introduced in the Getting Ready for Problem 4.2 in the next problem. It can be used a final summary to this problem and as a launch to Problem 4.2.

ACE Assignment Guide for Problem 4.1

Differentiated Instruction
Solutions for All Learners

Core 1–4
Other *Connections* 31, 32; *Extensions* 51–53; unassigned choices from previous problems

Adapted For suggestions about adapting Exercise 4 and other ACE exercises, see the CMP *Special Needs Handbook*.

Answers to Problem 4.1

A. 1. The height of the ball increases from 0 feet (ground level) to a maximum height of 64 feet at time equal to 2 seconds and then decreases in a way which is symmetric to the increase until the ball hits the ground at 0 feet at the end of 4 seconds. The differences between successive heights decrease from a difference of 15 after the first 0.25 second and then during each successive 0.25 second until it reaches its maximum height. For example, for each 0.25 second from 0 to 2 seconds the differences in the heights are 15, 13, 11, 9, 7, 5, 3, 1, 0. For each time interval the difference is 2 feet less than the previous difference.

2. The shape of the graph is an upside down U or a parabola with a maximum point. Its intercepts are $t = 0$ and $t = 4$. The maximum height is 64 feet which is reached after the ball has been in the air 2 seconds. The graph is symmetric around a line through $t = 2$. Be sure to use this data in class to make a sketch of the graph.

3. The data does represent a quadratic function. At this time the only evidence that students can give is its shape and possibly its pattern of change which is similar to those discussed in the last investigation.

B. 1.

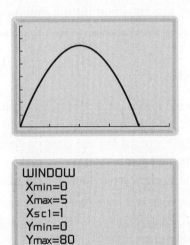

```
WINDOW
Xmin=0
Xmax=5
Xscl=1
Ymin=0
Ymax=80
Yscl=10
Xres=
```

2. The graph matches the description. (Note: Students may have adjusted their window setting to show parts of the graph beyond the given data.)

3. $t \approx 1.4$ seconds and $t \approx 2.6$ seconds; The ball is at a height of about 58 feet when $t \approx 1.4$ seconds and when $t \approx 2.6$ seconds. If $t = 1.4$, then
$h = -16(1.4)^2 + 64(1.4) = 58.24$ ft and if $t = 2.6$ seconds, then
$h = -16(2.6)^2 + 64(2.6) = 58.24$ ft.

4. $t = 1.6$ seconds; When $t = 1.6$ seconds,
$h = -16(1.6)^2 + 64(1.6) = 61.44$ ft.

5. The ball will reach the ground at 4 seconds because that is when the height is zero. This is assuming that when you throw the ball up in the air you started the throw at ground level. This can be seen from the table. Also when 4 is substituted into the equation $h = -16t^2 + 64t$ for t, we get $-16(4)^2 + 64(4) = 0$ ft for the height. The factored form of $h = -16t^2 + 64t$ is $h = -16t(t - 4)$. We can predict the x-intercepts from this form; $16t = 0$ or $t = 0$, and $t - 4 = 0$ or $t = 4$.

4.2 Measuring Jumps

Goals

- Examine patterns of change associated with quadratic situations that are represented by equations in expanded form, such as the height of a ball over time that is thrown in the air

- Predict the *y*-intercept from an equation, graph or table

- Interpret the information that the *y*-intercept represents

Mathematics Background

For background on modeling projectile motions, see page 10.

Launch 4.2

Use the Getting Ready to launch the problem. The projectile equation has a constant term, which is the *y*-intercept. Students should be able to interpret the information that the constant term represents and how its existence affects the maximum or minimum and *x*-intercepts. Be sure to put the graph of this problem on the overhead and discuss these points. The graph of

$h = -16t^2 + 64t + 6$ is similar to the graph of

$h = -16t^2 + 64t$ in Problem 4.1.The shapes are the same. The second graph could be shifted 6 units up to create the first graph. This shift will affect the *x*- and *y*-intercepts and the maximum point.

Suggested Questions

Start Problem 4.2 by asking:

- *How high do you think a professional basketball player can jump?*

- *How high do you think a frog or flea can jump?*

Write the equations for the frog, flea, and basketball player on the board. Discuss the similarities and differences in the context and equations with the class.

Have the class work in pairs.

Explore 4.2

Each pair could work on one equation and then the class can share data. Each student should have all of the data. You may want to have different groups put their tables and graphs on an overhead to use in the summary.

Summarize 4.2

Discuss the three equations, having students display their tables and graphs if they have copied them onto transparencies or large poster paper.

With the class you may want to display the graphs in all four quadrants to allow a more complete view of the parabolas. If you do this, discuss with students the facts that, in this context, negative time values have no meaning and negative height values cannot occur.

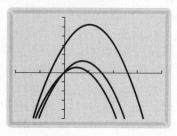

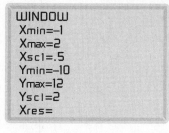

```
WINDOW
 Xmin=-1
 Xmax=2
 Xscl=.5
 Ymin=-10
 Ymax=12
 Yscl=2
 Xres=
```

• *Why are there negative values for height in the tables?* (A negative height means the jumper has reached the ground. If the jumper could continue below ground level, then the height would be negative.)

Talk about the meaning of the constant terms.

• *In the equation for the height of the basketball player, what does the constant term 6.5 mean?* (The equation records the player's height from the top of the head as time passes. This player is 6.5 feet tall, because at $t = 0$, $h = 6.5$.)

• *In the equation for the height of the frog, what does the constant term 0.2 mean?* (The equation records the frog's height from the top of the head as time passes. The frog's head is 2.4 inches from the ground at $t = 0$.)

• *Why is there no constant term for the equation of the flea?* (the flea's head is so close to ground level that it is assumed to be at 0 feet.)

• *What is the basketball player's vertical leap?* (the maximum height is 10.5 ft and the initial height is 6.5 feet, so the player's vertical leap is $10.5 - 6.5 = 4$ ft, or 48 in.)

• *Does this seem reasonable?*

To practice evaluating an expression, you can ask:

• *Use the equations to compute the height of each jumper after 0.15 seconds.* (Frog: 1.64 ft., Flea: 0.84 ft., Player: 8.54 ft.)

• *How do these answers compare to those obtained using a graph or calculator?* (The answers obtained with a calculator can usually be more accurate than those obtained by reading a graph.)

Be sure to discuss the profit situation in Question B.

• *How is this situation and equation similar to the jumping situations in Question A?* (Both are looking for a maximum. In one case it is height and the other profit. The profit equation is also similar to the height-time relationship for the frog. Neither have a y-intercept.)

Discuss the following:

• *What are other examples of situations where the maximum value is important?* (Some will remember the maximum area from Investigation 1. Pole vaulters are interested in maximum heights. Students may want to bring in some facts about their favorite basketball player.)

Transparency 4.2B displays four equations and their graphs that students have studied in the unit. The comparison will help students to more easily grasp the idea of maximum and minimum points.

• *Let's look back at some of the situations we have studied so far. Here are four equations, their graphs, and the related situation. What seems to determine whether the graph or quadratic relationship is a parabola with a minimum point or a parabola with a maximum point?* (They should quickly see that it is the coefficient of the x^2 term that determines whether a parabola will have a maximum or minimum point.)

If it is not obvious, take some conjectures, and have students test each of them by graphing on their calculators several equations that fit the conjecture.

The problem in the Check for Understanding has a minimum point.

Check for Understanding

After collecting data about cost factors, a jewelry company developed the equation $C = 0.01n^2 - 0.5n + 25$ to predict the cost to produce a necklace, C, for a given production level of n necklaces.

Suggested Questions

- *Make a table (in increments of 10) and graph for this equation for values of n from 0 to 80.*

- *How does the cost per necklace change as the number of necklaces produced increases from 0 to 80? Why is this pattern you observed reasonable?*

- *For how many necklaces is the cost per necklace the least? How is this number shown in the table and on the graph?*

- *Where does the cost graph cross the vertical axis? What does this point tell about the necklace-making situation?*

- *Use the equation to find the cost for producing 50 necklaces.*

Answers to Minimum Cost Problem

Note: By changing the table increment to 5 (Figure 1) instead of 10 one can see that for 25 necklaces the cost per necklace is $18.75.

The graph below shows $y = 0.01x^2 - 0.5x + 25$ for $0 \le x \le 100$ and $0 \le y \le 100$.

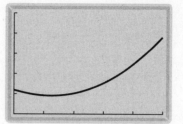

(As the number of necklaces increases from 0 to 80 the cost per necklace decreases to $18.75 when 25 necklaces are made and increases thereafter. The pattern is reasonable because a quantity price for materials without a substantial increase in labor cost should result in a lower cost per necklace. As the number produced increases beyond 25, the increased labor cost may outweigh any savings on materials so that the cost per necklace increases.)

[The cost per necklace is least for 25 necklaces. In the table that information is given by the lowest C (or y) value of $18.75 corresponding to an n (or x) value of 25. In the graph, information is given by the minimum point on the parabola that is the graph of $C = 0.01n^2 - 0.5n + 25$.]

(The cost graph crosses the vertical axis at 25, which indicates that there is a cost of $25 to operate the business even without producing any necklaces.)

($C = 6.25)

Figure 1

Production Cost of Jewelry

# of Necklaces	0	10	20	30	40	50	60	70	80
Cost per Item	25	21	19	19	21	25	31	39	49

4.2 Measuring Jumps

Mathematical Goals

- Examine patterns of change associated with quadratic situations that are represented by equations in expanded form, such as the height of a ball over time that is thrown in the air
- Predict the *y*-intercept from an equation, graph, or table
- Interpret the information that the *y*-intercept represents

Launch

Use the Getting Ready to launch the problem. Students should be able to interpret the information that the constant term represents and how its existence affects the maximum or minimum and *x*-intercepts. Put the graph of this problem on the overhead and discuss these points.

- *How high do you think a professional basketball player can jump? How high do you think a frog or flea can jump?*

Write the equations for the frog, flea, and basketball player on the board. Discuss the similarities and differences in the context and equations with the class. Have the class work in pairs.

Materials
- Transparencies 4.2A, 4.2B

Explore

Each pair could work on one equation and then the class can share data. Each student should have all of the data. You may want to have different groups put their tables and graphs on an overhead transparency to use in the summary.

Summarize

You may want to display the graphs in all 4 quadrants. Discuss how in this context, negative time values have no meaning and negative height values cannot occur.

- *Why are there negative values for height in the tables?*
- *In the equation for the height of the basketball player, what does the constant term 6.5 mean?*
- *In the equation for the height of the frog, what does the constant term 0.2 mean?*
- *Why is there no constant term for the equation of the flea?*
- *What is the basketball player's vertical leap? Does this seem reasonable?*
- *Use the equations to compute the height of each jumper after 0.15 seconds. How do these answers compare to those obtained using a graph or calculator?*

Be sure to discuss the profit situation in Question B.

- *How is this situation and equation similar to the jumping situations in Question A? Discuss the following:*

Materials
- Student notebooks

continued on next page

- *What are other examples of situations in which the maximum value is important?*

Summary Transparency 4.2B displays four equations and their graphs that students have studied in the unit.

- *Let's look back at some of the situations we have studied so far. Here are four equations, their graphs, and the related situation. What seems to determine whether the graph of a quadratic relationship is a parabola with a minimum point or parabola with a maximum point?*

ACE Assignment Guide for Problem 4.2

Differentiated Instruction
Solutions for All Learners

Core 5–8, 11–17
Other *Applications* 9,10; *Connections* 33–35; *Extensions* 54; and unassigned choices from previous problems

Adapted For suggestions about adapting ACE exercises, see the CMP *Special Needs Handbook*.
Connecting to Prior Units 33: *Covering and Surrounding, Stretching and Shrinking*; 34, 35: *Filling and Wrapping*

Answers to Problem 4.2

A. 1. Note the graphs below are shown with *x*-axes in increments of 0.1.

Flea

Time (seconds)	Height (ft)
0.0	0.0
0.1	0.64
0.2	0.96
0.3	0.96
0.4	0.64
0.5	0.0
0.6	−0.96
0.7	−2.24
0.8	−3.84
0.9	−5.76
1.0	−8

Frog

Time (seconds)	Height (ft)
0.0	0.2
0.1	1.24
0.2	1.96
0.3	2.36
0.4	2.44
0.5	2.2
0.6	1.64
0.7	0.76
0.8	−0.44
0.9	−1.96
1.0	−3.8

Basketball Player

Time (seconds)	Height (ft)
0.0	6.5
0.1	7.94
0.2	9.06
0.3	9.86
0.4	10.34
0.5	10.50
0.6	10.34
0.7	9.86
0.8	9.06
0.9	7.94
1.0	6.5

Graphs of:

$$h = -16t^2 + 12t + 0.2$$

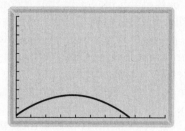

$$h = -16t^2 + 8t$$

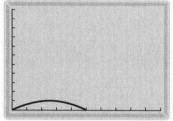

$$h = -16t^2 + 16t + 6.5$$

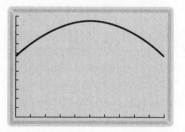

2. Maximum heights: Frog: 2.45 feet (after 0.375 seconds).;
   flea: 1.0 feet (after 0.25 seconds);
   Basketball player: 10.5 feet (after 0.5 seconds).

3. Time each jump lasts: frog: about 0.76 seconds; flea: 0.5 seconds; basketball player: about 1.3 seconds

4. The constant is the jumper's height. The frog is 0.2 feet tall (about 2.4 inches); the basketball player is 6.5 feet tall (about 6 feet 6 inches). In the graph, this information corresponds to the y-intercept.

5. For all the jumpers, the change in height for each 0.1-second increment decreases as the jumper approaches the maximum height and then increases as the jumper returns to the ground. This pattern is reflected in the tables in that the change in consecutive values for height decreases until the maximum height, and then increases until the height reaches its initial value. In the graphs, the parabola rises steeply, leveling out at the maximum point, and then decreases.

B. 1. **Profits From Jade Earrings**

Price	Profits
$0	$0
$5	$225
$10	$400
$15	$525
$20	$600
$25	$625
$30	$600
$35	$525
$40	$400
$45	$225
$50	$0

Profit From Jade Earrings

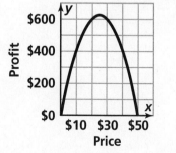

INVESTIGATION 4

2. The table shows that profit reaches its maximum of $625 when the price is $25. This can also be seen in the graph, as the maximum point occurs at (25, 625). The equation is similar to the equation for the height of the flea; if this is a quadratic equation, it should have a maximum value. This would mean that as price increases, profit would grow to a point and then, when the price gets too high for customers, the number of customers falls and the profit would start to fall.

3. The price of $25 will bring the greatest profit.

4. The equation is similar to those for predicting maximum height of frogs, fleas, and the basketball player in that it contains a term that involves the square of the variable preceded by a negative coefficient and a term that involves the variable multiplied by a constant amount. Like the equation for the height of a flea, this equation does not contain a constant term. Like the other equations in this unit, the graph of this equation is a parabola.

4.3 Putting It All Together

Goals

- Identify the first and second differences for a quadratic relationship represented in a table

- Summarize the understandings about quadratic functions

Students continue to use tables to find patterns characteristic of quadratic relations. By focusing on the first and second differences of the *y*-values in a table for a relation, they are able to determine whether or not it is a quadratic relation.

Launch 4.3

Put up the following table for a linear equation:

Table for a Linear Equation

x	y
0	1
1	4
2	7
3	10
4	13
5	16

Suggested Questions

- *Do the data in the table represent a quadratic relationship? Explain why.* (No, each successive *y*-value is increasing by 3. It is a linear relationship whose slope is 3 and *y*-intercept is 1. The equation for this relationship is $y = 3x + 1$.)

The constant difference, 3, is called the *first difference*. Let's look at the first differences for quadratic relationships.

Go over the example in the Getting Ready.

Put the equation $y = x^2$ and its table on the overhead.

- *Does this equation represent a quadratic relationship?* (yes)

- *Let's look at the first differences between successive values of* y.

Generate the table for values of *x* from −5 to 5. Then take the first difference.

- *Is the first difference constant?* (no)

- *What happens if you take the differences of the first differences?* (They are all equal to 2.)

This difference is called the second difference. For this quadratic function the second differences are constant; they are all 2.

In this problem we will investigate to see if other quadratic functions have a similar pattern.

Let the class work in groups of two to four.

Explore 4.3

You could ask different groups to put their work for one of the equations in Question A on poster paper for the summary. Ask a couple of groups to put the work for all of the equations for Question B on poster paper.

Going Further

Use your calculator to explore the effects of the *b* and *c* in the equation, $y = ax^2 + bx + c$. Start with the basic equation of $y = x^2$ and then add the parameters, *a*, *b*, and *c*, one at a time to determine their effects. (The coefficient, *a*, affects the width of the parabola and whether it is an upside down or an upright parabola. The constant, *c*, shifts the graph vertically up or down, while *b* shifts the graph horizontally to the left or right.)

Summarize 4.3

Suggested Questions As a class, discuss a few of the equations in Problem 4.3A.

- *In any of the tables, is there a constant rate of change for* y? (no)

- *What does this tell you about these equations?* (They are not linear.)

Each equation takes a second step to get the constant differences, and so none of the equations is linear.

- *If you were to graph these equations, what would the graphs look like? How does the equation or table help you predict the graph?* (Each one is a parabola. We expect a parabola if there is an x^2 term or if the second differences are constant.)

- *Which parabolas would open upward? Which would open downward?* ($y = 3x - x^2$ is the only one that opens downward. It has a maximum point. The others all have a minimum point. We expect a maximum if the coefficient of x^2 is negative, or a minimum if the coefficient of x^2 is positive.)

Be sure to discuss 4.3 B. See the answers for guidance. Then discuss another quadratic equation to check for understanding.

Check for Understanding

Recognizing patterns of change from tables: Put a few tables on the overhead or board and ask what relationship each represents.

- *What relationship does each set of data represent? Explain why.*
  [Linear, $y = 3 - 2x$; quadratic, $y = 1 - x^2$; exponential, $y = 2(3^x)$; quadratic, $y = x^2 - 1$]

- *Describe important features of the relationship, such as intercepts, maximum or minimum points, and symmetry.*

Tables of Various Relationships

Table 1		Table 3	
x	y	x	y
−1	5	0	2
0	3	1	6
1	1	2	18
2	−1	3	54
3	−3	4	162

Table 2		Table 4	
x	y	x	y
−1	0	−1	0
0	1	0	−1
1	0	1	0
2	−3	2	3
3	−8	3	8

Recognizing patterns of change from graphs: Each of the graphs represents a different relationship.

- *Analyze each graph below and indicate how the graph reflects the patterns of change for that particular relationship.*

- *For linear and exponential relationships, explain how the ratio of vertical change to horizontal change between two points on the graph is related to the pattern of change for that relationship.*

- *Does a similar pattern hold for quadratic relationships? Explain.*

These graphs and tables can be found on Transparencies 1.2C and 1.2D.

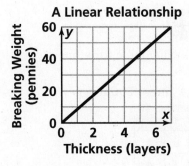

A Linear Relationship

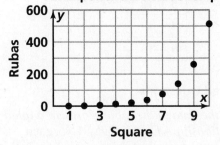

An Exponential Relationship

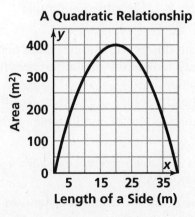

A Quadratic Relationship

Table For a Linear Relationship

Thickness (layers)	Breaking Weight (pennies)
0	0
1	8.4
2	16.8
3	25.2
4	33.6
5	42.0
6	50.4
7	58.8

Table For an Exponential Relationship

Square	Rubas
1	1
2	2
3	4
4	8
5	16
6	32
7	64
8	128
9	256
10	512

Table For a Quadratic Relationship

Length of a side (m)	Area (m²)
0	0
5	175
10	300
15	375
20	400
25	375
30	300
35	175
40	0

Going Further

You could have students examine the first, second, third (and so forth) differences for the power functions: $y = x$, $y = x^2$, $y = x^3$, and $y = x^4$, look for patterns and then predict what would happen for $y = x^5 \dots y = x^n$.

4.3 Putting It All Together

Mathematical Goals

- Identify the first and second differences for a quadratic relationship represented in a table
- Summarize the understandings about quadratic functions

Launch

Put up a table for a linear equation with a rate of change of 3:

- *Does the data in the table represent a quadratic relationship? Explain.*

The constant difference, 3, is called the *first difference*. Let's look at the first differences for quadratic relationships.

Use Transparency 4.3 for the Getting Ready.

Let the class work in groups of two to four.

Materials
- Transparency 4.3
- Poster paper (optional)
- Labsheets 4.3A and B (one per student)

Explore

Ask different groups to put their work for one of the equations in Question A on poster paper for the summary. Ask a couple of groups to put the work for all three of the equations for Question B on poster paper.

Summarize

As a class, discuss a few of the equations in Problem 4.3A.

- *In any of the tables, is there a constant rate of change?*
- *What does this tell you about these equations?*
- *If you were to graph these equations, what would the graphs look like? How does the equation or table help you predict the graph? Which parabolas would open upward? Downward?*

To check for understanding you might put a few tables on the overhead or board and ask what relationship each represents (for example table for $y = 3 - 2x$, , $y = 1 - x^2$, $y = 2(3^x)$ and $y = x^2 - 1$).

- *What kind of relationship does each set of data represent? Explain why. Describe important features of the relationship, such as intercepts, maximum or minimum points, and symmetry.*

Each of the graphs represents a different relationship.

- *Analyze each graph and indicate how the graph reflects the patterns of change for that particular relationship.*
- *For linear and exponential relationships, explain how the ratio of vertical change to horizontal change between two points on the graph is related to the pattern of change for that relationship. Does a similar pattern hold for quadratic relationships? Explain.*

Materials
- Student notebooks

Core 18–22, 25, 26

Other *Applications* 23, 24; *Connections* 36–40; *Extensions* 55; unassigned choices from previous problems

Adapted For suggestions about adapting ACE exercises, see the CMP *Special Needs Handbook*.

Answers to Problem 4.3

A. 1. a.

$y = 2x(x + 3)$

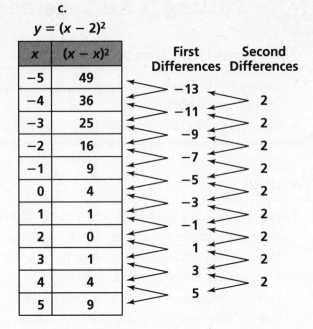

x	2x(x + 3)	First Differences	Second Differences
−5	20		
		−12	
−4	8		4
		−8	
−3	0		4
		−4	
−2	−4		4
		0	
−1	−4		4
		4	
0	0		4
		8	
1	8		4
		12	
2	20		4
		16	
3	36		4
		20	
4	56		4
		24	
5	80		

b.

$y = 3x - x^2$

x	3x − x²	First Differences	Second Differences
−5	−40		
		12	
−4	−28		−2
		10	
−3	−18		−2
		8	
−2	−10		−2
		6	
−1	−4		−2
		4	
0	0		−2
		2	
1	2		−2
		0	
2	2		−2
		−2	
3	0		−2
		−4	
4	−4		−2
		−6	
5	−10		

c.

$y = (x - 2)^2$

x	(x − x)²	First Differences	Second Differences
−5	49		
		−13	
−4	36		2
		−11	
−3	25		2
		−9	
−2	16		2
		−7	
−1	9		2
		−5	
0	4		2
		−3	
1	1		2
		−1	
2	0		2
		1	
3	1		2
		3	
4	4		2
		5	
5	9		

d.

$y = x^2 + 5x + 6$

x	x² + 5x + 6	First Differences	Second Differences
−5	6		
		−4	
−4	2		2
		−2	
−3	0		2
		0	
−2	0		2
		2	
−1	2		2
		4	
0	6		2
		6	
1	12		2
		8	
2	20		2
		10	
3	30		2
		12	
4	42		2
		14	
5	56		

2. For $y = 2x(x + 3)$, $y = (x - 2)^2$, and $y = x^2 + 5x + 6$, the y-value first decreases and then increases. For the equation $y = 3x - x^2$ the y-value first increases and then decreases. In all four equations, the first differences are not constant: for $y = 2x(x + 3)$, they increase by 4; for $y = (x - 2)^2$ and $y = x^2 + 5x + 6$, they increase by 2; and for $y = 3x - x^2$ they decrease by 2.

3. In all four equations, the second differences are constant.

B. 1. a. $y = x + 2$

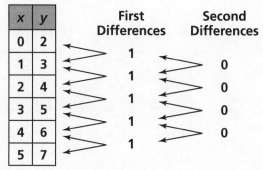

b. $y = 2x$

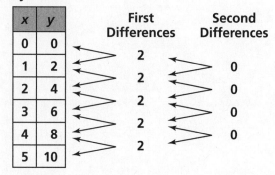

c. $y = 2^x$

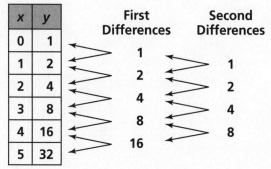

d. $y = x^2$

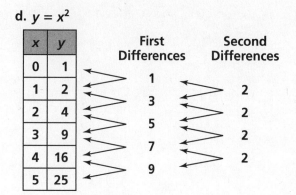

2. In all the tables, for $x > 0$, the y-value increases as the x value increases. For $y = x + 2$ and $y = 2x$, the change in the y-value is constant, which means that the y-value increases at a constant rate. For $y = 2^x$ and $y = x^2$, the y-value increases at an increasing rate. The second differences for $y = x^2$ are constant, while the second differences for $y = 2^x$ increase exponentially.

3. The equations $y = x + 2$ and $y = 2x$ fit the general form of linear equations, $y = mx + b$. In the table, the constant first differences tell that the equation is linear. The third equation, $y = 2^x$, fits the form of an exponential equation, $y = b^x$. Since the variable is in the exponent, the base 2 tells the factor by which the y-value grows. In the table, the growth factor of 2 shows up in the ratio of consecutive y-values: each difference is twice the previous difference. In $y = x^2$, the exponent is 2 and the base is the variable, so the y-values are the square numbers. In the table we note that first differences are not constant, but second differences are all 2.

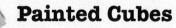

Painted Cubes

Goals

- Explore the "Painted Cube" situation, which has linear, quadratic, and cubic functions

- Compare linear, quadratic, and exponential functions

When a painted cube with edge length n is separated into n^3 small cubes, how many of these cubes will have paint on three faces? Two faces? One face? No face? To answer this question, students can consider cubes with smaller dimensions and then look for patterns in the data to make generalizations.

Launch 4.4

You can use a Rubik's™ Cube to launch the problem.

Note: Having a Rubik's Cube, a base ten block, or some other large cube to show students while you discuss it would be helpful. Also having small unit cubes or sugar cubes around so students can build some of the smaller cubes of length 2, 3, or 4 will be very helpful.

Suggested Questions Hold up a large cube:

- *How many faces, edges and corners does a cube have?* (A cube has six faces, 12 edges and 8 corners.)

- *Do the number of faces, edges and corners change from cube to cube?* (No.)

- *Suppose we paint a cube with edge length of 10 cm and then separate it into 1,000 small centimeter cubes. How many of the smaller cubes will have paint on three faces? Two faces? One face? No faces?* (Let students make some conjectures. Some might notice that the cube on a corner will have three faces painted.)

In this problem you will explore these questions for cubes of edge length 1 to 6 cm and then students will generalize for edge lengths of 10 cm or n cm. Note: you could leave the problem more open by posing the problem with a cube of edge length 10 cm and then have them generalize it to one with edge length of n cm.

Let the class work in groups of three to four.

Explore 4.4

If students are having difficulty getting started suggest that they study the sketches and build cubes like these to find the answers to these painted cube questions. Having a $10 \times 10 \times 10$ base 10 block and a large supply of 1 cm cubes for each group to examine while they work might be helpful.

Have one or more groups put their data table on a transparency to use in the summary.

Suggested Questions

- *Where are the unpainted cubes located?* (They are on the inside of the large cube; they are not visible from the outside.)

- *What shape does this set of unpainted cubes have?* (cube)

- *What are the dimensions of this cube?* (Its dimensions are two less the original cube.)

- *Where are the cubes that have only one face painted?* (They are on the faces of the cube but not along the edges.)

- *Within one face of the large cube, what shape is formed by the set of cubes with only one face painted?* (They form a square.)

- *How many faces are there?* (6)

- *Where are the cubes that have two faces painted?* (They form the edges of the cube but not the corners.)

- *How many edges are there?* (12)

- *Where are the cubes that have three faces painted?* (They form the corners of the cube.)

- *How many corners are there?* (8)

INVESTIGATION 4

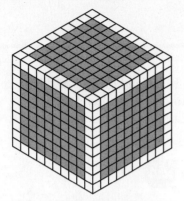

Cubes painted on one face

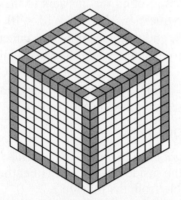

Cubes painted on two faces

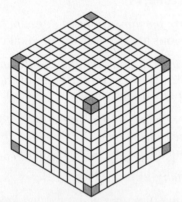

Cubes painted on three faces

If students are having trouble seeing patterns of change for Question C in the tables, ask them to look at the patterns of change.

- *What pattern in the differences would suggest a linear relationship?*

- *What pattern in the differences would suggest a quadratic relationship?*

Summarize **4.4**

During the discussion give students an opportunity to verbalize the patterns of change they have found in their tables. This will help them write symbolic statements for Question C.

Put up a transparency of a table of data that the students collected to refer to during the summary. Ask students to study the data they collected. Possible student responses are provided.

Suggested Questions

- *What kind of relationship—linear, quadratic, exponential, or other—do you observe in the plotted graph or table of data for the number of cubes with paint on 3 faces?* (This one seems to be linear since it is always 8.)

- *What kind of relationship—linear, quadratic, exponential, or other—do you observe in the plotted graph or table of data for the number of cubes with paint on 2 faces?* (This one seems to be linear since they seem to be in a straight line. Also, the table seems to be increasing by 12 each time.)

- *What kind of relationship—linear, quadratic, exponential, or other—do you observe in the plotted graph or table of data for the number of cubes with paint on one face?* (The relationship seems like it might be quadratic because the second difference is constant.)

- *What kind of relationship—linear, quadratic, exponential, or other—do you observe in the plotted graph or table of data for the number of cubes with paint on 0 faces?* [The pattern of change indicates this is *not* linear, nor quadratic, nor exponential. In fact the relationship is cubic, $P = (n - 2)^3$, though students will not necessarily see this without some discussion.]

- *Let's look closer at the pattern of change in the data for zero faces.*

- *When we look at the differences between y-values in tables where x changes by 1 each time, what tells us that a relationship is linear?* (First differences are constant.)

- *What tells that a relationship is quadratic?* (The second differences are constant.)

- *If we continued to take differences in each of these cases, what would happen?*

If you asked some groups to make tables of differences, have these students put up their tables of differences or demonstrate finding second differences. (Figures 2 and 3)

- Explain that once constant differences of 0 are reached it is pointless to go further. (Figure 4)

In this situation, the third differences are constant.

Figure 2

Edge Length of Large Cube	Cubes Painted on 2 Faces
2	0
3	12
4	24
5	36
6	48

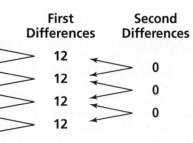

Figure 3

Edge Length of Large Cube	Cubes Painted on 1 Face
2	0
3	6
4	24
5	54
6	96

Figure 4

Edge Length of Large Cube	Cubes Painted on 0 Faces
2	0
3	1
4	8
5	27
6	64

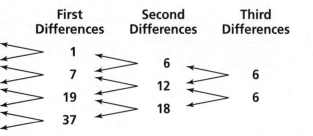

- *Let's use this information to work backward and find the number of cubes painted on 0 faces for an edge length of 7 centimeters. (Figure 5)*

- *What kind of equation do you think describes this relationship? (Students may not guess "cubic" yet.)*

To help students write the equations, go back to some of the questions from the *Explore*. For example, to write an expression for the number of cubes with no faces painted:

Suggested Questions

- *Where are the unpainted cubes located?* (They are on the inside of the large cube; they are not visible from the outside.)

- *What shape does this set of unpainted cubes have?* (cube)

- *What are the dimensions of this cube?* (Its dimensions are two less than the original cube.)

- *So how can we write this in symbols?* [$(n - 2)(n - 2)(n - 2)$ or $(n - 2)^3$]

- *We call $(n - 2)^3$ a cubic expression. What would you conjecture about the first, second, or third differences for a cubic relationship? (First and second differences are not constant. Third differences are constant.)*

Repeat these questions from the Explore for the pattern of cubes on the faces [$6(n - 2)^2$], on the edges [$12(n - 2)$], and on the corners (8).

Use your calculator to make sketches of the graphs of these relationships.

- *Describe the shapes of the graphs.*

- *How many different kinds of relationships did we explore in this problem? How can we recognize each relationship from its table, graph and equation? (For cubics they may only be able to say something about the equation containing a variable whose highest exponent is 3. They may also say something about the third difference.)*

You can end the summary by going back to the cube (10 × 10 × 10) and answering the original questions.

Figure 5

Edge Length of Large Cube	Cubes Painted on 0 Faces
2	0
3	1
4	8
5	27
6	64
7	125

First Differences: 1, 7, 19, 37, 61

Second Differences: 6, 12, 18, 24

Third Differences: 6, 6, 6

4.4 Painted Cubes

Mathematical Goals

- Explore the "Painted Cube" situation, which has linear, quadratic, and cubic functions
- Compare linear, quadratic, and exponential functions

Launch

Having a Rubik's Cube, a base ten block, or some other large cube to show students would be helpful. Hold up a large cube:

- *How many faces, edges, and corners does a cube have?*
- *Do the number of faces, edges, and corners change from cube to cube?*
- *Suppose we paint a cube with edge length of 10 cm and then separate it into 1,000 small centimeter cubes. How many of the smaller cubes will have paint on three faces? Two faces? One face? No faces?*

In this problem you will explore these questions for cubes of edge length 1 to 6 cm and then generalize for edge lengths of 10 cm or *n* cm. Let the class work in groups of three to four.

Materials

- Base ten thousands blocks (optional; 1 per group)
- Rubik's cube or other large cube (optional)

Explore

Suggest students study the sketches and build cubes like these to find the answers to these painted cube questions. To get started ask:

- *Where are the unpainted cubes located? What shape does this set of unpainted cubes have? What are the dimensions of this cube? Where are the cubes that have only one face painted?*
- *Within one face of the large cube, what shape is formed by the set of cubes with only one face painted?*
- *Where are the cubes that have two faces painted? How many edges are there? Where are the cubes that have three faces painted? How many corners are there?*

If students are having trouble seeing patterns of change for Question C in the tables, ask them to look at the patterns of change.

- *What pattern in the differences would suggest a linear relationship? A quadratic relationship?*

Materials

- Centimeter or other unit cubes (in four colors or with colored dot stickers, or sugar cubes and colored markers)
- Transparency 4.4

Summarize

Give students an opportunity to verbalize the patterns of change they have found in their tables.

- *What kind of relationship—linear, quadratic, exponential, or other—do you observe in the plotted graph or table of data for the number of cubes with paint on 3 faces (on 2 faces, on 1 face, on 0 faces)?*

Materials

- Student notebooks

continued on next page

● *When we look at the differences between y-values in tables where x changes by 1 each time, what tells us that a relationship is linear? Quadratic? If we continued to take differences in each of these cases, what would happen?*

If you asked some groups to make tables of differences, have these students put up their tables of differences or demonstrate finding second differences. Explain that once constant differences of 0 are reached it is pointless to go further.

● *Notice that when third differences are constant, the expanded form of the equation contains the variable raised to the third power. Or, it is the product of three terms that contain the variable x, like x · x · x or x³, or (x − 2)(x − 2) (x − 2). We call such a relationship a* cubic *relationship.*

To help students write the equations, go back to some of the questions from the *Explore*.

ACE Assignment Guide for Problem 4.4

Differentiated Instruction
Solutions for All Learners

Core 27–30
Other *Connections* 41–50; *Extensions* 56, 57; unassigned choices from previous problems

Adapted For suggestions about adapting Exercise 4 and otherACE exercises, see the CMP *Special Needs Handbook*.
Connecting to Prior Units 41, 43–45: *Covering and Surrounding*

Answers to Problem 4.4

A. 1. and **2.** (Figure 6)

B. 1. The number of centimeter cubes in a large cube is the edge length of the large cube

used as a factor 3 times, $x \cdot x \cdot x$ or x^3. The relationship is not linear, quadratic, or exponential.

2. The number of cubes painted on three faces is 8 regardless of the edge length of the large cube. The number of cubes painted on two faces is the edge length of the large cube minus 2 and then multiplied by 12. The number of cubes painted on one face is the edge length of the large cube minus 2, squared, and then multiplied by 6. The number of cubes painted on zero faces is the edge length of the large cube minus 2 then raised to the third power.

Figure 6

Painted Faces of a Centimeter Cube

Edge Length of Large Cube	Number of cm Cubes	Number of cm Cubes Painted on			
		3 Faces	2 Faces	1 Face	0 Faces
2	8	8	0	0	0
3	27	8	12	6	1
4	64	8	24	24	8
5	125	8	36	54	27
6	216	8	48	96	64

3. Three faces: the relationship is linear
Two faces: the relationship is linear
One face: the relationship is quadratic
Zero faces: Not linear, quadratic, nor exponential

C. 1. For the equations below; let n be the number of cubes and ℓ represent edge length of the large cube in cm.
For the relationship between edge length of the large cube and total number of cubes, $n = \ell^3$.
For three faces painted: $n = 8$
For two faces painted: $n = 12(\ell - 2)$ or $n = 12\ell - 24$
For one face painted: $n = 6(\ell - 2)^2$ or $n = 6\ell^2 - 24\ell + 24$
For zero faces painted: $n = (\ell - 2)^3$

2.

Edge Length vs. Total Number of Cubes

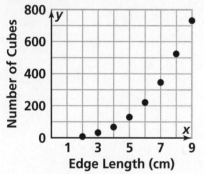

Edge Length vs. Cubes Painted on 3 Faces

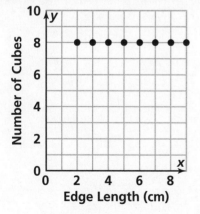

Edge Length vs. Cubes Painted on 2 Faces

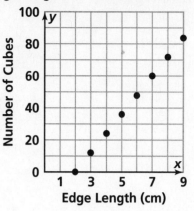

Edge Length vs. Cubes Painted on 1 Face

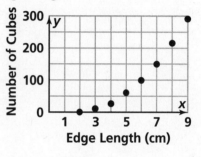

Edge Length vs. Unpainted Cubes

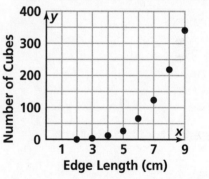

We can predict that (edge, 3 faces) and (edge, 2 faces) will be linear because the table indicates first differences that are constant. We can predict (edge, 1 face) will be quadratic because the second differences are constant.

INVESTIGATION 4

Investigation 4

ACE Assignment Choices

Differentiated Instruction
Solutions for All Learners

Problem 4.1
Core 1–4
Other *Connections* 31, 32; *Extensions* 51–53; unassigned choices from previous problems

Problem 4.2
Core 5–8, 11–17
Other *Applications* 9, 10; *Connections* 33–35; *Extensions* 54; unassigned choices from previous problems

Problem 4.3
Core 18–22, 25, 26
Other *Applications* 23, 24; *Connections* 36–40; *Extensions* 55; unassigned choices from previous problems

Problem 4.4
Core 27–30
Other *Connections* 41–50; *Extensions* 56, 57; unassigned choices from previous problems

Adapted For suggestions about adapting ACE exercises, see the CMP *Special Needs Handbook*.
Connecting to Prior Units 33: *Covering and Surrounding, Stretching and Shrinking*; 34, 35: *Filling and Wrapping*; 33: *Covering and Surrounding*; 34, 35: *Filling and Wrapping*; 41, 43–45: *Covering and Surrounding*

Applications

1. **a.** At 5 seconds, the flare will have traveled to a maximum height of 400 ft.

   b. The flare will hit the water when the height is 0 ft, which will occur at 10 s.

   c. In a graph, the maximum point represents the maximum height of the flare, and the right-hand *x*-intercept represents the point at which the flare hits the water. In a table, the entry for when the height is its greatest represents the maximum height reached by

the flare, and the entry for when the height is once again 0 represents the point at which the flare hits the water.

2. **a.** The rocket will travel to a height of 148 feet. It reaches this maximum height after 2 seconds.

   b. The rocket was launched at a height of 84 feet above ground level.

   c. It will take 4 seconds for the rocket to return to the height from which it was launched.

3. **a.** The ball is released at about 6.5 ft (the *y*-intercept).

   b. The ball reaches its maximum height, about 17.5 ft, at about 0.8 seconds.

   c. The ball would reach the basket just after 1.5 seconds.

4. **a. Height of a Diver After *t* Seconds**

Time (*t*)	Height (*h*)
0	10
0.1	10.441
0.2	10.784
0.3	11.029
0.4	11.176
0.5	11.225
0.6	11.176
0.7	11.029
0.8	10.784
0.9	10.441
1.0	10
1.1	9.461
1.2	8.824
1.3	8.089
1.4	7.256
1.5	6.325

b.

Diving From the Platform

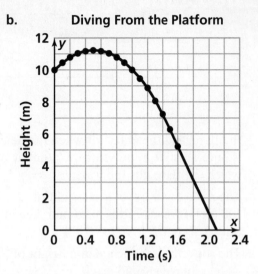

c. The diver hits the water's surface when the height is 0, which happens at between 2 and 2.1 seconds. In the graph, this is the *x*-intercept. In the table, it is the entry for when height is 0.

d. The diver will be 5 m above the water's surface between 1.6 and 1.7 seconds.

e. The diver is falling at the greatest rate just before hitting the water's surface. In the table, this is when the difference between successive height values is the greatest. In the graph, this is where the curve has the steepest downward slope.

5. a. The maximum height is about 15.06 ft, which occurs after about 0.56 seconds. (Note: Students can find this by making a table or a graph of the equations.)

b. Her feet hit the water when the height is 0, which occurs at about 1.53 seconds.

c. The board is 10 ft above the water's surface.

6. a. The maximum height is 44 ft, which is reached at 1.5 seconds. You could find this in a table of time versus height by locating the maximum height. You could find this in a graph by determining the height at the maximum point of the parabola.

b. The ball hits the ground just after 3.1 seconds. You could find this in a table of time versus height by locating the value for time when height is 0. You could find this in a graph by determining the time at the point at which the parabola crosses the *x*-axis.

c. The ball begins rising rapidly and then slows its ascent until it reaches the maximum height of 44 ft. It then starts to fall, slowly at first and gaining speed on the way down until it hits the ground.

d. The ball is 8 ft above ground when thrown.

7. $y = 9 - x^2$

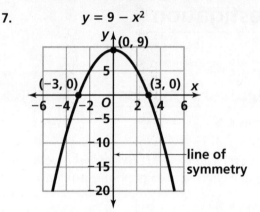

8. $y = 2x^2 - 4x$

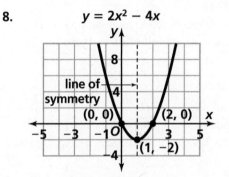

9. $y = 6x - x^2$

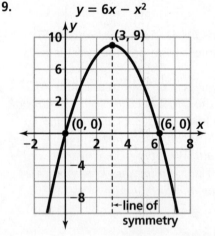

10. $y = x^2 + 6x + 8$

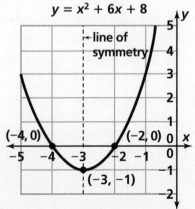

11. a. If the sign of the coefficient of the x^2 term is negative, the graph will have a maximum point. If it is positive, the graph will have a minimum point.

b. The x-intercepts are the values that make each factor in the factored form of the equation equal to 0. The y-intercept is the constant term in the expanded form of the equation.

c. If there are two x-intercepts, the distances from each x-intercept to the line of symmetry are the same. If there is only one intercept, it is on the line of symmetry. There is not any apparent relationship between the y-intercept and the line of symmetry.

12. We can predict that this is a parabola with x-intercepts and minimum at $(0, 0)$.

$$y = x^2$$

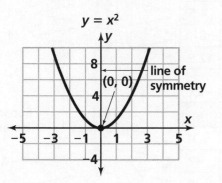

13. We can predict that this is a parabola with x-intercepts and maximum at $(0, 0)$.

$$y = -x^2$$

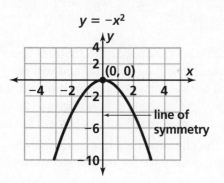

14. We can predict that this is a parabola with a minimum, and the y-intercept at $(0, 1)$.

$$y = x^2 + 1$$

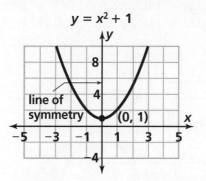

Note to the teacher: This graph does not have real roots; that is, it does not cross the x-axis. If $y = 0$, then $x^2 = -1$, so x is a complex number.

15. If we factor this we have $y = (x + 3)^2$. From this, we can predict this is a parabola with minimum and x-intercept at $(0, -3)$. We can predict the y-intercept from $y = x^2 + 6x + 9$; it is $(0, 9)$.

$$y = x^2 + 6x + 9$$

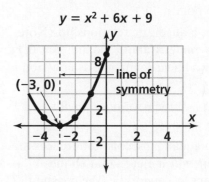

16. We can predict that this is a parabola with a minimum and y-intercept at $(0, -2)$.

$$y = x^2 - 2$$

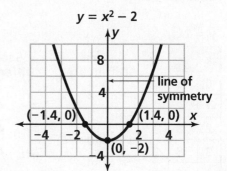

ACE ANSWERS 4

17. We can predict that this is a parabola with x-intercepts at 0 and 4, and a vertex at $(2, 4)$. From the expanded form $y = 4x - x^2$ we can predict there will be a maximum at $(2, 4)$.

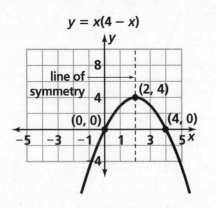

$$y = x(4 - x)$$

18. This is not a quadratic relationship. (Note: If the point $(5, -18)$ were $(5, -20)$, this would be a quadratic relationship.)

19. This is a quadratic relationship with a minimum point.

20. This is a quadratic relationship with a minimum point.

21. This is not a quadratic relationship. (Note: This has symmetry about the line $x = 0$, but this has two linear segments; its equation is $y = |x| + 1$)

22. This is a quadratic relationship with a minimum point.

23. a. In each equation, second differences are constant, which means that all the equations are quadratic. The constant second differences for each equation are equal to $2a$, where a is the coefficient of x^2. See tables below.

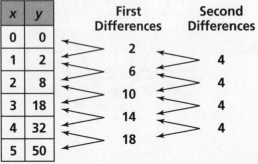

$y = 2x^2$

x	y	First Differences	Second Differences
0	0		
		2	
1	2		4
		6	
2	8		4
		10	
3	18		4
		14	
4	32		4
		18	
5	50		

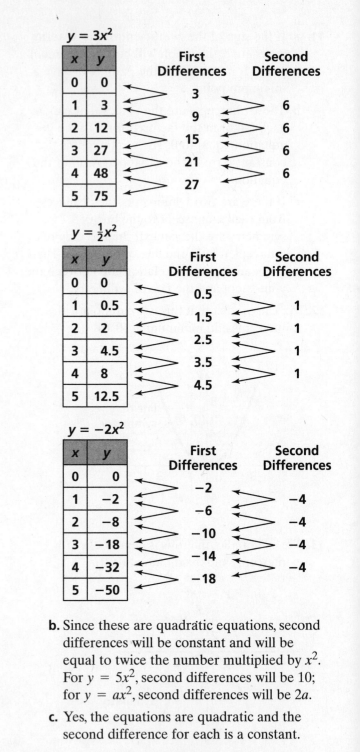

$y = 3x^2$

x	y	First Differences	Second Differences
0	0		
		3	
1	3		6
		9	
2	12		6
		15	
3	27		6
		21	
4	48		6
		27	
5	75		

$y = \frac{1}{2}x^2$

x	y	First Differences	Second Differences
0	0		
		0.5	
1	0.5		1
		1.5	
2	2		1
		2.5	
3	4.5		1
		3.5	
4	8		1
		4.5	
5	12.5		

$y = -2x^2$

x	y	First Differences	Second Differences
0	0		
		-2	
1	-2		-4
		-6	
2	-8		-4
		-10	
3	-18		-4
		-14	
4	-32		-4
		-18	
5	-50		

b. Since these are quadratic equations, second differences will be constant and will be equal to twice the number multiplied by x^2. For $y = 5x^2$, second differences will be 10; for $y = ax^2$, second differences will be $2a$.

c. Yes, the equations are quadratic and the second difference for each is a constant.

24. a.

Table of (x, y) Values

x	y
0	0
1	9
2	16
3	21
4	24
5	25

b.

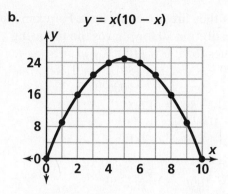
$y = x(10 - x)$

We know where the maximum point is, so we can find the line of symmetry and complete the graph by plotting a corresponding point on the right side for each point on the left side.

25. We know that the minimum point is where $x = 0.5$, so we can find the line of symmetry and complete the graph by plotting a corresponding point on the left side for each point on the right side. (Figure 7)

26. If you extend the table, you will get the following values: $(-1, 15), (-2, 24), (-3, 35), (-4, 48), (-5, 63)$. Note: The second difference is 2.

27. a. The 8 corners, or 8 cubes.

b. The cubes along the 12 edges that are not corner cubes, or $12 \times 10 = 120$ cubes.

c. The large cube has 6 faces, and each face contains $10 \times 10 = 100$ cubes with one face painted, a total of $6 \times 100 = 600$ cubes.

d. Removing the external cubes leaves $10 \times 10 \times 10 = 1,000$ unpainted cubes.

Figure 7

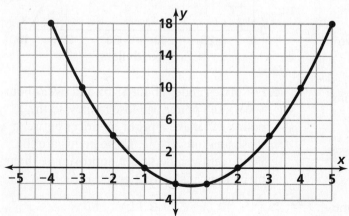

28. a. The unpainted cubes form a 10-by-10-by-10 cube on the inside of the large cube, which means the dimensions of the large cube must be 12-by-12-by-12, with 1,728 total cubes.

b. Each of the 6 faces on the cube contains $\frac{864}{6} = 144$ cubes with one face painted. There are 144 cubes arranged in a 12-by-12 square, which means the large cube must have the dimensions of 14-by-14-by-14, with 2,744 total cubes.

c. Each of the 12 edges contains $\frac{132}{12} = 11$ cubes painted on two faces, which means the large cube must have the dimensions of 13-by-13-by-13, with 2,197 total cubes.

d. Any cube would have 8 cubes painted on three faces, located at the 8 corners; we cannot tell the size of the large cube based on this information.

29. a. In the values for x, first differences are constant. In the values for x^2, second differences are constant. In the values for x^3, the third differences are constant.

x	x
1	1
2	2
3	3
4	4
5	5

x	x^2
1	1
2	4
3	9
4	16
5	25

x	x^3
1	1
2	8
3	27
4	64
5	125

b. In the table of value x, the pattern of change is similar to the pattern of the number of cubes with 3 or 2 faces painted because their first differences are constant. In the table of value x^2, the pattern of change is similar to the pattern of the number of cubes with 1 face painted because their second differences are constant. In the table of value x^3, the pattern of change is similar to the pattern of the number of cubes with 0 faces painted because their third differences are constant.

30. $y_1 = 2(x - 1)$ is similar to the relationship of the number of cubes painted on two faces because they are both linear. $y_2 = (x - 1)^3$ is similar to the relationship of the number of cubes painted on 0 faces or total cubes because they are both cubic. $y_3 = 4(x - 1)^2$ is similar to the relationship for the number of cubes painted on one face because they are both quadratic. (Note: Students can observe the similarity from the form of equations or the pattern of changes in tables.)

Connections

31. a. Table 1: Each y-value is twice the previous y-value. The missing entry is $(5, 800)$.

Table 2: Each y-value is 3 greater than the previous y-value. The missing entry is $(2, 18)$.

Table 3: Each increase in the y-value is 2 greater than the previous increase. The missing entry is $(7, 56)$.

Table 4: Each increase in the y-value is 2 less than the previous increase. The missing entry is $(3, 16)$.

b. Table 1; $y_6 = 25(2^x)$

Table 2; $y_5 = 3(x + 4)$

Table 3; $y_2 = x(x + 1)$

Table 4; $y_3 = 25 - x^2$

c. Tables 3 and 4. In Tables 3 and 4, the second differences are constant.

d. Table 4. $(0, 25)$.

e. The minimum is not visible in any of the tables, but if the tables are extended, there will be a minimum point.

32. a. The equations are equivalent. Possible explanation: When you graph the equations, the graphs are identical so the equations must be the same, or use the Distributive Property.

b. Possible answers: This equation is not equivalent to the other two because its graph is different. Or, substituting the same value for p into all three equations proves

that they are not equivalent. For example, substituting 20 for p gives the following values for I: $I = (100 - p)p = (100 - 20) 20 = (80) 20 = 1,600$. $I = 100p - p^2 = 100(20) - 20^2 = 2000 - 400 = 1,600$. $I = 100 - p^2 = 100 - 20^2 = 100 - 400 = -300$.

c. $M = (100 - p)p - 350$, or $M = 100p - p^2 - 350$.

d. A price of $50 gives the maximum profit, which is $2,150. Note: This can be seen in a graph or a table of the equation as shown below.

Profit From Art Fair

Price ($)	Profit ($)
10	550
20	1,250
30	1,750
40	2,050
50	2,150
60	2,050
70	1,750
80	1,250
90	550

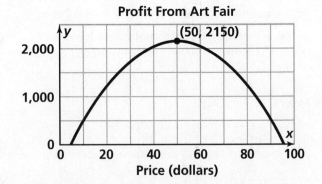

Profit From Art Fair

e. For prices under about $3.65 and over about $96.35, the potter will lose money, so the potter will make a profit on prices between these amounts. (Note: These points are the x-intercepts; students can approximate them by making a table or a graph.)

33. a. $A = x^2$; $P = 4x$

b. $A = (2x)^2 = 4x^2$, so the area would increase by a factor of 4. $P = 4(2x) = 8x$, so the perimeter would increase by a factor of 2. (Note: Students may solve this by testing several examples.)

c. $A = (3x)^2 = 9x^2$, so the area would increase by a factor of 9. Since $P = 4(3x) = 12x$, the perimeter would increase by a factor of 3.

d. Since $A = 36 \text{ m}^2$, $x = 6$ m, so $P = 4(6) = 24$ m.

e.

Side Length, Perimeter and Area of a Square

x	4x	x²
0	0	0
1	4	1
2	8	4
3	12	9
4	16	16
5	20	25
6	24	36
7	28	49
8	32	64
9	36	81
10	40	100
11	44	121
12	48	144

f.

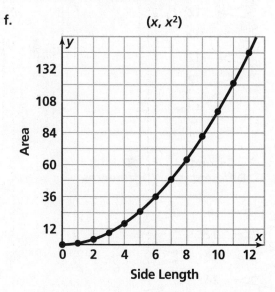

(x, x^2)

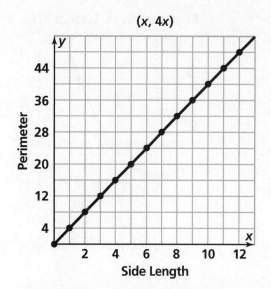

$(x, 4x)$

g. The relationship is quadratic between the side length (x) and the area (x^2). The relationship is linear between the side length (x) and the perimeter ($4x$).

34. a. $12 \times 12 = 144$ eggs in each layer.

b. $144 \times 12 = 1{,}728$ eggs in the container.

35. a. $V = x^3$

b. $V = (2x)^3 = 8x^3$; the volume would increase by a factor of 8.

c. $V = (3x)^3 = 27x^3$; the volume would increase by a factor of 27 and the surface area would increase by a factor of 9.

d.

Length, Surface Area and Volume of a Solid

Edge Length	Surface Area	Volume
0	0	0
1	6	1
2	24	8
3	54	27
4	96	64
5	150	125
6	216	216
7	294	343
8	384	512
9	486	729
10	600	1,000
11	726	1,331
12	864	1,728

e.

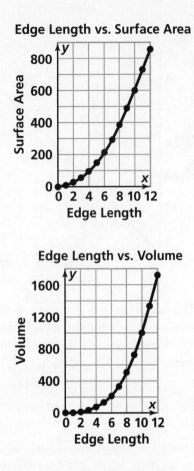

Edge Length vs. Surface Area

Edge Length vs. Volume

f. The relationship between edge length and surface area appears to be quadratic. The graph looks quadratic, and second differences are constant. (Figure 8)

The relationship between edge length and volume appears to be some new type of relationship because it is not a linear, quadratic, or exponential relation. (Figure 9)

36. a. $-3x(2x - 1) = -6x^2 + 3x$

b. $1.5x(6 - 2x) = 9x - 3x^2$

37. a. $(x + 1)(x + 1) = x^2 + 2x + 1$

b. $(x + 5)(x + 5) = x^2 + 10x + 25$

c. $(x - 5)(x - 5) = x^2 - 10x + 25$

The pattern is squaring a binomial, $(x + c)^2$ when the coefficient of x is 1. The square of a binomial is the square of x plus $2(c)(x)$ plus the square of c. Symbolically this is represented by: $(x + c)^2 = (x + c)(x + c) = x^2 + cx + cx + c^2$ or $x^2 + 2cx + c^2$. A similar pattern holds when the coefficient of x is not 1. $(ax + c)^2 = (ax + c)(ax + c) = (ax)^2 + acx + acx + c^2$ or $(ax)^2 + 2acx + c^2$.

Figure 8

Edge Length (cm)	Surface Area (cm²)	First Differences	Second Differences
0	0		
		6	
1	6		12
		18	
2	24		12
		30	
3	54		12
		42	
4	96		12
		54	
5	150		12
		66	
6	216		

Figure 9

Edge Length (cm)	Volume (cm³)	First Differences	Second Differences	Third Differences
0	0			
		1		
1	1		6	
		7		6
2	8		12	
		19		6
3	27		18	
		37		6
4	64		24	
		61		6
5	125		30	
		91		
6	216			

38. a. $(x + 1)(x - 1) = x^2 - 1$

  b. $(x + 5)(x - 5) = x^2 - 25$

  c. $(x + 1.5)(x - 1.5) = x^2 - 2.25$

  The pattern is multiplying the sum and difference of two numbers. The result is the difference of the squares of the two numbers. Symbolically, this is represented by:

  $(x + c)(x - c) =$
  $x^2 + cx - cx - c^2$ or $x^2 - c^2$. A similar pattern holds when the coefficient of x is not 1. $(ax + c)(ax - c) = (ax)^2 - c^2$.

39. a. $x^2 + 6x + 9 = (x + 3)^2$

  b. $x^2 - 6x + 9 = (x - 3)^2$

  c. $x^2 - 9 = (x + 3)(x - 3)$

  d. $x^2 - 16 = (x + 4)(x - 4)$

40. a. $2x^2 + 5x + 3 = (2x + 3)(x + 1)$

  b. $4x^2 - 9 = (2x + 3)(2x - 3)$

  c. $4x^2 + 12x + 9 = (2x + 3)(2x + 3)$

41. a. The areas are π square units and 4π square cm.

  b. The relationship is quadratic. The area increases by increasing amounts. Students might examine the differences in areas, or they might graph the radii and area to see if they get a quadratic, or they might use

symbols to justify that $y = 3.14x^2$ is a quadratic relationship. (Figure 10)

  c. The length of the smaller rectangle is the same as the circumference of the smaller circle or 2π. So the surface area of the smaller cylinder is $\pi + \pi + (2\pi)(2)$, or 6π square units. The surface area of the larger cylinder is $4\pi + 4\pi + 4\pi(2)$ or 16π square units.

  d. Yes; students might examine second differences and see that they are a constant 2π. Or they might identify the equation $y = 2\pi x(x + 2)$ as the equation of a parabola with x-intercepts at 0 and -2. (Figure 11)

42. B

43. a. (Figure 12)

  b. Yes; students might examine the second differences and see that they are a constant 8π or they might identify the relationship's equation of $y = 4\pi x^2$ as the equation of a parabola.

44. a. Each edge is 3 units.

  b. The surface area is 54 square units. The volume is 27 cubic units.

  c. Student drawings should show the flat pattern of a cube with edge 4 units, surface area 6(16) or 96 square units.

Figure 10

Relationship of a Radius to Area of a Circle

Radius	1	2	3	4	x
Area	π	4π	9π	16π	πx^2

Figure 11   **Surface Areas of Cylinders With Different Radius and Height**

Radius	1	2	3	4	x
Height	2	2	2	2	2
Surface Area	6π	16π	$[9 + 9 + (6)(2)]\pi = 30\pi$	$[16 + 16 + (8)(2)]\pi = 48\pi$	$\pi x^2 + \pi x^2 + (2\pi x)(2) = 2\pi x^2 + 4\pi x = 2\pi x(x + 2)$

Figure 12   **Surface Areas of Cylinders With Equal Radius and Height**

Radius	1	2	3	4	x
Height	1	2	3	4	x
Surface Area	$\pi + \pi + (2\pi)(1) = 4\pi$	$4\pi + 4\pi + (4\pi)(2) = 16\pi$	$9\pi + 9\pi + (6\pi)(3) = 36\pi$	$16\pi + 16\pi + (8\pi)(4) = 64\pi$	$\pi x^2 + \pi x^2 + (2\pi x)(x) = 4\pi x^2$

d. $V = x^3$. This is not quadratic (it is actually a cubic relationship). Students might make a table and examine how the volume grows, or they might graph $y = x^3$ and examine the shape, or they might refer to the symbols.

45. No; the surface area of Silvio's box is 1,536 sq. in, since $16^2 \times 6 = 1,536$. Ten sq. ft. of wrapping paper equals 1,440 sq. in since a square foot is 144 square inches and 10(144 in) = 1,440 sq. inches. There will not be enough paper.

46. H   **47.** C

48.

Building	1	2	3	4
Base	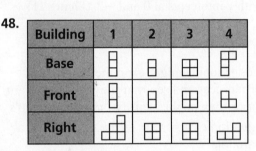			
Front				
Right				

49.

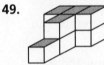

50.

Building 1   Building 2

Extensions

51.a. If only the 20 soccer team members go, the cost of the trip is $125 per student. The travel agent's profit is the difference between income and cost, or $P = 125n - 75n$, where n is the number of students:
$P = 125(20) - 75(20) = 2,500 - 1,500 = \$1,000$.

b. If 25 students go, the cost is $120 per student and the agent's profit is $P = 120n - 75n = 120(25) - 75(25) = 3,000 - 1,875 = \$1,125$.

c. If 60 students go, the cost is $85 per student and the agent's profit is $P = 85n - 75n = 85(60) - 75(60) = 5,100 - 4,500 = \$600$.

d. If 80 students go, the cost is $65 per student and the agent's profit is $P = 65n - 75n = 65(80) - 75(80) = 5,200 - 6,000 = -\$800$. For this many students, the travel agent would lose money.

52. (Figure 13)

a. price per student $= 125 - (n - 20)$, or $125 - n + 20$, or $145 - n$

b. income = price $\times n = [125 - (n - 20)]n$, or $125n - n(n - 20)$, or $125n - n^2 + 20n$, or $145n - n^2$

c. expenses $= 75n$

d. profit = income $-$ expenses $= [125 - (n - 20)]n - 75n$, or $125n - n(n - 20) - 75n$, or $-n^2 + 20n - 75n$, or $70n - n^2$.

Figure 13   **Pricing and Profit Scenarios for a Travel Agent**

Number of Students	Price per Student	Travel Agent's Income	Travel Agent's Expenses	Travel Agent's Profit
20	125	$20 \times 125 = 2,500$	$20 \times 75 = 1,500$	$2,500 - 1,500 = 1,000$
21	124	$21 \times 124 = 2,604$	$21 \times 75 = 1,575$	$2,604 - 1,575 = 1,029$
22	123	$22 \times 123 = 2,706$	$22 \times 75 = 1,650$	$2,706 - 1,650 = 1,056$
23	122	$23 \times 122 = 2,806$	$23 \times 75 = 1,725$	$2,806 - 1,725 = 1,081$

53. a. The agent's profit is greatest for 35 students.

b. If fewer than 70 students go on the trip, the agent will make a profit.

c. From 30 students to 40 students give the travel agent a profit of at least $1,200.

54. a. It takes 3 moves to solve the puzzle with 1 pair of coins. Starting with

the moves could be as follows:

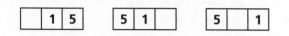

It takes 8 moves to solve the puzzle with 2 pairs of coins. Starting with

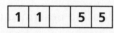

the moves could be as follows:

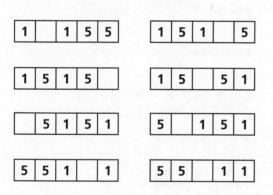

It takes 15 moves to solve the puzzle with 3 pairs of coins. Starting with

| 1 | 1 | 1 | | 5 | 5 | 5 |

The moves could be as follows:

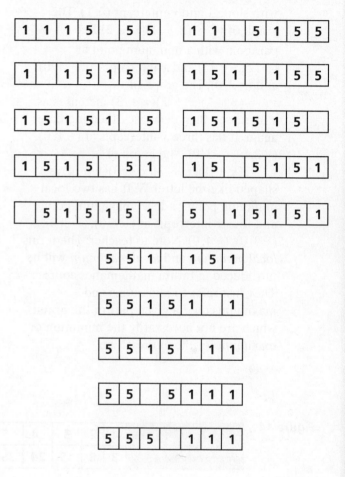

b. (Figure 15)

c. The numbers of moves calculated from the expression agree with the numbers found above. (Figure 14)

d. Second differences are a constant 2, so the relationship is quadratic. (Figure 15)

55. a. The graph of $y_1 = x + 1$ is a straight line with slope 1 and y-intercept $(0, 1)$. The graph of $y_2 = (x + 1)(x + 2)$ is a parabola with a minimum point at $(-1.5, -0.25)$ and x-intercepts at $(-1, 0)$ and $(-2, 0)$. The graph of $y_3 = (x + 1)(x + 2)(x + 3)$ increases as x increases, then decreases, then increases again. It has three x-intercepts at $(-1, 0)$, $(-2, 0), (-3, 0)$. The graph of $y_4 = (x + 1)(x + 2)(x + 3)(x + 4)$ is shaped like the letter W. It has two local minimum points, a local maximum point, and four x-intercepts at $(-1, 0), (-2, 0)$, $(-3, 0), (-4, 0)$. Note to teacher: The terms *local minimum* and *local maximum* will be introduced in future mathematics courses. They just refer to minimums and maximums over a given part of the graph, which are not necessarily the minimum or maximum for the entire graph.

b. The equation $y_1 = (x + 1)$ has constant first differences. The equation $y_2 = (x + 1)(x + 2)$ has constant second differences. The equation $y_3 = (x + 1)(x + 2)(x + 3)$ has constant third differences. The equation $y_4 = (x + 1)(x + 2)(x + 3)(x + 4)$ has constant fourth differences.

56. a. blue: 4
yellow: $4 \times 3 = 12$
orange: $3 \times 3 = 9$

b. blue: 4
yellow: $4 \times 8 = 32$
orange: $8 \times 8 = 64$

c. blue: 4
yellow: $4(n - 2)$
orange: $(n - 2) \times (n - 2)$ or $(n - 2)^2$

d. The relationship described by $(n - 2)^2$ is quadratic because it is formed by the product of two linear factors.

57. a. 0 cubes

b. 6 cubes

c. 16 cubes

d. 8 cubes

e. $8 + 16 + 6 = 30$ cubes, or $3 \times 2 \times 5 = 30$ cubes

Figure 14

# of Type of Coin	1	2	3	4	5	6	7	8	9	10
# of Moves	3	8	15	24	35	48	63	80	99	120

Figure 15

Number of Each Type of Coin	Number of Moves	First Differences	Second Differences
1	3		
		5	
2	8		2
		7	
3	15		2
		9	
4	24		2
		11	
5	35		2
		13	
6	48		2
		15	
7	63		2
		17	
8	80		2
		19	
9	99		2
		21	
10	120		

Possible Answers to Mathematical Reflections

1. Possible situations: (i) the nth triangular number. Question: What is the 20th triangular number? (ii) the height in a frog jump. Question: What is the highest height in a frog jump? (iii) the number of high fives. Question: How many high fives are there if everyone exchanges high fives with each other on a team with 10 members? (iv) rectangles with a fixed perimeter. Question: What is the greatest area for a rectangle with a fixed perimeter of 60 meters?

2. a. In tables of (x, y) values for quadratics the first differences are non-constant but the second differences are constant.

   b. The graphs of quadratics (if a view window including all four quadrants is used and if a big enough range of values for the x- and the y-values is used) are parabolas opening upward or downward depending on the sign of the coefficient of the x^2 term. The graph has a line of symmetry through the maximum or minimum point. The line of symmetry intersects the x-axis at the midpoint between the x-intercepts.

   c. The equations that match quadratic relations can be in expanded form or factored form. In the expanded form, $y = ax^2 + bx + c$, the highest exponent of the independent variable is 2. If a is positive, then there is a minimum point; if a is negative, then there is a maximum point. The y-intercept is c. In a factored form, $y = (x + b)(x + c)$, there are two factors, each of which has the independent variable raised to the first power. The x-intercepts are $x = -b$ and $x = -c$.

3. The patterns of change for *linear* functions are characterized by constant first differences. The patterns of change for *exponential* functions are characterized by consecutive differences either increasing without bound or approaching 0 but never achieving it. The patterns of change for *quadratic* functions are characterized by a constant second difference. Note to the teacher: These are only general trends and simply because consecutive

differences increase without bound does not imply that a function is exponential.

Answers to Looking Back and Looking Ahead

1. a. All graphs will be parabolas that are concave down with the y-intercept 0 and x-intercepts at 0 and $\frac{b}{16}$ and maximum point $\left(\frac{b}{32}, \frac{b^2}{64}\right)$. At this point in the students' learning about quadratic functions and equations we don't expect such complete abstract reasoning. Most students should know the general shape of the graphs and recognize in general that the maximum point will lie midway between the two x-intercepts.

   b. Table 1 was produced by the necessary quadratic, while Table 2 shows a constant rate of rise and fall in height, and thus cannot be quadratic. Students might notice that if one looks at the first and second differences of height values in Table 1, you get $5, 3, 1, -1, -3, -5$, and then $-2, -2, -2, -2, -2$. Constant second differences are another indicator of a quadratic relationship.

2. a. 16 feet. This answer can be found by tracing a table or graph of the height equation. Symbolic reasoning might be used to find that the ball comes back to its starting position when $t = 2$ and to infer that the maximum point occurs midway in that time interval.

   b. 2 seconds. Students might find this result by tracing a table or graph of the equation or by solving with symbolic reasoning.

   $$-16t^2 + 32t = 0$$
   $$-16t(t - 2) = 0$$
   $$t = 0 \text{ and } t = 2$$

   c. 0.5 seconds and 1.5 seconds. Again, students might answer this question by tracing a table or graph of the equation to find x-values for which $y = 12$. We do not really expect students to solve the equation $-16t^2 + 32t = 12$ by symbolic reasoning.

3. a. width $= 90 - x$ or width $= \frac{180 - 2x}{2}$

b. $A = x(90 - x)$

c. $x(90 - x) = 2{,}000$; so $x = 40$ and $w = 50$ or $x = 50$ and $w = 40$

Students will probably solve the equation by tracing a table or graph of the equation $y = x(90 - x)$ to find values of x that give an area of 2,000, not by formal reasoning with the symbols alone.

d. $x = w = 45$ gives a maximum area of 2,025 square feet. Students could use a calculator to find the x-value that corresponded to the largest y-value in the table. They could use the trace function to approximate the maximum point on the graph of the parabola or they could use the maximum function to find the maximum point on the parabola. Students might also reason that the figure with maximum area and fixed perimeter is a square, so each side would be $\frac{180}{4} = 45$ feet.

4. a. As x goes up by a constant value, the y-values either rise to a maximum and then decrease in a symmetric pattern or fall to a minimum and then increase in a symmetric pattern. The rate of change in y-values is not constant, but the second differences of y-values will be constant for a sequence of equally spaced x-values. In general, the rate of change in y-values is smallest near the maximum or minimum point and increases as x-values move away from that point.

b. Graphs of all quadratics are parabolas that are symmetric about the vertical line through their maximum or minimum point. The parabolas are concave up (open upward) if the coefficient of the x^2 term is positive and concave down if that coefficient is negative. The y-intercept of any quadratic graph is the constant term in the equation for that graph.

c. Any quadratic relation can be expressed with an equation in the form $y = ax^2 + bx + c$, though other equivalent forms are often useful. In particular, the factored form of $y = a(x - r)(x - s)$ can be used to find the x-intercepts $(r, 0)$ and $(s, 0)$ by inspection.

5. a. Differences include the following ideas: Equations of linear relations have exponents equal to one; the tables of linear relations show a constant rate of change in output values (y) as input values (x) change (either always increasing or always decreasing); and the graphs of linear relations are straight lines.

b. Equations of exponential relations are of the form $y = a(b^x)$; in tables of exponential relations $y = a(b^x)$ any increase of 1 in x corresponds to changes in y by the factor b (always increasing or always decreasing); and the graphs of exponential relations are curves that resemble half of a parabola. They do not have symmetry about a vertical line as parabolas do.

6. If a is positive the parabola will have a minimum point. If a is negative, the parabola will have a maximum point.

7. a. Find the value of x when $y = 0$ by tracing in a table.

b. Find the x-intercepts of the function graph.

C

constant term A number in an algebraic expression that is not multiplied by a variable. In the expanded form of a quadratic expression, $ax^2 + bx + c$, the constant term is the number c. The constant term in the expression $-16t^2 + 64t + 7$ is 7. The constant term in the expression $x^2 - 4$ is -4.

D

Distributive Property For any three numbers a, b, and c, $a(b + c) = ab + bc$.

E

expanded form The form of an expression composed of sums and differences of terms, rather than products of factors. The expressions $x^2 + 7x - 12$ and $x^2 + 2x$ are in expanded form.

F

factored form The form of an expression composed of products of factors, rather than sums or differences of terms. The expressions $x(x - 2)$ and $(x + 3)(x + 4)$ are in factored form.

function A relationship between two variables in which the value of one variable depends on the value of the other. The relationship between length and area for rectangles with a fixed perimeter is a function; the area of the rectangle depends on, or is a *function of*, the length. If the variable y is a function of the variable x, then there is exactly one y-value for every x-value.

L

like terms Terms with the same variable raised to the same power. In the expression $4x^2 + 3x - 2x^2 - 2x + 1$, $3x$ and $-2x$ are like terms, and $4x^2$ and $-2x^2$ are like terms.

line of symmetry A line that divides a graph or drawing into two halves that are mirror images of each other

linear term A part of an algebraic expression in expanded form in which the variable is raised to the first power. In the expression $4x^2 + 3x - 2x + 1$, $3x$ and $-2x$ are linear terms.

M

maximum value The greatest y-value a function assumes. If y is the height of a thrown object, then the maximum value of the height is the greatest height the object reaches. If you throw a ball into the air, its height increases until it reaches the maximum height, and then its height decreases as it falls back to the ground. If y is the area of a rectangle with a fixed perimeter, then the maximum value of the area, or simply the maximum area, is the greatest area possible for a rectangle with that perimeter. In this unit, the maximum area for a rectangle with a perimeter of 20 meters is 25 square meters.

minimum value The least y-value a function assumes. If y is the cost of an item, then the minimum value of the cost, or simply the minimum cost, is the least cost possible for the item.

P

parabola The graph of a quadratic function. A parabola has a line of symmetry that passes through the maximum point if the graph opens downward or through the minimum point if the graph opens upward.

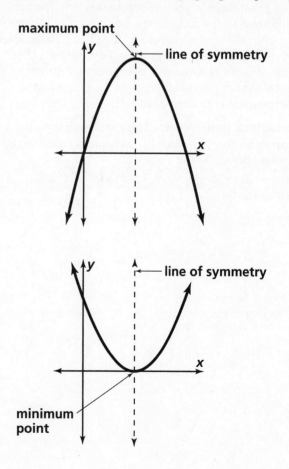

quadratic expression An expression that is equivalent to an expression of the form $ax^2 + bx + c$, where a, b, and c are numbers and $a \neq 0$. An expression in factored form is quadratic if it has exactly two linear factors, each with the variable raised to the first power. An expression in expanded form is quadratic if the highest power of the variable is 2. For example, $2x^2, 3x^2 - 2x$, and $4x^2 + 2x - 7$ are all quadratic expressions. The expression $x(x - 2)$ is also a quadratic expression because $x(x - 2) = x^2 - 2x$. In this unit, you used quadratic expressions to represent the areas of rectangles for a fixed perimeter, the number of high fives between members of a team, and the path of a projectile over time.

quadratic relationship A relationship between the independent and dependent variables such that, as the dependent values increase by a constant amount, the successive (first) differences between the dependent values change by a constant amount. For example, in $y = x^2$, as x increases by 1, the first differences for y increase by $3, 5, 7, 9, \ldots$ and then the second differences increase by $2, 2, 2, \ldots$. The graphs of quadratic relationships have the shape of a U or upside down U with a line of symmetry through a maximum or minimum point on the graph that is perpendicular to the x-axis.

quadratic term A part of an expression in expanded form in which the variable is raised to the second power. In the expression $4x^2 + 3x - 2x^2 - 2x + 1, 4x^2$ and $-2x^2$ are quadratic terms.

term An expression that consists of either a number or a number multiplied by a variable raised to a power. In the expression $3x^2 - 2x + 10, 3x^2, -2x$, and 10 are terms.

triangular number A number that gives the total number of dots in a triangular pattern. The first four triangular numbers are 1, 3, 6, and 10, the numbers of dots in Figures 1 through 4 below.

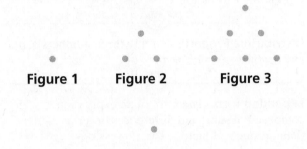

Figure 1   **Figure 2**   **Figure 3**

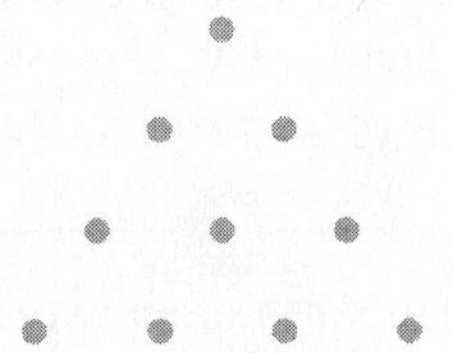

Figure 4

Labsheet 2.5 Graphs A–H

Graph	Graph A	Graph B	Graph C	Graph D	Graph E	Graph F	Graph G	Graph H
Equation-Factored Form								
Equation-Expanded Form								
x-intercepts								
y-intercepts								
Minimum or Maximum Point								
Opens Up or Down								
Equation of the Line of Symmetry								

Labsheet 3.3

....

Handshakes

Case 1

Equation _____

Table

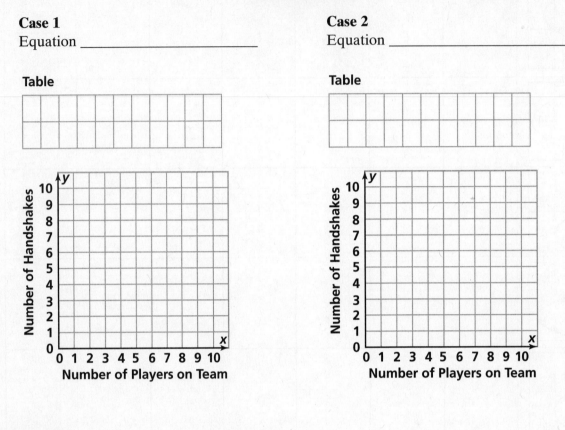

Case 2

Equation _____

Table

Case 3

Equation _____

Table

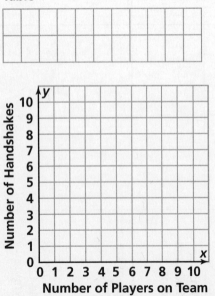

Labsheet 4.3A

First and Second Differences

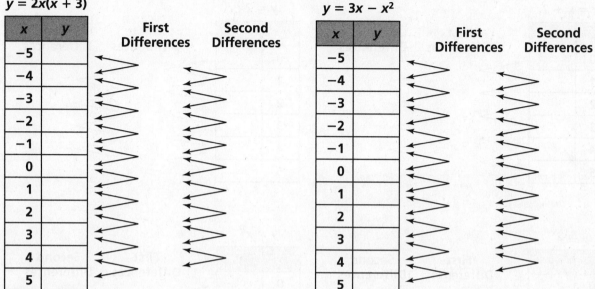

$y = 2x(x + 3)$

x	y	First Differences	Second Differences
−5			
−4			
−3			
−2			
−1			
0			
1			
2			
3			
4			
5			

$y = 3x − x^2$

x	y	First Differences	Second Differences
−5			
−4			
−3			
−2			
−1			
0			
1			
2			
3			
4			
5			

$y = (x − 2)^2$

x	y	First Differences	Second Differences
−5			
−4			
−3			
−2			
−1			
0			
1			
2			
3			
4			
5			

$y = x^2 + 5x + 6$

x	y	First Differences	Second Differences
−5			
−4			
−3			
−2			
−1			
0			
1			
2			
3			
4			
5			

Labsheet 4.3B

....

First and Second Differences

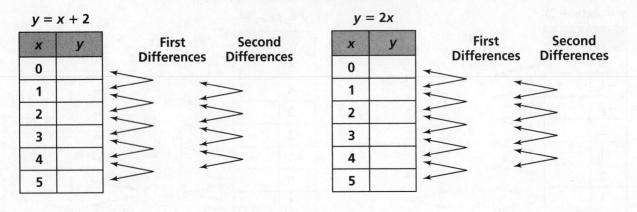

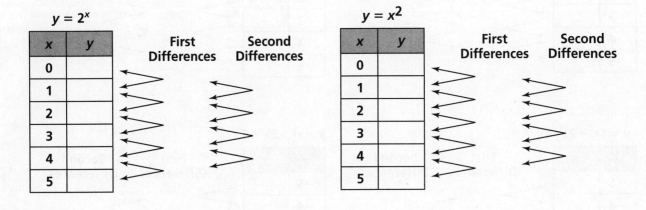

Centimeter Grid Paper

PACING: _____

Mathematical Goals

Launch

Materials

Explore

Materials

Summarize

Materials

Index

Acknowledgments

Team Credits

The people who made up the **Connected Mathematics 2** team—representing editorial, editorial services, design services, and production services—are listed below. Bold type denotes core team members.

Leora Adler, Judith Buice, Kerry Cashman, Patrick Culleton, Sheila DeFazio, Richard Heater, **Barbara Hollingdale, Jayne Holman,** Karen Holtzman, **Etta Jacobs,** Christine Lee, Carolyn Lock, Catherine Maglio, **Dotti Marshall,** Rich McMahon, Eve Melnechuk, Kristin Mingrone, Terri Mitchell, **Marsha Novak,** Irene Rubin, Donna Russo, Robin Samper, Siri Schwartzman, **Nancy Smith,** Emily Soltanoff, **Mark Tricca,** Paula Vergith, Roberta Warshaw, Helen Young

Additional Credits

Diana Bonfilio, Mairead Reddin, Michael Torocsik, nSight, Inc.

Technical Illustration

Schawk, Inc.

Cover Design

tom white.images